Climate Change & The Humanities

Also by Emil Morhardt

Climate Change & The Humanities

J. Emil Morhardt, Editor

CloudRipper Press

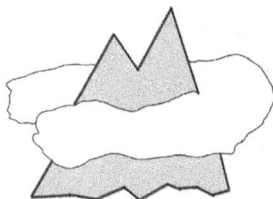

Cutting Edge Books

CloudRipper Press
    Santa Barbara, California
    www.CloudRipperPress.com
    Copyright © 2015 J. Emil Morhardt
    All rights reserved. No part of this
book may be reproduced in any form
without written permission from the author.

    Morhardt, J. Emil
        Climate Change & The
    Humanities
        J. Emil Morhardt, Editor.
    ISBN 978-0-9963536-2-5 (paper)

TABLE OF CONTENTS

FORWARD

Climate change, the result of global warming, which is in turn the result of our massive burning of fossil fuels, is the province of the natural sciences; the vast majority of the information we have about these topics is clearly the result of scientific research. On the other hand, climate change is caused by human behavior, driven by economic considerations and the universal human desire for a better life, and ultimately affects all aspects of human endeavor including the "imaginative practices from the arts and humanities [that] play a critical role in thinking through our representations of environmental change" (Yusoff and Gabrys, 2011).

Mike Hulme, writing in *Nature Climate Change*, one of the premier scientific journals dealing with climate change, in a 2011 opinion piece titled *Meet the Humanities*, asserted that "Although climate is inarguably changing society, social practices are also impacting on the climate. Nature and culture are deeply entangled, and researchers must examine how each is shaping the other. But they are largely failing to do so" (Hulme, 2011). This was likely the first time that many climate scientists thought much about the humanities as relevant to what they were studying.

That was true in my case, and stimulated me to propose a course at Claremont McKenna College entitled "The Human Response to Climate Change". My working definition of suitable material was any serious writing or research about climate change produced by non-scientists, and by that I meant people who were not some version of physicists, chemists, biologists, geologists, or engineers. In other words, I include the humanities and social sciences, but none of the natural sciences.

The idea was to have students scour the academic literature for relevant papers in these areas and write a weekly summary of a paper they found interesting with the instructions that the writing style would be journalistic; jargon-free, informative, and easy to assimilate. Along the way the selection criteria were relaxed a little to include a variety nonacademic writing, including that in newspapers, and various presentations in the arts, but the main focus remained academic output. The result is this book—a compilation of more than 200 such summaries which provide an interesting readible overview of the sorts of things non-scientists are writing about climate change.

The authors, as authors often are—or at least appear to be to editors—were somewhat intractable, with two of them sometimes writing about the same publication, or wandering over the humanities line I drew in the sand and reporting on scientific papers instead. I included all of these pieces under the general operating principal that more is better, as long as it is well-enough written, and I like to think that the students were practicing for one of my upper-division courses in which only papers by scientists are allowed.

To add a modicum of organization, I have grouped the summaries into eight sections; within each section the summaries are arranged alphabetically by author, making it easy for the reader to read everything by a specific author, but causing similar topics within a section to be separated, which is particularly disorienting when two authors have written about the same paper. *C'est la vie.* In addition, many of the papers could equally well have been inserted into a different section instead. For example, a paper about the behavior of religiously-motivated people written by psychologists could have been equally accurately placed into the religion or psychology section, so a reader interested only in religion will need to look in the psychology section as well (and *vice versa*) for complete coverage.

How well does the involvement of the humanities clarify the problem of climate change and what to do about it? The novelest Jonathan Franzen, writing in The

New Yorker recently (Franzen, 2015) identified the problem more clearly than most scientists would: "We're taking carbon that used to be sequestered and putting it into the atmosphere, and unless we stop we're fucked." Most scientists believe this; maybe people in the humanities like Franzen can get through to politicians better.

Another take on the value of the humanities in addressing climate change follows.

Franzen, J., 2015. Carbon Capture: Has climate change made it harder for people to care about conservation? The New Yorker, 56-65.
Hulme, M., 2011. Meet the humanities. Nature Climate Change 1, 177-179.
Yusoff, K., Gabrys, J., 2011. Climate change and the imagination. Wiley Interdisciplinary Reviews: Climate Change 2, 516-534.

Why Environmental Science Needs the Humanities
by Emily Segal

In the past, those working to combat environmental problems were generally thought of as natural scientists utilizing technology, economics, and policy to come up with solutions for reducing and preventing climate change. The truth is that humanist thinkers were an integral part of the first phase of the environmental revolution. They were early journalists, philosophers and historians writing and thinking about the environment and its relation to human beings. It seems that over time, these humanities scholars were pushed aside and took a back seat to natural scientists and economists who were at the front of the environmentalist movement. However, in contemporary society, people are still shaped by cultural values and political and religious ideals, each of which is a humanitarian, and not necessarily a scientific, issue.

So far, approaching climate change from a purely scientific or economic standpoint has not been successful in changing human behaviors, which is fundamental if we hope to protect the environment. Anthropogenic environmental degradation and climate change are specifically human issues, so we need to learn, think and talk about them from a humanitarian perspective as well as a scientific one.

As historian and environmentalist Sverker Sörlin (2012) writes, "After half a century of putting nature first, it may be time to put humans first." He summarizes the idea that because drastic climate change is caused by humans, it must also be solved by humans, and cannot be solved by nature itself. This is the moment that environmental science depends on the humanities in order to understand how humans think, behave and respond to one another and society as a whole. As Sörlin argues, environmentally relevant knowledge is changing because what environmentalists have found is necessary to save our planet is a better understanding of human behavior, an idea that is at the core of humanitarian studies.

Sörlin, S., 2012. Environmental humanities: why should biologists interested in the environment take the humanities seriously. BioScience 62, 9, 788-789.

THE ARTS, PUBLIC MEDIA, AND CLIMATE CHANGE

Satirizing Climate Change
by Brendan Busch

Observing that even believers in climate change are reluctant to take significant action against it, Dr. Inger-Lise Kalviknes Bore, a Lecturer in Media and Cultural Theory at Birmingham City University, and Dr. Grace Reid, an assistant professor at the University of Alberta, tried to determine if satire could be used as a mobilizing force to convince people to become active in the movement to halt climate change. In their article "Laughing in the Face of Climate Change? Satire as a Device for Engaging Audiences in Public Debate," Bore and Reid analyze a satirical play, entitled *U: The Comedy of Global Warming*, that attempts to use humor to inspire its audience to combat climate change. By interviewing the director of the play, examining surveys taken by audience members, conducting focus groups with select audience members, and analyzing the play itself, Bore and Reid were able to identify several strengths and weaknesses of using satire as a means to increase public engagement with climate change.

The first benefit that Bore and Reid identified is the idea that satire encourages reflection amongst audience members. While strictly scientific discourse may seem dry to the general public, Bore and Reid found that, for the most part, satirical humor helped to hold the audience's interest and keep them engaged in the material. In addition, it encouraged the audience to think about the message of the play long after leaving the theater and gave them a vehicle through which they could discuss their thoughts on climate change with friends and family. Another benefit to using satire in the discussion about climate change is that it helps to alleviate the fear, guilt, and helplessness people feel when confronted with the realities with climate change. These feelings tend to immobilize people and make them think that there is no action they can take to deal with a problem of such enormous scale. However, Bore and Reid observe that the humor associated with satire can diminish these negative emotions, allowing it to become a powerful enabler for climate change action.

In addition to these positives, though, Bore and Reid warn that there are dangers involved with using satire. For one, placing climate change in a humorous light (if done incorrectly) can trivialize the issue. If the humor overshadows the serious undertone of the material, then the audience may fail to get the correct message. Additionally, Bore and Reid point out that there is an issue with labeling works as "satirical" or "comedic." If audiences view works with these preconceptions, they expect to laugh and be entertained. However, if the audience does not find the material funny, then they may become unresponsive to it and either miss or ignore the underlying message entirely. Therefore, Borne and Reid conclude that satire is a good form of encouraging climate change activism, but only if these weaknesses are acknowledged and taken account for.

Bore I.K., & Reid G. 2014. Laughing in the Face of Climate Change? Satire as a Device for Engaging Audiences in Public Debate. Science Communication, 36, 454-478. http://scx.sagepub.com/content/36/4/454

YouTube—A Worthwhile Forum for Climate Change Debate?

by Brendan Busch

The emergence of the Internet has radically altered the nature of the climate change debate by providing a nearly unending source of uncensored (yet unverified) information for any interested individual. In their paper "More than entertainment: YouTube and public responses to the science of global warming and climate change," Matthew A. Shapiro, an associate professor of social science at the Illinois Institute of Technology, and Han

Woo Park, a professor of media and communication at Yeungnam University, tried to identify what kind of role one of the most popular sources of information on the internet– YouTube– plays in the climate change debate. After identifying several pertinent aspects of the website's nature and conducting a detailed analysis of the site's ten most popular climate change videos, Shapiro and Park were able to determine that, no matter the content of the individual video, the YouTube platform induced highly politicized climate change arguments in its comment section.

Shapiro and Park cite three distinct characteristics of the YouTube site that make it unique as a forum for discussing climate change. First, YouTube is not a self-selecting community. Unlike a conversation with selected friends or acquaintances, a conversation in the comment section of a YouTube video is open to people of all ideologies across the globe, forcing commenters to interact with people who have viewpoints that they are not used to encountering. Second, YouTube allows viewers to interact directly with the creators of website's content. While traditional media works in a much more linear fashion (in which the public either reads an article or watches a single video, with no further flow of information), YouTube viewers can ask a question or direct a comment at either the creators of videos or other commenters. Because viewers often receive a response, YouTube becomes more of an open debate than a one-sided lecture. Finally, YouTube provides a vast source of information that is largely exploratory in nature and is constantly updated.

After establishing YouTube's importance and distinctiveness as a source of information, Shapiro and Park performed an analysis of the site's ten most popular climate change-related video, studying both the content of the videos and the nature of the comments posted to the videos' feeds. Shapiro and Park observed that the comments (the discussion aspect of the YouTube forum) often did not pertain directly to the information presented in the video they were posted on. Aside from a general theme of climate change, it did not matter what the content of the video was; it could be scientific, political, pro-mitigation, or climate change denying and still produce a similar response in the comments. The comments did not discuss the merits of the video but, unfailingly, resorted to highly politicized arguments about climate change. Furthermore, the dissemination of misinformation is common in these disputes as there is no journalistic standard or vehicle for fact-checking YouTube comments. However, Shapiro and Park remain hopeful, as they acknowledge that the first step in creating a government policy for a problem is public debate, which is highly evident in the YouTube format.

Shapiro, M., & Park, H. W. (2014). More than entertainment: YouTube and public responses to the science of global warming and climate change. Social Science Information, Nov. 10, 2014, 1-31.

Telling the Story of Climate Change Well
by Juana Granados

How are the media and a storyteller similar? Grasping the attention of the audience is always the main objective. As scientists try to understand the climatic changes and the effects, there exists a prevailing issue of miscommunication and contradiction. Scientists agree that the earth is undergoing a global heating. However, no one is certain about the actual societal effects. Are there going to be slight problems like a warmer earth or major ones like a change in the social system of humans? While society understands that the climate's temperature is increasing, there is not yet a fear about its actual dangers. Some advances have been made to cope with global warming such as the Global Climate Coalition funding several groups aimed at climate change prevention. Nonetheless, there is no sense of committed dedication to an issue that is top priority, for the Global Climate Coalition ironically is funded itself by a fossil fuel industry. This lack of concern to the changing climate is due to the low priority of scientific, environmental concerns within the overall government.

Public policy is at risk if no one is informed. In a society where the newscast is our top informer of current events, people are vulnerable to misrepresentation of an event. News anchors have been found to focus their coverage more on emphasizing the drama of a story rather than its significance. Advances in preventing harsher, ecological effects can be accomplished if everyone focuses their time on listening to more than just the news on climate change but also understanding the science articles behind it. Based on a plethora of research polls and surveys, it was concluded that people are genuinely concerned about climate change. However, the number of concerned people concerned correlated with the amount of time the media gave attention to the issue during the timespan of the questionnaires. The way to have an informed society is based on how well the media accurately projects global warming because only through understanding will more people be willing to participate in efforts to prevent further climate change and amend public policy.

Trumbo, C.W., Shanahan, J. 2000. Social research on climate change: Where we have been, where we are, and where we might go. Public understanding of science 9, 199-204.

CABE Climate Change Festival
by Juana Granados

Can people see climate change engagement through a different, more positive perspective? Birmingham, a city in the United Kingdom, decided to showcase climate change in an interactive setting during an early summer climate change festival. Vandergert (2009) explains that half of all carbon emissions in the UK come from the city's built environment. Thus, Birmingham's citizens perceive climate change as a barrier restricting their lives. The festival was created to help the city's people realize that opting for a low-carbon life can result in a beautiful, more vivid environment. However, complete participation for climate change mitigation is required before the beautification goal is achieved. The Commission for Architecture and the Built Environment's objective was to inspire citizens and to advocate for climate change mitigation through a display of future Birmingham, along with interactive activities for people of all ages. At the festival, there was a 29-meter-high electricity pylon placed in the central festival's region. CABE constructed it to highlight the problem of energy consumption and distribution, while also being visible for the festival attendees. Different activities included tours of past, present, and future buildings, along with a claystation that outlined urban regeneration plans. There were even dance lessons as an alternative to carbon-consuming activities. Since there was only a focus on solutions for climate change instead of the negative effects, most visitors left the festival with a positive view for environmental engagement, making the objective a success.

Vandergert, P. 2008. The CABE Climate Change Festival. Places 20, 59-61. http://bit.ly/1RfglKS

Mass Media and Local Temperature Influence Twitter Discussion
by Juana Granados

Does the mass media have an influence over the trend of tweets related to climate change or are they the spontaneous result of us noticing changes in climate? Kirilenko *et al.* (2014) produced a study to investigate the relationship between the rate of tweeting on climate change and the number of climate change articles in the mass media. The researchers wanted to know if people connect weather deviations to climate change, creating climate change discourse, or whether the mass media is the source that initiates this discourse. Software was created that searched for the key terms "climate change" and "global warming" every 10 minutes. In order to avoid redundancy, several filters were included such as restricting the software to only US tweets and selecting only the most accurate actively tweeting urban areas. The Twitter feed was analyzed daily and weekly. According to the results of the daily cycle, there appeared to be more tweets on climate change during the daytime hours of 9 a.m. to 5 p.m. On the weekly cycle, there were more tweets during Monday-Thursday, the start of the work week, compared to only a few tweets on Friday-Saturday.

Researchers believe that there are more tweets during Monday-Thursday because a large proportion of tweets is published by bloggers, organizations, and journalists, who are essentially at work doing their jobs.

In an effort to determine the effect of local temperature on tweeting about climate change, there was another filter applied to focus on one location with extreme weather at a time. The results revealed that temperature had minimal influence on climate change tweets. However, there was a stronger tweeting rate in colder regions. The authors did not speculate why but perhaps people staying inside in the cold have more time to tweet. Overall, the results of the study indicated that the greater the presence of climate change in the media, the more the tweets on climate change were posted. Although temperature does not significantly affect the number of tweets, people living in extreme weather conditions did naturally feel that climate change was happening.

Kirilenko, A.P., Molodtsova, T., Stepchenkova, S.O., 2015. People as sensors: Mass media and local temperature influence climate change discussion on Twitter. Global Environmental Change 30, 92-100.

Climate Imagery in the US, UK, and Australia
by Juana Granados

The media uniquely uses visual framing, a method that shapes particular views of events, to influence the audience. O'Neill (2013) was interested in the concept of framing within images and created a study focused on the analysis of imagery in the US, UK, and Australia. He wanted to know what trends were behind the selection of climate change imagery because he realized that images shown by the news convey more than just a picture, but also a vivid experience that can be interpreted as the truth of an event. The objective of the study revolved around three questions: what images are used by online newspapers to communicate climate change, what variation is observed within these images, and what visual frames are used by online newspapers' climate change reportage? For each news-affiliated website, the terms "climate change," "global warming," and "green-house effect" were searched. Many of the 17,480 articles did not contain images, as expected. For Australia, *Courier Mail*, *Herald Sun*, *Age*, *Australian*, and *Telegraph* were used. For the UK, *The Sun*, *Daily Express*, *Daily Mail*, and *Times* were used. For the USA, the *New York Times*, *Wall Street Journal*, and *USA Today* were used. For the UK's *Guardian* website, there was a significantly larger representation of imagery. Thus, a different method was used in which every 10th article, within a total of 2,825 articles, was examined to determine total imagery coverage on climate change. The analysis of coverage was summed up as a percentage that included the total number of images found for the climate search terms for each site in comparison to all of the other websites. From these observations, it was concluded that media framing focuses a large portion of its climate change imagery on politicians, especially in Australia. This is known as contested visual framing and is very common among all thirteen newspaper websites, possibly because there might be more political and opinion journalists than science-focused journalists. The second part of the analysis consisted of an in-depth examination of the images. The literal meaning, including color, shape, and movement, was observed, and the connotative and ideological meaning was also analyzed, such as the image's relationship to the country's culture and underlying attitudes about climate change. It was concluded that although there is a diversity of meaning across every image, there is no common conceptualization of the meaning of climate change. The images still fall under the contested visual frame, where mostly in newspapers, societal and political instead of environmental imagery are used. O'Neill claims that specialist science sections and climate change imagery newspapers are slowly decreasing, and this is likely detract from the urgency for climate change mitigation presented in the media.

O'Neill, S. J. 2013. Image matters: Climate change imagery in US, UK and Australian newspapers. Geoforum 49, 10-19.

Twitter vs. Mainstream Media—How is Climate Change Communicated?
by JP Kiefer

Twitter has created a new way to share news and information, different from classic news sources. With somewhere near 2.8 million tweets per month related to climate change, social media clearly has an impact on the way news is communicated. Social media users frame content much differently, allowing them to highlight different points.

According to Olteanu *et al.* (2015), coverage of specific events is very different on Twitter versus mainstream media, with an overlap in peaks of attention of just 22%-25% of events. Only 7% of all climate change related tweets are about natural disasters, compared to 20% of all climate change-related coverage on mainstream media. Twitter spends more time covering media-triggered events, like the publication of an investigation by a newspaper (9% of climate change related tweets vs. 1% of climate change on mainstream media) or the coverage of an individual's actions (14% on twitter vs. 4% in mainstream media). The actions of Government and inter-governmental agencies receive the largest amount of coverage on both forms of media, however twitter users tend to focus on legal proceedings, while mainstream media focuses on publications and meetings.

Contrary to what one would assume, events involving conflict or referencing elite persons are not the majority of news about climate change. While individual actions appear prominently on twitter, about half of these individuals are not rich, powerful, nor famous. Twitter has allowed average individuals to generate peaks of attention as large as those obtained by large organizations or governments.

Olteanu *et al.* recommend that activists and advocates publicize works highlighting high-impact negative effects of climate change, as both types of media tend to pick them up. Public relations or for-profit corporations should be aware of how easily lawsuits involving corporations spread on social media. Media organizations should

31

consider looking at the gap in their coverage compared to social media, and might consider attempting to narrow this gap. There is clearly a desire for the information distributed on twitter, and media organizations could attempt to distribute this information themselves.

Olteanut, A., Castillo, C., Diakopoulos, N., and Aberer, K. 2015. Comparing Events Coverage in Online News and Social Media: The Case of Climate Change.

Climate Fiction Before Climate Change—the Work of J.G. Ballard
by Russell Salazar

Even before the coining of terms such as 'global warming' and 'climate change' came the climate-related dystopian fiction of J.G. Ballard. His work is considered to be the start of a genre known as climate fiction, or cli-fi. Clarke (2013) examines Ballard's work in depth, investigating the extent to which the writing aligns with more recent climate fiction. Furthermore, the paper delves into the exploratory nature of climate fiction with regard to the humanistic approach to climate change; Ballard's "fiction is as much psychological and ontological as it is physiological".

Given the lack of scientific knowledge with regard to climate change, Ballard's fiction has distinct differences from more recent works. A key feature is that novels such as *The Drowned World* and *The Crystal World* do not attribute the change in climate to human activity. Instead, the works are explorations of the human psyche in response to drastic changes in the environment. Essentially, these older novels are much less concerned with the causes of climate change, and much more interested in the way humans process and adapt to an inevitable scenario. Clarke argues that *The Crystal World* is a testament to Ballard's antipathy towards scientists; fictional scientific explanations are provided for the environmental changes, but mean nothing when considering the psychological response from the characters. Instead, the characters respond emotionally to drawings, religious inferences, and the inherent poetry of the changing environment. J.G. Ballard's writing suggests that the scientific way in which we approach climate change is unable to achieve emotional resonance that can be produced through art and theology.

On the other hand, Ballard's works have also set the precedent for many of the cli-fi works that followed. Clarke introduces an interesting observation: "the science of climate mitigation has given society a perhaps misplaced sense of confidence that anthropogenic global warming is not likely to lead directly to... human extinction." *The Crystal World* and *The Drowned World* both utilize extreme cases of mass extinction and dystopia, and deliver the emotional responses of characters in those unthinkable scenarios. This theme carried over into the genre, which delves into a plethora of extreme climate-related change.

Climate fiction is, in itself, a study of the human responses to climate change, albeit on a much more extreme level. Such a genre plays an important role in the multi-faceted push for climate change mitigation and adaptation.

Clarke, J., 2013. Reading Climate Change in J.G. Ballard. Critical Survey 25, 7-21.

Climate—7 Questions on 2 Degrees
by Abby Schantz

In "Climate: 7 questions on 2 degrees," aired by CNN on April 24th, 2015, John D. Sutter announces his plan to focus the rest of the year's reporting on the issue of global temperature increasing by 2°C. In recent years, 2°C has become the marketing mecca of climate change and is being used as the measure of our progress. Drought, rising sea levels and extinction of species are all associated with rising temperatures. Sutter sees more significance to these 2°C than are currently understood by the average person. Beginning with a Facebook post last week, CNN requested that people post questions about climate change and more specifically, the 2°C threshold. Sutter admits that he does not yet have all the answers to these questions but he has made it his goal to find them out over the next year. This first article to kick off the project attempts to explain the basics of the two-degree threshold. Sutter begins by explaining that the focus on a

2°C change is not a recent thing. An economist at Yale, William Nordhaus, suggested the threshold back in 1977. Nordhaus noted that this much of an increase would bring temperatures above any that have been measured for the past several hundred thousand years. Though at first it was a just an estimate, ongoing research is increasingly supporting the threshold. As research has advanced, the threshold has been put on political agendas. Germany was first in the 1990s, followed by the European Commission, the G8, and the US National Academy of Sciences. Finally, the Copenhagen Accord was signed by over 100 nations, including the United States, all agreeing that a 2°C increase would be too much for the world with withstand. The effects of a 2°C rise in temperature, as predicted by the National Research Counsel, the Intergovernmental Panel on Climate Change, and the World Bank include: a 400%–800% increase in wildfire size within the United States, 2%–8% more intense hurricanes, a 20%–30% higher risk of extinction for plants and animals, particularly amphibians, a 30% annual loss of average sea ice in the Arctic, a 10%–30% decrease in certain crop yields within the United States, India, and Africa, and a 20% decrease in availability of freshwater. Though 2°C is an accepted number amongst experts, it is by no means precise. Rather, there are numerous marketing reasons that 2°C has become the staple number of global warming. One explanation is simply that it is an even number: One degree is too low and 3°C seems too high. Recognizing that the effects will not necessarily be drastically different at 2.1°C, Katharine Hayhoe, a climate scientist at Texas Tech compared the 2°C threshold to cigarettes. There is no exact number of cigarettes guaranteed to give a person cancer. Rather, the more an individual smokes, the higher the risk. It is at a 2°C rise that experts believe we are in dangerous territory. Since the Industrial Revolution, our climate has warmed 0.85°C, and the average prediction for the future, based on our current pollution levels, is an increase of 1.5°C. The World Bank predicts that even with active efforts to reduce warming, this increase is nearly inevitable. This suggests the difficultly of keeping the increase below the critical 2°C. Jaeger of the Global°

Climate Forum stresses the immense degree to which we would have to reduce emissions with which we would have to reduce emissions in order to prevent an increase of 2°C. The global director of the climate program at the World Resource Institute, Jennifer Morgan, puts that number at around 80%–90% of emissions reduction by 2050. Without action to reduce emissions, it is predicted that the 2°C threshold will be reached before midcentury, and an increase of 3–5°C by 2100.

Sutter, J. "Climate: 7 questions on 2 degrees." CNN. April 24th, 2015

Poetry and the Environment
by Emily Segal

Because our emotions can be equally as important as rationality in decision-making, obstacles to living sustainably can relate to our feelings and attitudes as well as scientific and political issues. Ecocritics believe that approaching climate change from an interdisciplinary perspective, using literature to explore how humans relate to nature, can be helpful. Poets, for example, are experts at exploring the relationship between our internal and external worlds. This can be used to address one of the problems in understanding climate change—it is such a grand concept that it can be difficult to relate to on an individual level. As Garrard (2014) and climate scientist Mike Hulme suggest, it might be time for us to stop thinking about sustainable living and development as a 'fight against climate change' and rather deal with the idea of climate change from a more constructive and creative perspective. Poems are a good way to understand climate change because they have flexible structures and multiple levels of meaning, which can be useful in explaining the complex relationship between humans and the environment. Climate change involves intricate connections between ecological, political and socioeconomic issues, and because of this, a complex form of expression like poetry is successful because it allows people to explain how all these issues are related in a single, concise form. An important distinction in ecopoetry is between 'ecophenomenological poetry,' a style that aims to focus its readers on appreciating nature in its purest state, and 'environmental poetry,' which focuses specifically on the changing relationships between humans and the environment. Ecopoetry as a whole promotes the idea that humans should live *with* nature, and not abuse the Earth only to satisfy our needs. Anthropocentrism is currently a major problem with how people think; it reflects the idea that something only has importance in terms of its value to human beings. Instead, ecopoetry urges people to see past the world as a resource for consumption. Ecopoetry adopts biocentrism, the idea that human actions should be guided not solely by self-interest but rather by the fact that all natural life has value.

Garrard, G., and Lidström, S., 2014. Images adequate to our predicament: Ecology, Environment and Ecopoetics. Environmental Humanities 5, 35-53.

Ecological Consciousness and the Performing Arts

by Emily Segal

Performing arts such as puppet theatre, film, comedy and music can be useful in activating people's consciousness about the environment. Professor and environmentalist Andrew Mark (2014) explains this through his own first hand experience watching Bob Wiseman perform his piece *Uranium,* about the tragedy of nuclear mining, as well as through analysis of others' response to the performance. *Uranium* is ecomusicological because it explores how music and sound relate to ecology and the natural environment, but it also incorporates a visual component. It is an example of how art can help people relate to, make sense of, and think about a topic that they otherwise would try to avoid because it is difficult to accept. When Wiseman performs *Uranium,* he narrates and plays guitar as a silent film plays showing puppets that interpret what he is saying. Wiseman starts the piece introducing a main character in the story, a country girl, as simply "She." The chords he plays on the acoustic guitar allude to echo and wide ecosystems. A sense of nostalgia and a vast horizon are implied. The audience finds the girl puppet likable. She is curious and drawn to the city, and as she travels south past Ontario's most industrial mining towns, Wiseman's choruses feature an E minor chord. Mark notes this is the only minor chord in the song so far and combined with Wiseman's lift in pitch in the sung melody, it creates a sense of lament. "She" then meets another character in the story, Joe Blow, and they fall in love. However, the second half of the song starts out on a different note. "She" appears to be in pain and has black moles all over her body. The audience is suddenly silent and melancholy as "She" can hardly lie on her side because of the pain, and Wiseman narrates "the cancer took her in its arms." A human hand emerges on the stage, signifying the taking of her soul after death. The hand also takes Joe Blow's guitar and the audience learns he can no longer sing anymore out of grief for his loss. Joe blow begins to think that people are evil. At this point, though the story is tragic, Wiseman's intentions are not entirely clear. However, what happens next explains the purpose of his performance. The scenery on stage retraces the girl character's journey from the city back to her home in the country. Wiseman's lyrics narrate Joe Blow's confusion: "Why was the woman that he loved, taken so young? She was only from a small town, where they mine uranium." The audience is shocked not only by the dark turn the performance takes but also by the connection that "She" died because contamination from the uranium mines in her town gave her cancer.

Wiseman here is describing a prominent issue in Canadian history that is also relevant on a global scale: major urban centers have been responsible for the unrelenting exploitation of resources in the countryside. In 1953, the world's largest uranium deposit was found in Northern Canada, and for the next forty years, the town of Elliot Lake produced most of the world's uranium. Filling this global demand for Uranium came at the expense of actual human lives, which Wiseman showed through *Uranium*. Wiseman is able to link these facts to the sentiments of the audience. When then audience is engaged in the story by laughing, moaning, sighing or crying they are relating to the characters and events occurring. This in turn engages the audience in the environmental issue of radioactive contamination resulting from uranium mining. The audience is able to transcend their individual experience and as a whole community experience the pain of the characters who suffer because of a way in which we alter our environment through mining. Wiseman creates cognitive connections between the audience and environmental concerns that the natural sciences cannot achieve in the same way.

Mark, A., 2014. Refining Uranium: Bob Wiseman's Ecomusicological Puppetry. Environmental Humanities 4, 69-93.

Concerts and Composting
by Emily Segal

Bonnaroo Music and Arts Festival, in addition to its reputation as one of the largest music festivals in the world, has become a model for on-site composting at large events. The festival is held on a 700 acre farm in Manchester, Tennessee, and was attended by over 80,000 people in 2014. By partnering with Clean Vibes, a company focused on effective waste management, in 2014 the festival generated 120 tons of compostable material that was processed on-site. In addition, Clean Vibes hosted a booth at the festival that rewarded attendees with small prizes like t-shirts, artist merchandise, and free tickets to other events in exchange for collecting and turning in littered recyclable items. The event's Concessions Team made sure vendors used only compostable utensils and threatened to kick out any of the food stands that did not comply with their sustainable demands. In 2006, Bonnaroo organizers bought the farmland the festival takes place on so they could implement on-site composting rather than continue to pay the environmental cost of fuel consumption and pollution required to transport organic materials to compost sites.

Composting begins before the festival has ended. A tractor mixes leftover food scraps, compostable tableware and wood chips continuously, forming a pile that will be placed on a large compost pad on the farm. When the festival ends and everyone clears out, an employee is responsible for mixing the compost pile once every few months. Once everything is turned to compost, the biggest challenge is sorting out small non-compostable items like plastic butter packets.

Not only is Bonnaroo's compost used on-site, it is also used in the community by the non-profit Keep Coffee Country Beautiful, an organization that focuses on reducing litter and encouraging sustainable practices in Manchester's Coffee County. Other large-scale events can learn from Bonnaroo's composting system and encourage the same commitment to sustainable living within their businesses as is shown by the Bonnaroo festival's organizing team.

Katsaros, 2014. Music Festivals Keep Beat With Composting. BioCycle 55, 8, 80-86.

Artists, Scientists, and the Environment
by Emily Segal

A growing number of artists are using their work to solve ecological challenges and communicate with the general public about environmental science and sustainability. The US National Science Foundation (NSF) and the U.K. Arts and Humanities Research Council (AHRC) have funded an international research project exploring the benefits of collaboration between artists and scientists who use their work to address climate change issues. Art can be a motivator for social action and participation, and these artist-scientist collaborations serve as models for encouraging public-private relationships, educating the public about environmental issues, including the youth population in environmental conversations, raising awareness about environmental justice, and promoting ideas about green infrastructure and sustainable technology.

Digital design researcher Lone Koefoed Hansen and choreographer and writer Susan Kozel claim the NSF/AHRC project has shown an "affective, embodied nature of scientific learning," as a major theme in artist-scientist collaborations (26). Examples of artist-scientist collaborations studied by the NSF/AHRC project include the international nonprofit Cape Farewell, which brings artists and scientists together to view evidence of climate change in locations such as the Arctic and the Amazon, and the Swiss artists-in-labs project, which implements artist residencies in various laboratories.

There are also many examples of artist-scientist collaborations in the US Artist Lillian Ball used sustainable technology in her project WATERWASH ABC, a project along the Bronx River dealing with excess storm water, when she created a permeable pavement for her instillation out of recycled glass. Artist Francis Whitehead worked with the City of Chicago's Department of Environment to come up with sustainable solutions for abandoned gas stations. After researching over 400 gas stations in Chicago, Whitehead collaborated with soil chemist A. Paul Schwab and geologist David S. Graham to create her project *Slow Cleanup*, a system of using phytoremediation, the use of plants to reduce underground contamination, to transform empty lots.

Combining art and science allows people to relate to environmental issues on a more intimate level. Artist Jackie Brookner makes the comparison that by only repairing ecosystems, we are continuing to apply a Band-Aid solution to environmental problems. The only way to achieve a fundamental change towards sustainable behavior is to reach people on a deeper, emotional level, which art can be used to do.

Ingram, 2012. Sculpting Solutions: Art–Science Collaborations in Sustainability. Environment, 54, 4, 24-34.

Reduce, Reuse, Recycle, and Rap
by Emily Segal

An education program that incorporated environmentally themed (green) hip-hop was able to facilitate learning in an environmental science classroom. Environmentalist Michael J. Cermak argues that the urban cultural landscape can be used to help people relate to environmental issues. For example, he explains how rap artist Mos Def's track "New World Water" combines the ecological theme of fresh water scarcity with the cultural theme of racial injustice. Green hip-hop helps disprove the stereotype that rap is only about material wealth, drugs, violence, and misogyny. Cermak's four years of incorporating green hip-hop into classrooms has helped him redefine the term ecological literacy. Cermak used a curriculum in which he replaced traditional lectures about lakes and forests with conversations about urban environmental injustices using green hip-hop as part of his curriculum during that time.

Intertwining raps about race, social justice, and the environment not only changes the voice of who is speaking to students about environmental change, but it also increases student engagement as a whole. Environmentalist and civil rights leader Van Jones calls for a need to make the environmental movement "less white," and focuses on promoting the environmental dialogue within and coming from urban communities of color. Green hip-hop can change the idea that environmental education has to come predominately from a white author educated in the natural sciences. Expanding the sources of education about the environment increases the likelihood students will be involved in the conversation about environmental science and climate change. When Cermak had his students write their own green hip-hop verses, concepts about environmental science suddenly became personal creations and had a greater meaning for students.

> Cermak, M, 2012. Hip Hop, Social Justice, and Environmental Education: Toward a Critical Ecological Literacy. The Journal of Environmental Education, 43, 3, 192-203.

What Images Evoke Climate Change?
by Phoebe Shum

Getting people to do something about climate change can be a tough feat. Eleri Evans, PhD candidate at Swansea University UK, explores how a community arts program was designed with the hopes of involving more people in taking action against climate change in Wales (Evans 2014). She elaborates on theories of critical realism and how our actions are affected by the way we think. She introduces the theory of *internal conversation* and explains how people actively converse with themselves to define their values and actions. To demonstrate her point, she focuses on a particular community arts project organized by Awel Aman Tawe (AAT), a community wind farm project in Southern Wales. AAT, founded in 2000, is a renewable energy activist group that has faced both success and hostility from their community. Their aim in developing an arts program was to engage people on a deeper, personal level with climate change and initiate change-oriented intervention. The program features film, drama, poetry, and a project named "Postcards from the Future," in which people submit original images of what a climate-changed world would look like. Competitions like their bilingual climate change poetry competition received over 700 received entries worldwide. The arts program was successful in providing the community with a platform to bring the community together and initiate change.

According to Evans, the majority of our population recognizes the emerging issue of climate change, but the issue still remains as a problem too distant from us. Media coverage on climate change is decreasing more and more. Climate change is becoming something we're tired of hearing about—but its effects on our environment are intensifying day by day. Creative arts may not be a typical approach to promoting climate change activism, but they undoubtedly help push a larger circle of people to take action and generate productive conversation.

Evans, E. 2014. How Green is my Valley? The Art of Getting People in Wales to Care about Climate Change. Journal of Critical Realism, 304–325.

Is a Cartoon Worth a Thousand Words?
by Phoebe Shum

Relaying issues of climate change through black and white text can begin to seem monotonous after a while. Kate Manzo, a senior lecturer in human geography at the University of Newcastle, advocates for the efficacy of cartoons in relaying the different perspectives on climate change geopolitics (Manzo, 2012). In her article, she focuses on a few cartoons from Earthworks, an international political cartoon competition that took place in 2008. The various cartoons embody different geopolitical climate change visions, and demonstrate the influence that visual commentary can have on climate change awareness. The judges based their decisions on the shock value and clarity of the cartoon's message. The winning cartoon entries were easy to understand—no matter your culture, religion, language or political stance.

Currently, cartoons are not being used at an optimum level. Manzo warns us that while cartoons often convey serious issues through humor, this does not mean that they should be taken lightly. What makes cartoons different from other forms of art, such as paintings? Cartoons are usually simple and feature caricatures, allowing them to be accessible to people of all ages and intellectual levels. Through visuals, cartoonists assist in heightening awareness, portraying different perspectives, providing exposure and deepening our understanding of climate change. However, while cartoons spread awareness and allow people to grasp the happenings of climate change, they create room for a misunderstanding towards the actual time-sensitivity and complexity of climate change.

During a time of skepticism towards climate change, it may seem odd to push for unscientific forms of climate change promotion. However, Manzo introduces the term 'knowledge paradox' to explain why this approach works. The theory is that the more informed people are towards climate science, the less they care about climate change. An influx of information will not persuade skeptics to take action. Rather, we must find ways to connect climate change with their current morals. The accessibility of cartoons allow for audiences to engage with the issue, even if there is a lack of scientific knowledge imparted during the process.

Manzo, Kate. 2012. Earthworks: The geopolitical visions of climate change cartoons. Political Geography. November 2012, 481-494.

Climate Change in the Media
by Phoebe Shum

How are people from different countries publicly responding to the global issue of climate change? Seung Mo Jang and Phillip Sol Hart (2015), assistant professors at University of South Carolina and University of Michigan, examine two years worth of climate-change Twitter conversations in order to see how different regions and political environments affect the way people communicate about climate issues. The way mass media presents and interprets global issues like climate change can play a big role in defining public perceptions, which is why it's extremely important to research and assess these patterns of communication. Most people do not have the means to accurately assess the climate change information they are exposed to.

Jang and Hart discovered that Republican-leaning states tend to use the term "global warming" instead of "climate change." While these terms seem interchangeable, "global warming" is usually used by skeptics who do not believe in the scientific theories behind climate change. By focusing on the way people treat climate change issues in everyday conversations, especially in the US, UK, Canada, and Australia. Apparently, climate change skepticism is much more prevalent in the US than in the UK. The American media still present climate change as a highly contested topic, while media in the UK have accepted the reality of climate change and choose to focus on environmental action plans instead. Australian and Canadian media mirror theUK's views, focusing on the *how* as opposed to questioning the reality of climate change. The UK, Australia and Canada are all focusing on ways to minimize the economic and environmental impact of climate change, while the US is still struggling to garner a more enthusiastic attitude towards climate change mitigation efforts. By understanding the different sentiments countries have towards climate change, we can better create and "personalize" mitigation approaches and policies so that they are more effective amongst different populations.

Climate change is a global problem, and a unified global effort towards this ever-intensifying issue will definitely bring many benefits.

Jang, S.M., Hart, P.S., 2015. Polarized frames on "climate change" and "global warming" across countries and states: evidence from twitter big data. Global Environmental Change 32, 11-17

Theater as a Medium for Communicating the Consequences of Climate Change
by Sarah Whitney

The National Science Foundation funded Steve Cosson and the Civilians theatre company to create a play about global climate change, and investigate the effectiveness of public engagement around the project. The Civilians is an investigative theatre company that uses research to tackle and communicate complex and undeveloped subjects. Steve Cosson collaborated with composer Michael Friedman to explore the topic of global warming through a play called "The Great Immensity". This medium of the arts is yet to be fully explored as a method for public outreach about major issues like climate change. The process of research for the play, the balance of fiction and facts within the plot, the inclusion of research and scientists in the creative process, and the efforts to engage a wide array of people though a multi-platform media approach are noteworthy in regards to future methods of public engagement.

Steve Cosson uses fiction to present mitigation methods and the wide variety of effects caused by climate change in a directed and straightforward manor so as to not overwhelm the audience. "The Great Immensity" tells the story of a woman named Phyllis who has to retrace the steps of her sister Polly after she goes missing while on an assignment for a nature show. After consulting scientists, activists, and educators it seems that her sister's disappearance revolves around a conspiracy involving climate change and culminates at the international Auckland Summit. Cosson used extensive research to construct "The Great Immensity", and based his characters on real individuals he interviewed. Steve

Cosson traveled to Barro Colorado Island (BCI) to ask its current resident scientists about their work and conclusions regarding climate change. He used this information primarily to create the backbone of research for the play. Cosson and the Civilians theatre company pride themselves in recalling all interviews from memory to make for a more humanistic and passionate approach to producing and directing. Therefore, "The Great Immensity" takes a more personal approach to presenting facts about climate change in which people are genuinely interested, hopefully leading to greater engagement. Cosson also incorporates media footage in the play from the locations to which he traveled.

Straying away from NSF's idea of creating a website for public engagement, Cosson thought a multi-platform outreach program would be much more effective. The goal of the platform was to engage a diverse audience, and make the subject of the play understandable, accessible, and intriguing. This plan consisted of witty YouTube videos, radio program appearances, creating and distributing educational materials, connecting the audience to local resources, creating a website and various social network accounts, and holding discussions after the play. The show had an overall positive response but was not significantly more engaging than any other play the Civilians put on. However, the play gained extreme momentum and nationwide recognition after Cosson presented it at a TED Talk in 2012. Cosson says that the project itself serves as a baseline for both limitations and effective methods on public engagement with climate change.

Wasserman, S., Young, M.F., 2013. The Great Immensity: A Theatrical Approach to Climate Change. Curator: The Museum Journal 56, 79-86.

The Dilemma of Climate Change Theatre
by Sarah Whitney

Jason Zinoman, in his New York Times article "Fate of the Earth Takes Center Stage" (2013), asks the question why is there not a great American play about climate change? As global warming may lead to the end of civilization as we know it, it's quite odd that more American play writers have not utilized this dramatic topic. Zinoman states that it is the complexity of the issue that is the root of the problem. It is difficult for one to find a personal connection because we are not directly experiencing its full effects. The variety of topics within the umbrella of climate change and their impacts on humanity are distressing and terrifying, leaving an average audience feeling numb and overwhelmed. American audiences want upbeat productions that leave them feeling happy rather than paralyzed by the subject matter. Thus, climate change theater is not an easy sell. Says American playwrite Cynthia Hopkins, "the challenge is to communicate that there's also hope and agency" within the topic of global warming.

While there have been a few small off-Broadway productions touching on the effects of climate change, there is no popular drama that explores one of the greatest challenges of our time. Jason Zinoman spotlights Cynthia Hopkins's "This Clement World" as the innovative and engaging work that may spark the fire to a climate change theater movement. Hopkins has created a play that is out-of-this-world, with a plot line crossing time, space, and mediums while incorporating a variety of eccentric characters. Yet the play is still extremely personal to the author. After becoming inspired by a speech from Jeffery Sachs at a 2009 conference on climate change, Hopkins decided to use her talents to publicize a significant issue. She was funded by the Cape Farewell project, an organization that fosters relations between scientists and artists, to go on an expedition in the Arctic for research. The trip is the backbone of her work as she uses her footage from the trip, and creates characters from the people she encountered in her play, one in which is a German scientist who claims there is beauty in the death of humanity. The work itself pushes to persuade the audience of the severity of the issue and communicate difficult topics through symbolism. For example, one of the most significant characters of her play is the ghost of a Native American who delivers a monologue that warns those who do not think their way of life will ever change.

The image of the American Indian is the living example of how a people's way of life has almost completely diminished. She also incorporates her personal struggle with alcoholism as a metaphor for the climate change crisis, as "we're addicted to behavior that is making us sick". Jason Zinoman regards the play as a revolutionary and groundbreaking American work.

Zinoman, J., 2013. Fate of the Earth Takes Center Stage. New York Times. Theater.

Rise of the Cli-Fi Literary Genre
by Sarah Whitney

Angela Evancie of NPR News (2013), reports that a new genre of literature is growing in popularity. Publicist Brian Gittis returned to his job after the east coast storm Sandy to find a book with Manhattan submerged on his desk. The novel, Odds Against Tomorrow by Nathaniel Rich, tells the story of a young genius who figures out worst-case environmental scenarios and sells his calculations to large corporations. Odds Against Tomorrow is just one example of a new literary genre that has emerged over the last decade called Cli-fi. Climate Fiction is the latest trend that captures its readers by depicting current challenges and fears of climate change.

Cli-fi novels are constructed in a world like ours, yet the Earth's systems are somehow in trouble. This concept is not exactly unique, as some of these concepts have been addressed in Science Fiction. However, the difference between Sci-fi and Cli-fi is that Sci-fi takes place in a dystopian future, while Cli-fi depicts a dystopian present. Climate change can be the central theme of the novel, or an outlying condition. In addition, Cli-fi authors do not use the phrase climate change or global warming as they say it seems too clichéd for their writing and distracts from their ideas. Instead, these authors strive to depict how humans deal with relationships, emotions, and actions in a Cli-fi setting.

By adding emotional depth and a human element to the topic of Climate Change, novelists can reach the public in a way that other mediums cannot.

Instead of presenting the facts in a direct and almost

condescending way as some Scientists can, novelists are able to bridge the gap between different ideologies and explore topics within their work. They do not need to bluntly address their audience, but subtly hide facts about climate change within the ebbs and flows of a riveting story. Books like Daniel Kramb's show that the Cli-fi genre is not limited to this methodology. In his novel "From Here" (2012), Kramb is extremely direct and political in his approach, as he wants a strong reaction from his audience. However, regardless of the approach it seems that fiction is a fairly untapped way to explore and communicate the topic of climate change to the public. This new kind of novel mirrors our current and approaching reality, and with growing popularity, could be called the genre of the 21st century.

Evancie, A., 2013. So Hot Right Now: Has Climate Change Created A New Literary Genre. National Public Radio.

Film Industry Pushes to Mitigate its Effects on Climate Change through Film4Climate
by Sarah Whitney

On it's 30th Anniversary, the Guadalajara International Film Festival (2015) invested in making the film industry more environmentally friendly by committing to Film4Climate. Film4Climate is an organization sponsored by the World Bank Group Connect4Climate. With it comes a commitment to create mitigations for the environmental impact of film production, and to raise awareness through cinema. Film4Climate held screenings and discussion about the obstacles, challenges, and possible strategies for action. One of the most significant proposals encouraged film industries around the world to allocate a percentage of their budgets to reduce their carbon footprint in production. There is also a "Film4Climate declaration" which includes a social and environmental responsibility to biodiversity conservation, proper waste disposal, and climate change action and awareness. The declaration strives to reduce, mitigate and even compensate the film industries' actions to become more sustainable.

The Guadalajara International is considered Latin America's most significant film festival, and reaches a worldwide audience. It served as the perfect platform to introduce Film4Climate. In addition, the festival also presented the winners of the Action4Climate film competition that engaged over 230 filmmakers worldwide. It is vital to engage those in the film industry as they have a huge influence over pop culture. Cinema is a fantastic medium for this purpose in that it can easily raise awareness and call for action from the general public on social issues. The festival also hosted a forum that included several presentations from high profile industry speakers including Ivan Trujillo Bolio, Director of the fesitval; Blanca Guerra, Actress and Director of the Mexican Academy of Motion Picture Arts and Sciences; and Eduardo Santana Castellón, Director of the Museum of Environmental Science of University of Guadalajara.

The Guadalajara International Film Festival made the commitment to be environmentally friendly over seven years ago and has created over a hundred environmental films since then. During this year's festival, the panel explicitly pushed climate-sensitive practices like reducing the amount of printed materials and reducing the environmental impact of the event itself. The festival director, Ivan Tujilo, says that the Guadalajara International Film Festival coalition with the World Bank has been magnificent and has created a strong response in the film industry. Film4Climate films and message will be delivered around the world at several other film festivals, including the Cannes International Film Festival, in years to come.

Braga, G., 2015. Film4Climate, the first film forum to take on climate change, debuts at the 30th Guadalajara International Film Festival. The World Bank. http://bit.ly/1KtoXN4

Visual Imagery and Climate Change
by Yijing Zhang

A review by O'Neill (2014) studies the visual representation of climate change and public's reaction on visual imagery. O'Neill begins by outlining three essential qualities of image that are different from text: analogical quality, a lack of an explicit propositional syntax, and indexicality (unlike words that are understood as a particular way of portraying the world, images are seen as direct representation of reality). These three qualities are related when O'Neill discusses three moments of communication cycles. The moment of production is about how climate visual are made, in what form, by and for whom, when and why. The moment of the visual text is about the context of the visual climate discourses. The moment of consumption is about how does the public read the visual climate discourses.

When reviewing the moment of the visual text, O'Neill looks at newspapers, TV and film, NGO, advertising and marketing, science, and art. In newspapers, not only have the number of climate change imageries increased, the contents of these imageries has also diversified. During the process of visualization, personification of climate imagery plays an important role. Personification allows many people, particularly politicians, to be the cover. Also, there is a difference of preference between newspapers owned by News Corporation and those under other ownerships. News Corporation prefers to use imagery of people, while other newspapers like to use visuals of climate impacts. In terms of TV and films, researchers find out that because visual images have the indexicality quality, documentary films aim to earn the trust from viewer and let them believe in the truthfulness of the films. Television has another advantage of portraying multiple visual in sequence so that comparisons can be made.

Non-governmental organizations, like Greenpeace, utilized visual imagery for campaigns, and according to media studies scholar Julie Doyle, they undergo five phases. In the first phase, images emphasize on dangers of global warming by describing future as catastrophe. The second phase shifts emphasis to causes of climate change and possible solutions. Phase three captures evidence of a warming world. Phase four focuses on geopolitics of oil. The last phase returns to the melting glaciers in polar areas. Businesses use visual marketing strategies to relate their products to climate issues. For instance, automotive companies claim to produce high fuel efficiency by using green and scenic landscapes as advertising images. In contrast to these different fields, scientists use distinct figures to convey more complex data using simpler images. In addition, art exhibition often uses climate change as a theme to arouse more attention to climate issues.

When considering the moment of consumption, O'Neill has three key findings in the social science perspective: images of climate impacts could promote feelings of salience but reduce one's self-efficacy; images of future might enhance one's self-efficacy; images of people can undermine feelings of saliency.

Reviewing the moment of production, probably the main scheme is 3D landscape visualization. It adds a vivid virtual to climate projections, enabling participants in interact with imagery of the landscape in future conditions. Although such mechanisms allow the public to have accurate perceptions of climate change, the visualization can be problematic.

O'Neill, S. J. and N. Smith (2014). "Climate change and visual imagery." Wiley Interdisciplinary Reviews: Climate Change 5: 73-87.

How Artists and Scientists Engage the Public with Climate Change
by Yijing Zhang

David Buckland (2012) argues that climate science needs a broader platform to engage the public in the discussion of global warming. In his opinion, the Cape Farewell project is such a perfect means for scientist to work on cultural factors of climate, together with filmmakers, writers and poets. Cape Farwell is a good fit because it involves all the people, including artists, architects, and musicians, who know how to measure and evaluate climate changes in terms of topics most interesting to the public. The project consists of many journeys into areas most susceptible to climate change, in order to let participants see and examine how human activities are influencing our habitats. According to Buckland, these expeditions provide "a different language of climate change with which to engage the public." As an international affair, more than 140 participants have taken part by writing down their stories, creating their artworks, or videoing their experiences. These practitioners use their own artsy ways to offer public a cultural explanation of cause and effects of climate changes.

To both scientists and artists, voyages are filled with unknowns, but the unpredictability allows participants to meet unexpected elements that might be shed light on climate changes. The combination group of scientists and artists are mutually beneficial, as they share the same objective that the earth is exploited by human activities. Artists are able to understand complicated hard science and in turn, incorporate their understanding into their artworks concerning our planet. To scientists, works of art, including songs, books, films and paintings, can effectively relate to public's emotion, thus engaging people and transforming their perception on climate issues.

One expedition in 2011 witnessed an island community striving to undergo a sustainable cultural change, by installing an electricity grid that would mainly powered by renewable resource. Buckland points out that Cape Farewell has switched its attention from raising awareness to searching for solutions. In the end, Buckland concludes that the expedition itself is becoming part of the solutions required to boost optimism of moving forward in the climate change movement.

Buckland, D. (2012). "Climate is culture." Nature Climate Change 2: 137-140. http://www.capefarewell.com/downloads/nclimate1420.pdf

Climate Change Mitigation in Children's Poems
by Yijing Zhang

By analyzing children's poems, Peter Makwanya (2014) argued that the young generation should be placed on the center of the climate change adaptation and mitigation, because they are the most important stakeholders in the environmental issues. They are not only the inheritors of the world, but also the designers who shape the present form. Makwanya started by pointing out that although most people recognize that children play a role in climate change adaptation, children are not officially involved in the issue. Most of the climate issues are articulated for adults instead of modified for children's views. The paper offers a general background for poetry analysis, bringing focus on how children's participation can improve environmental sustainability.

According to Makwanya, there are two theories that are significant to the poetry study, eco-criticism and eco-linguistics. Eco-criticism is defined as the study of relationship between poetry and natural environment. Eco-linguistics is the study of relationship between language used and environment. As poetry device is designed to create a moving effect and to evoke feelings, images and thoughts, analysis of children's poem was focused on its communicative functions.

In Makwanya's research, critical discourse analysis (CDA) and eco-criticism were used to explain children's poems and to clarify the hidden assumptions behind these poems. Six poems were selected for analysis. The poems "Worry Mother Nature" and "Vegetation and Environment" both pointed out that children have conservation ideas, and they care about the environment as well. In the poem "Mother Nature", children talked about land degradation and the possible solutions. Another poem complained about the overwhelming propaganda of environmental protection while there were little real actions taken. Therefore, children showed a strong commitment to coordinate activities and work as initiators of a change. The analysis indicated that children's participation is critical for a sustainable future.

To conclude, children deserve the recognition of capable analyzers and indispensable communicators of risk in the climate change because their literature can promote climate change mitigation awareness among their young readers.

Makwanya, P., & Dick, M. (2014). An Analysis of Children's Poems in Environment and Climate Change Adaptation and Mitigation: A Participatory Approach, Catching Them Young. American Journal of Social Science and Humanities,1, 43-49.

Power of Mass Media in Climate Change
by Yijing Zhang

According to Corbett (2015), as the power of media lies in the complicated interactions among news-shapers, journalists, and readers, it is better to analyze news at a macro-level in both production and consumption.

Most scholars currently focus their research on media-effects, which they study how news content has an influence on audience, although its effect is very limited. The only condition for media effects to be effective is when the content is relatively unfamiliar to readers. For instance, climate change is the topic that most readers do not have direct experience with. Another effect tested is agenda setting. It points out that the news does not tell audiences what to think but tells readers what to think about. Thus, media has the power of shaping people's ideas and enlarging social concern, even though the effect lasts for short time duration. However, news produced by journalists is not independently set up. Instead, institutions with powerful social status usually supply news agenda to feed journalists.

Framing theory indicates that the way news is framed can affect readers' understanding and viewpoints. Researches on climate change media coverage show that keywords for climate issues are uncertainty, blame, and responsibility. Yet, Corbett argues that those studies on framing theories only tested the correlations between media content and framing schema, but not between readers and framing. Therefore, it would be inaccurate to conclude that media power is solely due to framing theories.

In addition, there is a lack of research on what or who is shaping news production. Corbett thinks that there is a mixture of people with various degrees of economic and social resources. In an analysis studying factors influencing the US public's opinion on climate change, most media coverage is related to economic and political elements. Politicians and others with an economic agenda people have put pressure on newsrooms to report news in their interest. Although media has long been considered as a guard dog for the public, Corbett suggests that half of the news content is the production of some interested party. The news institute, taking the role of guard dog, faces the difficulty of finding equilibrium between reporting news for interested group and reporting in the public interest. Only when the media finds the equilibrium, can it play at its greatest power to push social change.

Corbett, B. Julia (2015). "Media Power and Climate Change" Nature Climate Change 288-290.

ETHICS, RELIGION, AND CLIMATE CHANGE

Unexpected Ethical Limits to Climate Change Adaptation
by Caroline Chmiel

Typical analysis of the limits to adapting to climate change revolves around biological, economic, or technological thresholds. Interestingly, the latest research acknowledges that limits may largely revolve around society, "contingent on ethics, knowledge, attitudes to risk and culture". Adaptation to climate change is an ever-changing conversation, but a crucial one. The UN Framework Convention on Climate Change created the objective of showing that adaption to climate change in relation to food, ecosystems, and economic development will happen. This paper argues, first, that adaptation limits depend on goals, which are truly dependent on diverse values. So, the ethics and values held by actors in society affect their decision-making around adaption, and can act as limits. Next, a lack of knowledge and foresight of future climate changes may inhibit adaptation. Social and individual factors may also limit adaptation in the form of risk denial and perception. Lastly, culture can be a huge threat to adaptation in the undervaluation of involuntary loss of places and culture. Cultural assets are unique, so loss of assets that are irreversible, but culture values also change over time so may become less limiting.

Typical scientific limits of adaptation stem from the assumption that successful adaptation to the changes in our climate will be restricted by limiting factors beyond which acclimation will not be possible. But, the challenging view here is that society and its perceptions, values, structures, and ways prevent adaptation can be changed. Depending on standards and values in one country versus another, there may be different limits. The role of ethics and its diverse goals, the lack of exact knowledge about the future, the risk perceptions society holds, and the extent to which places and cultures have value all contribute to different factors of adapting. The crucial understanding here revolves around not being limited by just exogenous forces like physical and ecological limits. The ability to adapt can be determined by availability of technology and capacity to learn, but even more so by the treatment of people and places through ethics.

Adger, W. Neil, Suraje Dessai, Marisa Goulden, Mike Hulme, Irene Lorenzoni, Donald R. Nelson, Lars Otto Naess, Johanna Wolf, Anita Wreford. "Are there social limits to adaptation to climate change?" Climatic Change Volume 93, Issue 3-4 (2009) 335-354.

Climate Change and Meat Consumption Values
by Juana Granados

With the increase of greenhouse gas production every year and the growth of industrialized animal production, climate change mitigation in Western countries has become overly expensive. The world population continues to grow as farms resort to animal production increase because it provides the most income. Bread, once the protein of the west, has now been replaced by high demands of meat, the new protein. De Boer (2012) argues that climate change mitigation costs can be reduced by as much as 50% in 2050 if people choose at least one meal without meat weekly. The objective of de Boer's study was to see how consumers respond to eating less meat in the hopes of improving climate change mitigation. The study was focused on Netherland consumers who, on average, consume 87 kilograms of meat with bones per capita per year. Of the three hypotheses, the first predicted that there will be a negative correlation between the frequency of meat consumption and "universalism". Research has shown that "universalism," nature-related values, is strongly associated with vegetarians and people who consume very little meat. The second hypothesis was that the meat-free idea will be more accepted by those who value care for nature than those who do not. The last hypothesis was that the meat-free idea will be more accepted by those who do not question the seriousness of climate change in comparison to those who are skeptical and unaccepting. Survey participants consisted of a nationwide sample of 1,083 participants from the Netherlands. The results supported the first hypothesis, in which almost all of the participants were meat eaters not associated with a "universal" attitude. The second hypothesis supported the idea that the meat-free meal idea would be received more positively by consumers who value nature than those who do not. The third hypothesis was not supported because those who were serious about climate change did not significantly support the meat-free idea. Overall, the study concluded that although a change in meat-eating habits can lead to cheaper climate change mitigation, there can still be negative responses from consumers who are skeptical about climate change. Thus, there needs to be more specificity between climate change and meat consumption because it is not yet perceived as urgent. People do not want to self-sacrifice without a good reason.

De Boer, J., Schosler, H., Boersema, J.J. 2012. Climate change and meat eating: An inconvenient couple? Journal of Environment Psychology 33, 1-8.

Morality, Food Choices, and Climate Change
by Juana Granados

Is the concern for climate change a moral issue and can the intensity of your morality have an effect on your environmental engagement? Mäkiniemi *et al.* (2013) conducted a study to test how the environmental concern for food choice is affected by moral intensity. Moral intensity is measured through an evaluation of the positive or negative cost of the consequence, the probability of the effect, social correctness of the effect, time between the present and the time of the consequence, nearness (social, cultural, psychological, or physical) of the consequence, and the concentration of people affected by the effect. Generally, it was discovered that those who perceive climate change as a moral issue are more likely to support climate change mitigation. The present study measured how the six components of moral intensity positively influenced one's view and the overall likelihood of making climate-friendly food choices. A total of 350 Finnish students, 21% being vegetarian and 79% meat consumers, were given a questionnaire that measured the six components of moral intensity. Each statement was positively framed for climate change. Each component was ranked on a 1-7 scale of agreement, in which 1 meant completely disagree and 7 meant completely agree. The results indicated that the probable seriousness of consequences was the strongest measure of moral intensity. Unsurprisingly, the students who viewed making climate-friendly food choices as a serious consequence for the climate were more likely to make climate-unfriendly food choices. Furthermore, making climate-friendly food choices was strongly associated with moral evaluation, intention, and action. Thus, it was more likely that the magnitude of the perceived consequences is the most effective component in increasing participation for making climate-friendly food choices.

Mäkiniemi, J. P., Vainio, A. 2013. Moral intensity and climate-friendly food choices. Appetite 66, 54-61.

Is Relocation of Biota an Ethical Response to Climate Change?
by Brina Jablonski

As global warming continues to impact daily life for organisms on planet earth, organisms attempt to survive in these changing conditions by adapting or moving into a new environment but highways and cities prevent some species from crossing into higher latitudes and altitudes unaided. Habitat destruction, overhunting, and pollution also play a role in the destruction of certain species.

When animals and plants are not able to adapt quickly enough to the fluctuating environmental conditions caused by climate change, they perish. Humans have attempted to stop the extinction of species by creating parks and reserves but managed relocation (also known as assisted colonization, assisted migration) appears to be the more likely solution.

Managed relocation is a conservation strategy that involves the translocation of species to novel ecosystems in anticipation of range shifts forced by climate change. Ecologists and conservationists have concerns because of possible invasion and future genetic risks of relocating a species to a completely new environment. And, of course, there are many ethical and policy challenges that would come with moving an entire population.

Although managed relocation appears to be a more effective solution rather than no relocation whatsoever, this method of conservation is costly and could divert limited resources from more traditional conservation strategies. Furthermore, managed relocation will tax conservationists' financial and political capital. It is also important to note that there is no guarantee that the relocated species will survive in the new environment, which leaves the question if this method is actually an ethical way to deal with the situation at hand.

Minteer and Collins (2010) conclude that the only way to deal with the rapidly changing environment is to take a more hands-on approach to species conservation which involves redirecting funds towards more pragmatic and interventionist programs for conservation action. They believe the term "planetary manager" is an appropriate word to describe the role of human conservationists in the future. Overall, the two authors believe the key ethical and policy questions for the future of managed relocation should revolve around determining which are the appropriate candidate species, what legal actions are needed, how authorization will be obtained, what the motive is exactly, and what environmental responsibilities are at stake.

Minteer, B., Collins, J. 2010. Move it or lose it? The ecological ethics of relocating species under climate change? Ecological Applications, 20, 1801–1804.

Can Religion Help Save the Environment?
by JP Kiefer

Clingerman (2014) believes that geoengineering has the potential to solve the disaster of climate change. Geoengineering is the process of changing the environment through any one of many diverse methods, like solar radiation management or fertilizing the ocean to create algae blooms as a means of combating climate change. Each of these methods has unintended side effects, but can be summarized as cheap, fast, and imperfect ways of reducing the effects of greenhouse gasses on the environment.

A major criticism of geoengineering is that it is a form of man attempting to "play God" by directly manipulating the atmosphere. Another is that some religious individuals protest the idea that man cannot live in harmony with nature without technology. Clingerman states that while this may or may not be true, religion needs to play a larger, more informed role in this debate. Scientists and political leaders must realize the way religion might influence public perceptions of scientific progress. While most scientists stay away from religion professionally, as it exists outside of their area of expertise, Clingerman believes that religion needs to play a larger role to morally guide scientific progress.

One need to look no farther than Galileo to see how religious institutions have stood in the way of science in the past, but this calls for a more careful engagement between the two in the present. Clingerman believes that religion can help the wider public engage the science of climate change as it is currently understood, and geoengineering as mankind might undertake it if properly integrated into the discourse. Instead of religion pitting individuals against science, it could motivate them to endorse it if viewed from the right frame. Mankind's adjusting of the climate could be easily classified as a theological justification of human skill. When discussions of penance and conversion are added to the geoengineering debate, religion and science might come to a true consensus and properly motivate the public to act to solve this problem.

Clingerman and Obrien 2014. Playing God: Why religion belongs in the climate engineering debate. Bulletin of the Atomic Scientists, May 2014: 27-37

Our Responsibility to Regulate the Emissions of Airlines
by JP Kiefer

The governing body responsible for regulating greenhouse gas emissions in aircraft, the International Civil Aviation Organization, has not passed any significant greenhouse gas regulation over the past fourteen years despite the industry's contributions to climate change. Liu (2011), recognizes that there may be some technical reasons the ICAO has chosen not to do so, but ultimately states that the ICAO would be the proper organization to implement regulation if not for political issues within its leadership.

The ICAO's current policies regarding greenhouse gas emissions consist of improving fuel efficiency by two percent annually to 2050, capping greenhouse gas emissions from international aviation from 2020, and setting a global efficiency standard for aircraft engines in 2013. However, the two percent ICAO target "represents little above what is already happening," and the target to cap aviation emissions from 2020 is "merely a non-binding, aspirational goal." Furthermore, the ICAO disregards many factors contributing to the fuel efficiency of an aircraft, like weight, and focuses only on the engines of each plane.

The ICAO may choose not to regulate emissions due to the impact that constraining total emissions would have on the world. Reducing flying would affect individuals who must travel for business as well as harming international trade. This would especially impact the US and Japan, where about thirty percent of internationally traded merchandise is transported by air. Reducing the number of flights would also decrease job opportunities provided by airlines, airports, air manufacturers, and other related employers. Perhaps most significantly, the fuel efficiency of aircraft has steadily increased, with planes today seventy percent more fuel efficient than aircraft developed forty years ago. Despite this, the growth of the aviation industry has surpassed these technological improvements, and further steps need to be taken, according to Liu.

The ICAO has already set standards for environmental issues like aircraft noise, making it suitable to take a step towards establishing significant emission standards as well. Furthermore, the ICAO is one of the few organizations with enough scientific resources to implement policy effectively. It also is one of the few organizations with enough authority to regulate emissions without adversely affecting aircraft safety. The only problem with the ICAO's ability to proceed is its management. New standards can be proposed only by bodies within the ICAO, or other aviation-focused international organizations, with no room for environmental bodies to participate. These bodies within the ICAO are composed of 36 council members who represent the countries of most importance in air transport or who otherwise contribute significantly to the air transport industry. This not only leaves out any representation from countries that have little air travel but would be effected by climate change, but enables the council to avoid this environmental issue altogether. According to Liu, this shows that additional bodies need to join and pressure the ICAO in regulating greenhouse gas emissions in the future.

Liu, J., 2011. The Role of ICAO in Regulating the Greenhouse Gas Emissions of Aircraft. Carbon & Climate Law Review 4, 417-431

Dangers of Climate Change Denial
by JP Kiefer

While conspiracy theories are relatively common and well studied, very little research has been done investigating climate change conspiracy theories and their especially harmful nature. According to Douglas (2015), conspiracy theories tend to develop around global-scale events with enormous significance that individuals have trouble believing can be explained by mundane or ordinary details. Climate change fits this description perfectly, as science has shown that it is caused by small, common actions such as driving a car. Because of this, a number of climate change conspiracies have developed, such as that scientists have made up climate change for political reasons, to get research grants, or to help those who invested in green energy technology profit.

People have multiple, deep-seated reasons to believe in climate change conspiracies. Most people have an innate desire to believe they are moral beings with a bright future, a belief that is challenged by climate change. This problem is compounded when individuals who have a conspiracist view of the world are exposed to scientific evidence about climate change; researchers have shown that such exposure is more likely to polarize opinion, rather than informing it in the rational way. Climate change conspiracies are also more effective due to the few authoritative personalities who have backed them, such as professor of atmospheric science at Colorado State University, Bill Gray, or US Senator James Inhofe.

An additional unique factor of climate change conspiracies is that they exist on two different fronts. The better-known front of denying climate change exists on one side, while some conspiracies claim that climate change is underreported and covered up to some extent. No matter how plausible, the very existence of counter-conspiracies displays the corrosive and recursive nature of conspiracy theorizing.

Climate change conspiracies create a climate of uncertainty and mutual distrust, which undermines the possibility of rational debate and discourse about the appropriate policy response to scientific findings. At an extreme level, such conspiracies can paint a picture of being forced to pick between one of two extreme climate change conspiracies. While the average person might scoff at conspiracy theories, research has shown that people can be influenced by such theories without being aware that they have been persuaded. Exposure to conspiracy theories reduces people's intentions to reduce their carbon footprint. To help prevent this, Douglas suggests altering the factors associated with conspiracy belief. By removing the feelings of uncertainty, powerlessness, and political cynicism the reliance on conspiracy explanations could greatly diminish.

Douglas, K., and Sutton, R., 2015. Climate Change: Why the Conspiracy Theories are Dangerous. Bulletin of the Atomic Scientists 71, 98-106.

Aerospace Engineer Receives Corporate Funding to Create Climate Change Confusion
by Chloe Rodman

Justin Gillis and John Schwartz (2015) write for the New York Times about recently released documents that connect Aerospace Engineer Wei-Hock (Willie) Soon's scientific findings on climate change to $1.2 million he has received from a variety of fossil fuel corporations in the past ten years. Many climate-denying politicians in Congress cite Soon's research papers when arguing against emission reduction legislation. Soon, a scientist at the Harvard-Smithsonian Center for Astrophysics declares that the varying energy of the sun is causing climate change and not human created greenhouse emissions. Even though Soon has always denied the link between his work and corporate funding, in the recent publicized documents, he refers to many of his papers, as well as a few congressional testimonies, as deliverables—works he completed for money.

Because the Smithsonian is a government agency, two allied organizations, Greenpeace and the Climate Investigators Center, were able to obtain these documents through the Freedom of Information Act. Shortly after they obtained these documents, the two environmental groups shared them with the press. These documents showed that approximately $409,000 of Soon's funding came from Southern Company Services, one of the biggest utility holding corporations in the United States, which also has enormous investments in coal burning power plants. The Aerospace Engineer has also received $230,000 from the chartable foundation of Charles G. Koch, whose affluence arouse from oil refining. While Exxon and the American Petroleum Institute no longer support Soon, he receives large sums from DonorsTrust, an organization that receives money from anonymous donors and then distributes it to conservative causes.

While many of Soon's supporters refer to him as a 'Harvard Astrophysicist,' he is not an employee of Harvard University, nor is he an astrophysicist—Soon is an aerospace engineer with little climatology experience. Climate experts who have reviewed Soon's work argue that he uses old data, completely disregards greenhouse gases created by humans, and publishes false correlations between the sun and climate change. While Soon argues that the sun is the primary cause of climate change, The Goddard Institute of Space Studies, a division of NASA that specializes in climate change, maintains that variation of the sun's output is accountable for a mere 10% of global warming.

The fact that Soon's funding was not disclosed in any of his works, which is required by the modern standard of publishing, angered not only the many journals that published his work but also Soon's associates at the Harvard-Smithsonian Center. The Center has released a statement saying that they agree with the scientific consensus regarding climate change and plan to continue the investigation regarding Soon's work and funding.

Gillis, J., Schwartz, J. 2015. Deeper Ties to Corporate Cash for Doubtful Climate Researcher. http://nyti.ms/1LzSaDM

Pope Francis Plans to Tackle Climate Change
by Chloe Rodman

John Vidal (December, 2014) reports for The Guardian on the Pope's future plans to combat climate change around the world. This year, Pope Francis will address his fellow Catholics as well as the ambassadors of the United Nations regarding climate change. The Pope also plans to attend and play an influential role in the Paris climate talks held in December. This convention has the lofty goal of ending 20 years of controversy about climate change and hopes to finalize a solution to stop global warming from spiraling out of control. In addition to attending the conference, Pope Francis also wishes to meet with various religious leaders around the world so that both political and religious realms will be informed about upcoming changes. He will spend time in New York City during his UN address lobbying these two spheres.

The Pope will write a 60-page encyclical addressing climate change. His message is simple: science has proven that climate conditions are getting worse, and everyone needs to do their part to fight against global warming because it is the ethical thing to do. He will distribute this message to his priests and bishops so all Catholics will hear this message.

Other bishops around the world are begging wealthier countries to start the movement, warning that if action isn't taken soon, there will be dire, global consequences. However, not all Bishops feel this way. It is anticipated that there will be much opposition by conservative Catholic United States politicians as well as conservative members of the Vatican. Many important Republican congress members are climate change skeptics, as are members of the Vatican such as Cardinal George Pell, head of the Vatican's budget. These people believe that the Pope shouldn't be meddling in political or environmental affairs. Even more extreme groups like the Cornwall Alliance for the Stewardship of Creation believe the words of Pope Francis are going against the bible and against God.

Vidal, J. 2014, Pope Francis's Edict on Climate Change Will Anger Deniers and US Churches. The Guardian. http://bit.ly/1IY50vM

Morality, Ethics, and Values of Climate Change-Related Decision-Making
by Russell Salazar

What must a socially responsible organization do in the midst of a changing climate? Besio and Pronzini (2014) write that discourse on climate change has been transforming into a moral debate, and businesses and organizations must react. They take a closer look at the use of morality as a communicative tool, and analyze its relationship with the decision-making processes of organizations with regard to sustainability.

Reactions to moral pressures, are not as straightforward as one may think. Morality has essentially become a communicative tool; society communicates disapproval of particular behaviors to firms, and firms respond and change to place themselves back into a good light. This communication can sometimes result in profound differences in the operations of businesses, contributing greatly to the mitigation of climate change. On the other hand, firms can utilize this form of communication as a means of gaining popularity, employing a façade that does not work directly toward (and could, in some cases, work against) mitigating climate change.

There is clear heterogeneity in the responses of businesses to the societal push for sustainability as a moral practice. The authors attempt to understand these responses by providing a theoretical framework for the interactions between a firm's decision-making and changing moral values. They state, "One can observe that these entities transform values into something with which they can cope." Companies will take on sustainability practices if they result in greater efficiency and saved costs in the long term. Businesses will also publish their 'responsible' efforts and present them as a marketing strategy, if it can have the effect of raising demand. However, if a moral value runs against economic logic, other tactics may be employed to divert the attention of the masses; the use of morality could incentivize potentially detrimental outcomes. The use of morality as a mechanism for societal momentum toward climate change mitigation is not necessarily an effective strategy. Besio and Pronzini therefore argue for a more sociological approach to investigations on the risks and benefits of morality in the fight against climate change.

Besio, C., Pronzini, A., 2014. Morality, Ethics, and Values Outside and Inside Organizations: An Example of the Discourse on Climate Change. Journal of Business Ethics 119, 287–300.

Who's to Blame for Climate Change?
by Breanna Sewell

Blame is one aspect of global climate change that is a bit of a touchy subject. In Peter Rudiak-Gould's 2014 article, "Climate Change and Accusation: Global Warming and Local Blame in a Small Island State," he addresses the two types of blame for climate change. Specifically, he looks at the potential causes and effects for the accusation that occurs regarding climate change in the small, Pacific Marshall Islands.

The author first points out the two accepted types of blame for what is happening to our planet. The first is "industrial blame"— the indictment of developed countries and their citizens, specifically the Northern, Western civilizations. The second being "universal blame"— the viewpoint that we are all contributors to climate change and therefore we are all equally responsible for what is occurring.

The Republic of the Marshall Islands has only 60,000 citizens and was responsible for only 0.0003% of the world's carbon emissions in 2008. However, the author points out that surveys and studies have been done showing that the Marshellese surprisingly take the side of "universal blame." One of the countries in the world that could most objectively be seen as a victim of climate change is taking equal blame for climate change and the ugly effects that go along with it, such as sea levels that will eventually drown their home, the destruction of their coral reefs, increased intensity of droughts and extreme weather, and much more.

After many studies of the Marshall Islands and surveys taken by ethnographers of its citizens, the conclusion has been drawn that the Marshallese are so inclined to take the blame for climate change and the destruction of their home as a method to get their citizens to realize that following western civilization will result in their downfall. They are desperate to get back to their roots and pick up traditions that were tossed aside when they were introduced to the western ways and their cultural decline began. If Marshall Island citizens take equal blame for climate change, it means making a connection between their relatively new western ways and the effects on their cherished islands and will urge them to get back to their old, eco-friendly lifestyle. Mitigating the effects of climate change would just be the icing on the cake, while restoring their beloved traditions is the main goal.

Rudiak-Gould, P., 2014. Climate Change and Accusation: Global Warming and Local Blame in a Small Island State. Chicago Journals. http://bit.ly/1MWzlMQ

Why Enviroethics?
by Breanna Sewell

Marjan Laal lays out the basic concepts and the historical background of environmental ethics in her 2009 paper, "A Brief History of Enviroethics and Its Challenges." Laal begins by defining environmental ethics as a branch of environmental philosophy which accounts for more than just the typical ethical concern; extending to the ethics of the non-human world. She then explains that traditional views on ethics as a whole are anthropocentric, which means they are centered on humans and their wants and needs; something's importance can be measured by its utility to us.

According to Laal, the distinction between intrinsic and instrumental value has been of great import to the enviroethic discussion. Instrumental value is a measure of a thing's worth based on its usefulness; its capability and utility. Intrinsic value, on the other hand, is a measure of a thing's worth regardless of its usefulness to us.

Laal explains that after the scientific community's recognition of the varied and catastrophic effects that had and would result from climate change, along with their acknowledgement of a need for a change of values of society in regards to the environment back around the 1970s, resulted in a new branch of philosophy known as environmental ethics. Environmental ethics, according to Laal, has been known to advocate for the image of one's self in connection with the environment so as to bring about both an awareness of and an appreciation for it.

71

The author also states in her conclusion that traditional western ethics has the tendency to "wrongly" evaluate a thing's value in terms of its utility to us. She asserts that environmental ethics takes the proper approach to measuring worth, as it places an emphasis on the intrinsic value, rather than the instrumental value, of the non-human world, paying no mind to its usefulness to us humans.

Laal, M., 2009. A Brief History of Enviroethics and Its Challenges. Journal of Medical Ethics and History of Medicine. http://bit.ly/1DDxLxJ

More Consideration for Non-Humans in Public Health

by Breanna Sewell

Johan Mackenbach advocates for non-humans and for a new approach to public health in his 2007 article, "Public Health Ethics in Times of Global Environmental Change: Time to Look Beyond Human Interests." He begins by pointing out the immense decrease in biodiversity of our planet (i.e. the mass extinction of species) due to "habitat destruction, introduction of invasive non-native species, pollution of air, water, and soil, and over-harvesting by hunting and fishing." He provides stats which show that if "current trends of habitat destruction continue, half of all living species may disappear in the coming 50 to 100 years." This is a reminder that the pressure we as a society are putting on the environment is causing not only global warming, but also a shockingly high extinction rate for our planet's non-human inhabitants.

Mackenbach then addresses the anthropocentric nature of our public health system, writing that utilitarianism is the basis for our medical and public health ethics. He sees this as a flaw because of utilitarianism's inherent goal to promote "the greatest happiness of the greatest number." According to the author, since human health seems to count for more than non-human health per being, utilitarianism is not ideal for the well-being of other species.

Mackenbach then explains that it is part of our nature to put our own interests in mind, that we are programmed to populate the earth. This makes it so that we weigh everything else's value in terms of its utility to us, unfortunately. No matter what, humans will always come first, because of our inherent survivalist mentality.

The author concludes with a proposal that public health ethics should be reconstructed in an ecologically friendly way. He also asserts his opinion that if we are to preserve our global environment and protect its biodiversity, we must put the brakes on human development.

Mackenbach, J., 2007. Public Health Ethics in Times of Global Environmental Change: Time to Look Beyond Human Interests. Scandinavian Journal of Public Health. http://bit.ly/1b8L90t

Relationships Between Religion and Climate Change
by Sarah Whitney

The Journal of Religious History (2013) reviewed a collection of several articles and volumes by Sigurd Bergmann and Dieter Gerten describing the importance of engagement with religion from the global climate change community. The authors state that these selected volumes provide valuable evidence that the climate change community should consider cultural and ethical values represented in local religions. These subjects are currently excluded from the Intergovernmental Panel on Climate Change and most other discussions on global climate change efforts. These volumes also offer significant insight into the relationship between religion and climate change by showing that communities who are immediately threatened by climate change are adapting their beliefs and actions.

The Parliament of World's Religions was held in December of 2009 at coincidentally the same time as the United Nation's Climate Change Conference in Copenhagen. This occurrence prompted religious leaders from all over the world to directly address political leaders as they wrote about their reassurance and concerns regarding climate change. Even though the outcome may not have been effective, connecting these two groups was beneficial as it united people with an extreme diversity of beliefs to think about one common problem. It demonstrated the potentially large role of religion to promote sustainability and various green practices. Both Sigurd Bergmann and Dieter Gerten believe that an interdisciplinary approach is fundamental to addressing the complex issue of global climate change.

Since the interaction of this conference, studies and classes have developed regarding religion and the environment. In their works, Bergmann and Gerten focus on climate change with an anthropological lens. They state that the United States Evangelist church shelters conservatives. Noting specific incidents, like the number of degrees the global temperature has increased and its effects, help conservatives join the cause as they see exactly how communities are hurting. Conservatives focus on the impact of climate change on vulnerable local communities who are currently experiencing the effects of global warming. Such evidence is prompting different interpretations of Christian ideology and traditions, and sparking interest in the community.

Bergmann, S., Gerten, D., 2013. Religion and Dangerous Environmental Change: Transdisciplinary Perspectives on the Ethics of Climate and Sustainability. Journal of Religious History, Religious History Association. http://bit.ly/1KtnZjR

Why do Museums Censor Climate Change Exhibits?
by Sarah Whitney

Anna Kuchment (2014) analyzes the lack of information of climate change in natural science museums across the nation through the incident at Perot Museum of Nature and Science in Dallas, Texas. The Perot Museum omitted a panel display in the air and water geology exhibit that explained how the burning of fossil fuels and increased concentrations of carbon dioxide in the atmosphere contribute to global climate change. The Vice President of the museum, Steve Hinkley, says that the panel went missing sometime in the bustle before the opening of the museum in 2012. Kuchment is skeptical of the Perot Museum's actions and uses this occurrence to explain the reasons why natural science museums across the nation avoid the topic of climate change.

According to Kuchment, there are three key barriers of presenting climate change to the public. First, climate change is a progressing topic that is constantly changing with new information and statistics. The rapid pace of new findings in comparison to the time it takes to fund and create an exhibit is impractical for most museums. Second, museums find that presenting global warming in a clear and engaging way an enigma. The issue of climate change is so vast and overwhelming that it leaves viewers upset and confused. Natural science museums are designed to be fun and engaging institutions, in which the public can interact and learn about natural processes. Climate change is such a broad and inherently negative subject that it does not fit with this style of public engagement. Finally, museums do not want to present controversial subjects because of their dependencies upon donors, visitors, and even political representatives. The Perot Museum of Nature and Science was given millions of dollars by both Trevor Rees-Jones, Chief Oil and Gas founder, and the Exxon Mobil CEO. Not to mention, Texas has economically boomed for its natural gas and oil industry. Museums do not want to upset their audience or donors who support their business.

On the other hand, a study conducted by Anthony Leiserowitz states that 73% of museum visitors want to know more about climate change from these trusted institutions. After receiving this statistic, Leiserowitz started the Yale Project on Climate Change Communication to increase the content of global warming in museums across the country. Other organizations like the National Network for Ocean and Climate Change Interpretation have increased the content in displays, such as incorporating ocean acidification from carbon dioxide absorption, in over 70 institutions around the US Some museums have begun educating their staff about global warming to be able to inform inquisitive attendees. They also have found it beneficial to post about the subject in detail on their websites. Museums have utilized the topic of climate change in traveling exhibitions or as small nuggets of information that are apart of larger exhibits. Kuchment says the key is to frame the subject positively with humans' use of innovation and creativity to adapt as the backbone to each display.

Kuchment, A., 2014. Museums Tip-Toe Around Climate Change. The Dallas Morning News. General News.
http://bit.ly/1Q59MIf

PERCEPTIONS OF CLIMATE CHANGE

NASA Claims the Earth has a Fever
by Jordan Aronowitz

Even though NASA has been seeing diminished funding for space exploration, they are using their well-respected position in the world of science to educate the country about climate change. NASA's specialized YouTube channel, titled "NASA Climate Change," combines their global outreach and household name to connect with people about climate change in a more entertaining form than most media. One of their recent videos, titled "NASA's Earth Minute: Earth Has a Fever," highlights the effects of the planet's recent temperature changes. Using animations, they articulate how these seemingly small changes will drastically affect the earth in the near future. Overall, these new strategies by NASA are a good answer to informing the general population about the dangers of climate change in a stimulating and straightforward fashion.

Simple analogies are the easiest way to connect with audiences of all ages and backgrounds. The narrator from NASA explains that as snow and ice melt: "What's left behind are darker patches of land and water." The narrator then compares these dark patches to a man wearing a black shirt on a hot day. They both attract more heat than if they were a light color. In effect, the earth heats up more overall, harming the planet through a rise in the sea level and an increase in the severity of hurricanes. A parallel like this connects the viewer to the issue and enables him to actually comprehend the meaning of the changes in the earth's climate.

NASA's goal is to help us understand the hazards our planet will face if we continue to ignore global warming.

Videos like "Earth Has a Fever" are released about every two weeks and receive an average of 10,000 views. Hopefully NASA will continue to use their well-respected position in the world of science to inform our country about the dangers caused by climate change.

NASA Climate Change. (2014, October 2). NASA's Earth Minute: Earth Has a Fever [Video file]. Retrieved from http://bit.ly/1cV9R4P

Decision Makers—the Keys to Corporate Involvement in Climate Change
by Brendan Busch

As the effects of climate change become more visible in everyday life, some businesses are preparing to adapt to the new challenges that climate change will bring. However, some companies still deny the existence of climate change and have failed to prepare for its effects. This begs the question, why are some companies more likely than others to prepare for climate change adaptation? In their article "Executives' engagement with climate science and perceived need for business adaptation to climate change," Martina K. Linnenluecke and Andrew Griffiths (professors at the University of Queensland Business School), along with Peter J. Mumby (a professor at the University of Queensland School of Biological Sciences) highlight the importance of powerful executives in the management of business, and hypothesize that executives who are willing to read scientific literature are more likely to perceive their company's vulnerability to climate change and propose adaptation action.

In order to test this hypothesis, Linnenluecke, Griffiths, and Mumby conducted a survey of 125 executives from Australia's top 500 companies. After asking these executives about their exposure to scientific literature, their opinions on climate change, and their perceived risk of climate change as a threat to their business, Linnenluecke, Griffiths, and Mumby concluded that there is a significant correlation between the utilization of scientific information sources by decision-makers and their perceived vulnerability of their company

78

to the effects of climate change. While this result may at first appear trivial, Linnenluecke, Griffiths, and Mumby believe that it could be the key to increasing business's involvement in climate change issues. By making it easier for important corporate executives to access accurate scientific research about climate change and by showing the negative impacts that climate change will have on their companies, the scientific community has the opportunity to greatly increase the business world's involvement in climate change issues. This presents a promising opportunity to climate change activists; instead of changing the minds of the masses, as is necessary in politics, activists only need to persuade a select few executives to have an effect in the business world. Therefore, Linnenluecke, Griffiths, and Mumby strongly recommend working towards more effective communication between the academic and business worlds.

Linnenluecke, M. K., Griffiths, A., & Mumby, P. J. (2015). Executives' engagement with climate science and perceived need for business adaptation to climate change. Climatic Change, March 2015, 1-13.

Climate Change Adaptation—Lessening the Perceived Risk of Climate Change?

by Brendan Busch

As the future effects of climate change become more certain, it is clear that adaption to new climate conditions will be a necessity. However, will these plans for adaptation dissuade people from trying to prevent climate change? In their article "Does Learning About Climate Change Adaptation Change Support For Mitigation?" Amanda R. Carrico, Heather Barnes Truelove, Michael P. Vandenbergh, and David Dana (researchers and professors at the University of Colorado at Boulder, University of North Florida, Vanderbilt University Law School, and Northwestern University School of Law, respectively) attempt to determine if a focus on adaptation has adverse effects on the public's support of preventative climate change measures. Through psychological experimentation, this study tests the hypothesis held by some policy makers and scholars that learning about potential adaptation techniques may reduce the public's perceived risk about climate change, and thus lessen their willingness to fight against it.

In order to test this theory, Carrico, Truelove, Vandenbergh, and Dana assembled three different groups of random test subjects and gave each group a different fake news article. The three articles were nearly identical, with the exception that the first group's article had a focus on climate change prevention, the second group's had a focus on adaptation to climate change, and the third group's had no mention of climate change at all (so that they could serve as a control group). After reading their article, the members of each group answered an identical survey that determined their demographic information (such as political identification and age), the level of their support for climate change mitigation policies, and their perceived risk of climate change. Carrico, Truelove, Vandenbergh, and Dana then compared the results of these surveys to identify if exposure to adaptation policies had a significant on people's support for climate change mitigation. The experiment was performed twice, with two different sets of articles.

The results of the experiment showed very little difference in support for climate change mitigation policies between the group reading the adaptation-focused article and the group reading the mitigation-focused article. However, the demographic information on the survey did reveal one important distinction in the results: regardless of their assigned group, liberals had much more support for climate-change related policies than conservatives. This suggests that political affiliation had a far greater effect on the subjects' opinions than the researchers' attempts to prime the subjects with exposure to different types of climate change literature. However, in no subset of political affiliation did exposure to climate change adaptation cause a decrease in support for climate change mitigation (and in political moderates, a slight increase in support was indicated), effectively debunking the theories of those fearful of wide publication of climate change adaptation strategies.

Carrico, A.R., Truelove, H. B., Vandenbergh, M. P., & Dana, D., 2014. Does learning about climate change adaptation change support for mitigation? Journal of Environmental Psychology, 41, 19-29.

Climate Change Denial and the Great Recession
by Brendan Busch

In spite of the desperate efforts of the scientific community, public belief in the reality of climate change has been declining over the past few years. While several possible causes have been attributed to this phenomenon, Lyle Scruggs and Salil Benegal believe that the Great Recession is the root of the issue. In their article "Declining public concern about climate change: Can we blame the great recession?", Scruggs (a political science professor at the University of Connecticut) and Benegal (a graduate student researching political science at the University of Connecticut) analyzed the effects of economic conditions on the public's views on climate change in both the United States and Europe. Their research revealed a striking correlation between the condition of the economy and the prevalence of climate skepticism in society.

By studying the Gallup survey, a series of climate change-related questions asked at regular intervals over the past two decades, Scruggs and Benegal were able to gauge the change in people's opinions of climate change over time. They found that, regardless of the wording of the question, people's certainty of climate change plummeted between 2007 and 2011, coinciding perfectly with the timing of the Great Recession. Furthermore, looking at a broader history of the United States, Scruggs and Benegal discovered there was a strong negative correlation between the unemployment rate and American's belief in climate change; as the job market grows more bleak, people become less willing to believe in climate change. After examining similar studies in Europe, Scruggs and Benegal realized that this trend was not confined to the United States. Even though Europe tends to have a higher level of support for action on climate change-related issues than the United States, they experienced a similar downturn in climate change belief following the 2007-2008 economic crisis, indicating that this could be an international issue.

Scruggs and Benegal have come up with a theory as to why climate change belief could be tied to a country's economic wellbeing. First, they refute the idea that Americans are being swayed by climate-denying media output on an intellectual basis alone. Instead, they contest that the grim economic state of the nation has forced Americans to reconsider their priorities. Their immediate need for economic security causes them to devalue their support for climate change action, as they view these two prospects as mutually exclusive. In order to morally justify this change in priorities, Americans have to change their beliefs as well, and actively look for evidence to support the idea that climate change is not a real threat. Therefore, because Americans view an economic crisis as a bigger threat than climate change, they will try to deny the existence of climate change, so as not to conflict with their urgent need for economic recovery. Therefore, failing to recognize the economic element of climate change denial and trying to sway people's opinions with only scientific evidence could hinder the climate mitigation movement. Instead (although they believe that support for traditional climate change action will eventually increase as the economy improves), Scruggs and Benegal recommend crafting new climate change policies in ways that will either positively or negligibly affect the economy, as this will not conflict with Americans' temporarily shifted priorities and will be more likely to be passed into law.

Scruggs, L., & Benegal S. 2012. Declining public concern about climate change: Can we blame the great recession? Global Environmental Change, 22, 505-515.

Australia's Nuclear Power Dilemma
by Caroline Chmiel

Environmentalists in Australia strongly see nuclear energy as a crucial alternative to burning fossil fuels, especially because of its low-carbon emissions. A study conducted in in 2010, and then again in 2011 reveals the

Australian public's changing views on nuclear power in relation to climate change. Post-Fukushima, the majority of respondents (40%) said they would not accept nuclear power as an option to help tackle climate change, though most Australians still believed nuclear power to be a cleaner, more efficient option than coal which dominates their energy production. Previously, the survey in 2010 showed a majority (42%) responding with a sentiment of willingness to accept nuclear power if it would help address climate change.

Australia's apparent distrust in nuclear power will make the country as a whole more vulnerable to climate change because of the reliance on fossil fuels. Australia is extremely susceptible to disruption due to changing climate, recently experiencing drought, bushfires, floods, tropical cyclones and heat waves. Impacts of these events have been extreme water restrictions and huge government spending on repairing and supporting victims and affected areas. Ironically, as nearly three-quarters of Australians believe the climate of the world is changing, citizens seem less concerned with taking new measures against climate change. Surveys find Australians becoming more favorable towards the use of coal for energy than in past years. Again and again, studies find people will not allow a reduction of standard of living to help reduce future harm. Interestingly in the case of Australia, the fear of nuclear energy comes from the potential for its harm in the future, while climate change will most definitely cause harm to the future. The benefits of nuclear energy should therefore practically outweigh the risks, but polling suggest otherwise.

Finally, Australia continues to be the world's largest exporter of coal, providing many jobs and economic growth to the country. This stability is difficult to abandon and leaves scientists looking for new technological options in fighting climate change. Scientists believe that, despite the reliance on coal, Australia has many gas, wind, solar and high grade uranium oxide options that will cost much less than in most countries.

Bird, Deanne K., Katharine Haynes, Rob Van Den Honert, John Mcaneney, and Wouter Poortinga. "Nuclear Power in Australia: A Comparative Analysis of Public Opinion regarding Climate Change and the Fukushima Disaster." Energy Policy 65 (2014): 644-53. Print.

Changing Mindsets on Carbon Sequestration Technologies
by Caroline Chmiel

As "decarbonization" as a worldwide initiative continues to spread, scientists and governments have an increased interest in Carbon Capture and Storage (CCS) technologies. CCS technology involves capturing CO_2 emissions at the industrial combustion sources, compressing it for transportation and transporting it (via pipelines) to an appropriate geological site into which it is injected for long-term storage. Focus groups in London reveal the psychology behind differing opinions on energy. Nuclear power strongly shapes the critical argument in these studies. The general consensus of these findings argues there is little public anxiety concerning this technology, but in private, opinions are overall negative. To start, research shows awareness of CCS amongst non-specialist groups is small. Once briefly introduced to the concept, perceptions immediately took a negative attitude revolving around the risks being higher than benefits. In addition, this paper defines the concept of a 'moral hazard' in regards to CCS as risks associated with technology or continued reliance on fossil fuels when investment needs to completely shift to renewable technologies. The UK national planning policy says that "CO_2 emissions are not reasons to prohibit the consenting of projects which use these technologies" therefore endorsing the potential for technology beyond the demonstration stage. Returning to public opinion, when CCS is perceived in this manner of bridging technology that will not reduce invests in renewable technology, acceptance is at its highest. When people believe the government doesn't have an interest in the outcome and public involvement is valued on the topic of climate change and CCS, people are also more open.

Making the psychological task of opening people to CCS more difficult is the concept that knowing more about a particular technology does not necessarily mean that someone will be more supportive or enthusiastic about it. Regardless, researchers know few people will ever interact with this technology, but still be able to have an opinion. To change and influence these semi-blind thoughts, scientists note the need of opinion makers and rise of family and friend conversations. Currently, people interviewed tend to make opinions on CCS in the manner of trade-offs in comparisons to other renewable technologies. The public must engage with CCS technology to give it a wide role in energy conversation. Lastly, a mental dichotomy appeared in the public where technologies are split between 'good', 'natural' and commonsense technologies (i.e. wind turbines) and 'bad', 'unnatural' and industrialized technologies (i.e. nuclear power). CCS being pushed into the 'nuclear' category automatically impedes its potential power and image.

Lock, Simon J., Melanie Smallman, Maria Lee, and Yvonne Rydin. "'Nuclear Energy Sounded Wonderful 40 Years Ago": UK Citizen Views on CCS." Energy Policy (2014): 428-35. Web. 5 Apr. 2015.

Just How Pristine *Are* Virgin Rainforests?
by Jackson Cooney

There has been recent controversy over the state of many pristine rain forests. Those that have previously been called "virgin" due to the absence of human interaction are now being reviewed. It seems that humans have inhabited forests such the Amazon Basin, the lowland Congo basin, and the Indo-Malay region of Southeast Asia for many years. Evidence of human presence in these virgin forests includes pottery fragments, charcoal soil lairs, and iron tools. Because of this, there is little doubt of the presence of human civilizations in these lands. The question becomes: how has their presence affected the forests ability to prevail. These natives have used slash and burn techniques to create agriculture space, which has been largely thought of as the most harmful deforestation methods in recent times. It seems that the presence of humans on these lands about 2,500 years ago has actually enhanced the soil fertility due to this burning method. Human intervention and management of the land may have also caused an increase in tree diversity.

The human intervention seems to have given the forests a better advantage with "terra preta" soil, a soil with an abundance of nutrients that fosters tree growth. The one factor that is needed to increase the forests wellbeing seems to be time after human interaction. The forests need adequate time to recover form the loss of hectares due to the slash and burn methods. However, as proven by these virgin forests, the current forests occupied by humans should be able to regrow to their full potential with sufficient time. These newly discovered facts could help rainforest conservationists by providing them with information on the time it takes for forests to regenerate after humans leave and the likely composition of the new forests. These findings should give some relief to conservationists; however, it should not be used as an excuse to give up on rainforest conservation. Finally, rainforests being cleared should be allowed sufficient time to regenerate.

Willis, K. J., Gillson, L., Brncic, T. M. 2004. How "Virgin" Is Virgin Rainforest? Science, 304, 402-203.

NASA's Climate Change Awareness Program
by Jackson Cooney

NASA has been making an effort to bring awareness to climate change by hosting public events. For their 45th annual Earth Day celebration on April 17-22, NASA will be providing live and online activities to encourage the public to engage in these issues that are threatening our planet.

There are four events. The first, sponsored by Earth Day Network, involves a talk from NASA's administrator as well as hands on activities. The second event features satellite images of earth that display its beauty and NASA's data collection methods. At the end of the week, on April 22, NASA encourages people all over the world to go outside and take photos of the environment and post them on social media using the hashtag #NoPlaceLikeHome. This is their attempt to get people to appreciate the natural world and to become interested in protecting he environment. Later on April 22, The Global Learning and Observations to Benefit the Environment (GLOBE) hosts an online conversation for the public with scientists and educators to inform people of climate issues.

NASA has a unique ability to inform the public about climate problems. Their vantage point from satellites in space produces solid data on changes in global climate patterns, which allows us to increase our understanding of our planet. NASA is able to observe the Earth's interconnected natural systems and compare them to complete data sets from the past, allowing them to monitor changing conditions. They also collaborate with institutions around the world to obtain insight into how our planet changes and evolves. This information can then be shared with the public, furthering education on the realities of climate change. NASA's initiative to provide public events is a great way for people to learn about these issues.

Cole, S. (2015, April 14). NASA celebrates Earth Day with public events, online activities. Retrieved April 19, 2015, from http://climate.nasa.gov/news/2270/

Communicating Scientific Consensus on Climate Change
by Juana Granados

In a review of 12,500 scientific abstracts by Van der Linder *et al.* (2014), 97% accept the consensus position that climate change is caused by humans. On the other hand, only 42%, of Americans believe the idea that scientists regard global warming as real concern. To sort this out, the authors conducted a randomized online survey consisting of 1,104 people, aimed at reflecting the entire United States' population. Participants were told that they were going to be focusing on popular topics. Thus, a mix of topics were presented to hide the study's real objective. Two separate tests, both asking the same question about the certainty of climate change's occurrence were conducted. The first was in the form of a simple opinion poll while the second consisted of descriptive text, belief vs. action metaphors, and pie charts. This experiment was done with the thought that the communication of climate change using the three forms of presentation could significantly increase people's understandings of the scientific consensus. The highest percentage of agreement was evident in the pie charts and descriptive text compared to a bland research paper. The descriptive text generated a slight increase in agreement of the scientific consensus with an increase of 17.88% that was not statistically significant. The metaphor, which is frequently used in climate change discourse, led to an increase of 11.91% that was also not significant and was ultimately the lowest of the three forms in both tests. The pie chart also resulted in an increase of 14.38%. This increase was not significant but on average, the pie chart generated the highest pre-test and post-test percentage. Thus, a pie chart is the most useful way of communicating the scientific consensus on climate change because audiences like visuals, like a pie chart, and information that is easy to understand.

Van der Linden, S. L., Leiserowitz, A. A., Feinberg, G. D., & Maibach, E. W., 2014. How to communicate the scientific consensus on climate change: plain facts, pie charts or metaphors?. Climatic Change 126.1-2, 255-262. http://bit.ly/1GxuFLt

Climate Change Education Intervention
by Juana Granados

Can educating children about measures to mitigate climate change prevent it from becoming worse? In a study by Taber *et al.* (2009), 29 primary school students in Australia were taught about the causes of climate change and evaluated through an individual pre- and post-test. The authors of the study hypothesized that if young students are educated about actions that help reduce carbon emissions, they may feel empowered, and as a result be able to alleviate climate change. In the experiment's education intervention, the goal was to remove any misconceptions the students had about climate change and replace them with knowledge of the causes and possible solutions. Students were first tested about their knowledge of climate change, and they were then taught about the cost of energy in food transportation as well as more conceptual subjects like the greenhouse effect. There were a total of eight educational units relating to climate change causes, and each unit involved hands-on methods, presentations, and problem resolution posters. In the pre-test, only 47% of students were concerned about global warming but after studying this material, 73% of the students chose answers in the post test that could be categorized as concerned or very concerned about global warming. It was concluded that although some climate change misconceptions are too difficult to clarify for primary school students, there was generally more awareness and concern for climate change at the end of the study, making the effort seem worthwhile.

Taber, F., & Taylor, N., 2009. Climate of Concern-A Search for Effective Strategies for Teaching Children about Global Warming. International Journal of Environmental and Science Education 4, 97-116. http://1.usa.gov/1FJpFTr

The Most Effective Way to Deal with Climate Change
by Brina Jablonski

A major issue for America is the lack of public interaction and engagement on the matter of climate change. Although most people are educated in climate changes' causes, impacts, and solutions, many still refuse to take action and instead ignore the problem at hand. Communication researchers believe that outlining climate change in terms of public health could be a more effective method for convincing the community that climate change truly is a serious concern.

In 2010, a study was conducted to evaluate the most successful way to reach out to American citizens about climate change. The test involved dividing subjects into six different categories ranging from most concerned and motivated subjects to the least concerned and least motivated subjects. The six categories were labeled as alarmed, concerned, cautious, disengaged, doubtful, and dismissive. Subjects were classified by their previous knowledge and reaction to climate change. The testing itself required the subjects to read three distinctly framed news articles that highlighted the risks to either public health, environment, or national security due to climate change and the benefits of taking action. The subjects were then asked to underline which sentences in the article made them feel hopeful versus angry.

The results of the testing indicated that when public health was introduced as the primary issue at hand, subjects usually found the information convincing and valuable. This positive emotional feedback stands as a promising strategy for climate change communication.

Interestingly, the authors mention how negative emotions, such as anger or fear, can also motivate people to get active and seek clarification on the issues at hand. However, these negative emotions can backfire and instead result in less concern and more hopelessness. For example, highlighting how national security is at risk due to climate change actually angered some subjects and left them more doubtful or dismissive about climate change.

Overall, the health frame created the most feelings of hope and is thus the most promising method for engaging the public in the issue of climate change.

Myers, T., Nisbet, M., Maibach, E., Leiserowitz, A. "A public health frame arouses hopeful emotions about climate change." Climatic Change 113, 3-4,1105-1112. http://bit.ly/1AoOZiZ

Reaching Out to Today's Youth
by Brina Jablonski

A major issue in the twenty-first century is the lack of youth involvement in climate change discussion. The members of today's youth are the future leaders of tomorrow. If they have no interest or understanding of the severe climate problems at hand then they will never take the initiative to make a change.

Senebel *et al.* (2014) explain how people tend to honor set goals, pay close attention to what their peers are doing, and are strongly persuaded by people they like. Thus they concluded that social media is the most effective form of persuasion and communication with the public. With the use of digital media, information will be able to reach many, diverse populations as well as shift social norms, and reduce climate change. The article analyzed the results of a test designed to understand how social media can help encourage today's current youth to play an active role in preventing further climate change through energy reduction.

The test was conducted in the form of an energy reduction competition between university campuses in British Columbia. Focusing on college students for an energy reduction competition is ideal because the large amount of change in a college student's life can help grow new habits and improved energy reduction behavior.

Six thousand five hundred students participated in the competition. Results showed that students joined the competition when they had access to multiple forms of social media. Students were also found to pay attention only to the actions of their friends and usually ignore the actions of strangers. Students reduced energy use the most when they felt like they had complete control of their own energy reduction goals. The final result was that the most effective way to encourage students to take action in reducing energy was to employ entertainment that allows multiple methods of participation.

Senbel, M., Douglas, V., Blair, E. 2014. Social mobilization of climate change: University students conserving energy through multiple pathways for peer engagement. Journal of Environmental Psychology, 38, 84-93. http://bit.ly/1Q5aiGk

Is Climate Change Really Our Fault?
by Brina Jablonski

It is a well-known fact that humans play the largest role in global warming. Humans and the excessive amount of green house gas (GHG) emissions that they create stand as a main problem of the twenty first century. Now the real question is, who is to blame? Is the average American responsible for the suffering and/or death of (at least) one future person? Anders Schinkel, through his open peer commentary article, analyzes the different viewpoints on this matter and clearly states his own personal opinion as well.

Schinkel makes a point by saying that the harm done to planet Earth by global warming depends on the total greenhouse gas emissions, not an individual's personal emissions. He clarifies that even if GHG) emissions by an average American is responsible for the suffering and/or near death of one future person, that does not mean that the American is personal morally responsible for the death of a future person. Schinkel fights for the idea that "no-one creates the society, the economic structures, the culture and the institution in which one is born an raised" and thus one is not responsible for the effects of green house gas emissions. It would require a dramatic change of lifestyle, with huge social, financial, and emotional consequences for one to change the norms of their lifestyle and adjust to being climate change friendly for the future benefit of everyone. People's ability to avoid (collectively) harmful behavior is beyond their (individual) control. Thus this does not mean individuals have no moral responsibility with regard to climate change but it does mean they cannot be held morally responsible for their share of the total harm done.

Schinkel concludes by stating how as an individual, he has good moral reasons to change his own behavior to adjust to the demands of global warming but not to the point where this requires unreasonable sacrifices.

Schinkel, A. 2011. "Causal and Moral Responsibility of Individuals for (the Harmful Consequences of) Climate Change." Ethics, Policy, and Environment, Vol 14, No.1, 35-37. http://bit.ly/1LzCAIf

Should We Call it Climate Change, or Global Warming?
by JP Kiefer

Despite scientists' general preference for the term "climate change" over "global warming," Americans have historically used global warming more frequently than climate change as a search term in Google. Americans are also twice as likely to say they personally use the term global warming in their own conversations. According to Leiserowitz *et al.* (2014), this is significant because the two terms are not synonymous. Aside from the technical differences of the two terms, the term global warming is almost always more engaging than climate change.

Leiserowitz *et al.* discovered this by conducting a survey of 1,657 American adults and randomly assigning half a questionnaire using the term "global warming." The other half was given an identical questionnaire with the exception of "global warming" being replaced with "climate change." The different words have different effects on different categories of people due to different levels of understanding and preconceived notions.

For almost all people; the words "global warming" generate a higher percentage of associations to extreme weather along with stronger ratings of negative affects. The term also brings with it a greater certainty that the phenomenon is happening and a greater understanding that human activities are the primary cause. It also causes a greater sense of personal threat and of a threat to one's own family.

Politically liberal individuals feel a greater certainty that the phenomenon is happening, more intense worry about the issue, and a greater willingness to join a campaign to convince elected officials to take action when using the term "global warming" instead of "climate change." Conservative individuals feel a stronger belief that weather in the US is being affected a lot, but are not particularly affected in any other measured way. Politically independent people feel the most significant affects, as the term "global warming" provides a greater understanding that human activities are the primary cause of climate change, a greater understanding of scientific consensus on the issue, a greater sense of threat to future generations, and brings about higher issue priority ratings for action by the president and Congress.

According to Leiserowitz *et al.*, scientists should be aware of the different interpretations these two terms have. The results suggest that the different terms tend to be fairly synonymous for Republicans, and neither term would be more effective at engaging them in discourse. To Democrats and Independents it is possible that "climate change" will come to acquire similar connotative meanings as "global warming," but the results of this study strongly suggest that the two terms will continue to mean different things to many Americans.

Leiserowitz, A., Feinberg, G., Rosenthal, S., Smith, N., Anderson, A., Roser-Renouf, C., and Maibach, E. 2014. What's in a Name? Global Warming Versus Climate Change. Yale University and George Mason University. New Haven, CT: Yale Project on Climate Change Communication.

Yale Attempts to Produce Environmentally Conscious Graduates
by Margaret Loncki

Administrators at Yale University strongly believe that something needs to be done about imminent threats it faces as a result of climate change. Rachelle Dejong, a research associate at the National Organization of scholars, describes the importance of behavioral manipulation and social psychology in changing the behavior of college students. Yale administrators believe that appealing to one's moral side is not enough to change student's behavior in the long run. Instead, students must want to engage in sustainable behavior rather than being forced into it. When forced to make these changes, resulting behavior appears to be temporary rather than the long lasting changes that Yale hopes to produce.

Years prior, Yale attempted to become more green by creating trayless dining halls. The theory behind this mandatory change made total environmental sense. By not using large trays, water needed to clean them would be saved and students would be less likely to fill their tray with more food that they would be able to consume. This change however, did not go over as well with students as administrators had hoped. Unlike a reaction to a similar decision at the Claremont Colleges, Yale students revolted against the change and trays were soon brought back to the dining halls. Administrators admit that the most likely reason this change didn't stick is because it was a forced change rather than a voluntary one, something that the students would want to be a part of. The dining director at Yale now plans to "seduce students with plant-based foods" rather than forcing changes upon university students. Administrators believe that if they can infuse sustainable practices into students everyday lives, these changes will influence their environmental decisions for the better long after they graduate and will push them towards "solar paneled houses and vegan only restaurants." We shall see.

Dejong, Rachelle., 2014, An ivy league nudge-ucation. Commentary 134(4), 43-46.

"Purity" Versus "Harm" in Framing Climate Change
by Margaret Loncki

Rottman *et al.* (2015) explore the effectiveness of harm-based, as well as purity-based, framing in initiating behavioral change. Often, people do not engage in environmentally friendly behavior due to its uncertainty and temporal distance. Many studies have demonstrated that morality has been a powerful tool used to encourage environmentally friendly behavior, although conservation does not inherently have a moral association. Rottman *et al.* determine that both harm-based as well as purity-based framing have proven to be rather useful tools in bringing about environmental change, but both are accompanied by potential drawbacks.

Harm-based framing focuses on drawing attention to the harm caused by global climate change and its consequences for society. One common association with harm-based framing is the damage done to future generations, although temporal distance from these victims results in little change. The authors suggest that drawing attention to more specific victims, victims that are more easily related too, will result in increased environmentally friendly behavior. This study also suggested decreased environmentally conscious behavior when non-human subjects are affected. The authors determined that through anthropomorphism, attributing human qualities to non-human entities, people would be more willing to support the conservation of non-human subjects. Rottman *et al.* also point out the potential downsides of harm-based framing including the requirement of individualized victims as well as the restriction of concerns to humans. Often, those who focus solely on the impacts of climate change on humans tend to be less supportive of environmentally friendly behavior.

Purity-based framing focuses on drawing attention to the need to restore the purity of our environment, which we have so drastically contaminated. A previous study conducted in 2013 by Feinberg and Willer demonstrated that purity-based framing was often more powerful than harm-based framing. Violation of purity is often associated with the emotion of disgust. When environmental matters are framed in this way, they elicit strong feelings of disgust and result in increased environmentally conscious behavior. The authors also explain that intent plays a large role in harm-based framing, whereas purity violations evoke an emotional response no matter the intent of that violation. Similarly, people often label what is natural as being pure, and unnatural things as being a violation of that purity, again evoking a strong emotional response of disgust. Some religious audiences are very positively affected by purity-based framing as it elicits a strong desire to protect the purity of God's creation. However, purity-based framing can be detrimental in some religious audiences, as they believe that mankind was created to dominate and should be able to exploit all that our world has to offer. Unfortunately, people who are more focused on purity, tend to not be concerned with conservation and climate change. Although both harm-based as well as purity-based framing having potential drawbacks, if used effectively, they both have the potential to result in increased effectiveness and success in shifting behavior in a more environmental direction.

Rottman, J., Kelemen, D., Young, L., 2015. Hindering harm and preserving purity: how can moral psychology save the planet?. Philosophy Compass 10, 134-144.

Proximity to Coast is Linked to Climate Change Belief
by Sam Peterson

Despite increasingly contrasting and polarizing environmental beliefs between major political parties in many developed countries, there has been diminishing speculation in recent years regarding the existence of climate change as a scientific consensus builds. Though politicians may argue the merits of recognizing climate change as an immediate problem, the individuals bearing the brunt of the effects of climate change are those in regions that are reliant on specific weather patterns and temperature limitations. To examine how belief in climate change within the populace of developed countries is affected, in 2013, Milfont *et al.* (2014) analyzed the relationship between indvidual's physical proximity to coastlines in New Zealand and their belief in climate change. They found that in a national probability sample of 5,815 New Zealanders, people living in closer proximity to shorelines exhibited greater belief in climate change and "greater support for government regulation of carbon dioxide emissions," and found that the proximity effect "held when adjusting for height above sea level and regional poverty," in addition to respondent's sex, age, education, political orientation, and wealth. The authors conclude that proximity to coastlines directly correlates with ones belief in climate change, possibly the direct effects are more "concrete and local."

Like many other developed nations, New Zealand is split about the cause and existence of climate change:

"53% of the New Zealand public believe climate change is real and caused by humans...10% do not believe in climate change, 7% believe it [climate change] is real but not caused by humans, and a large proportion (31%) remain undecided" (Borick 2003, cited by Milfont 2013).

Many New Zealanders (64%) believe citizens should exert more effort to combat climate change, compared to 68% of citizens in the US (Horizon Poll 2012, Leiserowitz 2012, cited by Milfont 2013). Though a majority of citizens are generally for a more aggressive stance in combatting the sources and effects of climate change, there are evidently attitudes and psychological barriers to perceiving and acting on climate change, such as "uncertainty, skepticism, distrust in information sources, externalizing responsibility and blame, optimism bias, attention to other priorities" in addition to a "reluctance to change lifestyles" (Gifford 2011, Lorenzoni 2007, Pawlik 1991, cited by Milfont 2013). Formulating solutions to these psychological obstacles is one of the most important parts of climate change research.

The authors used data from the New Zealand Attitudes and Values Study (NZAVS), collected in 2009 from roughly 40,500 people, or approximately 1.36% of registered voters, were invited to participate in the study, of which 16.6% responded. The sample of 5,185 people was 60% women, had a mean age of 47.72, and 23.0% had or were studying for a undergraduate degree. These respondents were nested into meshblocks, with an average area of 9.66 km², whose centroids were used to measure the distance to the nearest coastline. As predicted, there was a significant correlation between the distance from the nearest coastline and belief in climate change and support for government regulation of emissions. This trend held for adjustments in poverty and other variables, including sex, education and wealth. Though the study was unable to determine the causal direction (whether believers in climate change seek out coastal areas, or if other variables are in play), they were able to determine that there is a significant correlation between physical proximity to areas most affected by climate change and belief in the phenomenon, which strongly suggests that a more concrete understanding of climate change comes from constant experience with the occurrence.

Milfont, T.L., Evans, L., Sibley, C.G., Ries, J., Cunningham, A., 2014. Proximity to coast is linked to climate change belief. PloS one 9, e103180.9(7): 1-8.

Social Norms and Preferences towards Climate Change Policies — A Meta-Analysis
by Sam Peterson

While climate change consensus has been growing in the last two decades, response to the alarming effects of it has not kept pace. There are various explanations for this societal inertia, including misinformation, lack of trust in government, and knowledge gaps (Norgaard 2009). Alló *et al.* (2014) examined, by way of meta-analysis, preferences regarding climate change action based on factors incorporating social norms and temporal restrictions in different countries. The study assessed data from completed analyses regarding climate change action preferences and measured several dependent variables, including whether the study proposed mitigation or adaptation strategies, households' willingness to pay (WTP), and forms of monetary support proposed by the included studies. Alló concludes that mitigation actions are preferred over adaptation actions, countries with long-term outlooks have higher WTP, and preferable policies encourage the prevention of disasters, like heat waves, as opposed to creation of and investment in greener technologies.

Climate change could impact global gross domestic product by 5% to 20% in many countries (Hallegatte and Corfee-Morlot, 2011, cited by Alló 2014), but despite warning signs like an increased frequency of severe storms, very few countries have imposed restrictive emissions caps. Global emissions have grown by 50% since 1990, spurred by the rapid expansion of the Chinese and some South American economies. In order to assess preferences regarding climate change mitigation and adaptation strategies, the study used willingness to pay (WTP) as an indicator of social inclination toward policies. The rapidly expanding field of behavioral economics provides some insight into consumer decision-making regarding climate change. If one considers effective halting of climate change as a public good, the economic free-rider problem arises, where there is no restriction on who can partake in the benefits of said good (Brekke and Johansson-Stenman 2008a, 2008b, cited by Alló 2014). In theory, this would incentivize those who did not have to pay for climate change policies to support them. This factor was included in the meta-analysis, as traditional economic models would predict individuals to be extremely self-serving in decision-making.

The analysis included 58 studies from multiple continents, but found that over half of existing climate policy preference research is done in America (52.18%), followed by Europe (34.15%) and Asia (9.03%). On average, studies included 6.1 observations, and were separated by the way they were conducted (face to face, telephone, internet). In order to account for changes in WTP by currency value, a Purchasing Power Parity Index (PPP) was used ($USD 2012). The authors then analyzed the number of climactic disasters in each country where a study was conducted, in order to test whether being near effects of climate change would correlate with a higher WTP. The researchers also accounted for political orientation in each country, as it has been demonstrated that "people with left-wing tendencies have a higher WTP for environmental programs than those who have a more conservative view" (Carlsson *et al.*, 2010; Solomon and Johnson, 2009; Wiser, 2007; Berrens *et al.*, 2004, cited by Alló 2014). The final variable controlled for was temporal outlook, defined by Hofstede (2001). Societies with long term orientation are those that "show an ability to adapt traditions to changed conditions, a strong propensity to save and invest, thriftiness, and perseverance in achieving results."

After running several regressions on the data set, including Ordinary Least Squares (OLS), Generalized Least Squares (GLS) and Random Effects Model (RE), the authors concluded people who have had more cumulative experience with climate change-caused weather conditions and those who were contacted for studies over the internet generally have a higher WTP than others. People are generally more likely to want to pay for preventative policies (mitigation) over adaptive policies or even a mix of both. This conclusion is useful for continued use in global climate policy growth, as societal preferences will generally determine whether legislation is effective and worthwhile, as well as providing a possible explanation for apathy regarding climate change action.

Alló, M. and M. L. Loureiro (2014). "The role of social norms on preferences towards climate change policies: A meta-analysis." Energy Policy 73(0): 563-574.

Climate Change or Nuclear Power in Britain?
by Sam Peterson

Policymakers have been challenged to formulate and introduce innovative new legislation following major international environmental awareness agreements, such as the Kyoto Protocol of 1992 (a treaty created by the United Nations Framework Convention on Climate

Change), but public opinion shifts have frequently trailed a growing scientific consensus regarding climate change. Pidgeon *et al.* (2005) find that when presented with the options of a transition from burning carbon-based fuels to the daunting spectacle of nuclear power or an increased rate of climate change, much of the British public is indecisive. The study finds that the British public is "prepared to accept nuclear power if they believe it contributes to climate change mitigation," but this is a "highly conditional view." There is only "reluctant acceptance" of utilization of nuclear power by policymakers, mostly due to the risks of nuclear power production.

While the Kyoto agreement committed the United Kingdom to a 12.5% reduction in the six primary anthropogenic greenhouse gas (GHG) emissions by 2012, the UK government has set a loftier goal of a 60% decrease in GHG emissions by the year 2050, when compared to 1990 levels. This environmental concern is coupled with the realization that by 2020, a majority of British oil will be imported, mostly from "potentially politically unstable" states. Policymakers have thus framed the issue of nuclear power in this uncertain context. While the UK was the first nation to open a commercial nuclear power station at Calder Hall in 1956, the 1986 Chernobyl accident in Ukraine led to a drastic shift in energy consumption composition toward North Sea oil. A 2003 Labour Government White Paper regarding energy policy reinforced the commitment of the UK to a "low-carbon economy," the paper was careful not to comment on the goals for the composition of UK energy creation.

Public opinion of nuclear power has shifted several times in the last half-century. Many studies have shown public wariness in the UK regarding nuclear power due to military uses and secrecy (Waynne 1992, cited by Pidgeon 2005) and major nuclear accidents (Van der Pligt 1992, cited by Pidgeon 2005). Building on previous public opinion surveys in the UK, the researchers found that while only 62% of 1491 respondents indicated "every possible action" should be taken against climate change, only 3% indicated no action should be taken, giving evidence to public opinion aligning with scientific consensus regarding climate change. However, when given a policy question, such as "How favourable or unfavourable are your overall opinions or impressions of the following energy sources for producing electricity currently," nuclear power ranked last in favorability (36%) behind solar (87%), wind (81%), hydroelectric (76%), biomass (54%), gas (55%), oil (39%) and coal power (38%). Additionally, 25% of respondents selected an option that for nuclear power, the "risks far outweigh benefits." These findings can be interpreted as an ongoing public relations battle policymakers will have with nuclear power sentiment until they are able to change public perception regarding the energy source. While many believe "nuclear power will make a significant contribution to energy production" in the future, policymakers will have to contend with wavering support for policies that include nuclear power as an option for climate change mitigation.

Pidgeon, N. F., Lorenzoni, I., & Poortinga, W. (2008). Climate change or nuclear power—No thanks! A quantitative study of public perceptions and risk framing in Britain. Global Environmental Change, 18(1), 69-85.

Catching Two European Problems with One Renewable Energy Stone

by Sam Peterson

Many studies support the finding climate change is deemed a relevant and important issue by the public, but frequently disappears from the public consciousness when individuals are not directly impacted by its effects, supplanted by more immediate economic and geopolitical issues. Rather than removing it from public concern, Creutizig *et al.* (2014) aim to attack environmental concerns and socioeconomic problems concurrently, with a sweeping energy policy change. Creutzig *et al.* argue climate change and the European Union (EU) periphery's economic recession could be mitigated and solved, respectively, by having member country legislators focus efforts on a policy transition toward sustainable, nonconventional sources of energy. The study argues that an energy conversion of this magnitude would have several net positive effects for a plurality of EU member countries on pressing issues such as employment, trade deficits and GDP growth, with focuses on "technical and economic potential for renewable electricity generation across Europe," "potential co-effects of a European energy transition," "barriers to a (periphery-focused) European energy transition," and "the issue of a European energy transition in the periphery to the larger context of a common project for Europe." The entirely new approach to energy policy implementation outlined in the study may not only be integral to lessening the European economic recession but also to significantly improving governmental efficiency in peripheral EU countries.

The study cites a triad of rationales for focus on changes in peripheral EU country energy production infrastructures: peripheral economic depression affects all EU member states, investment in peripheral member states' energy security may increase wealth parity across the EU, and a successful recovery from the recession may lead to willingness to contribute to an energy transition. While there would be certain tangible effects of a transition to renewable energy sources in periphery countries (Ireland, Italy, Poland, Spain, Greece), including a projected 0.5%-1.0% increase in GDP due to the multiplier of fiscal spending in Europe being between 0.8 and 21 (Baunsgaard *et al.* 2012, cited by Creutzig *et al.* 2014), the most important byproduct may be "a renewed solidarity between European citizens...even if hard to quantify in monetary or other economic units." A more noticeable change would be that of European employment, particularly in the industrial manufacturing sector. In the European Renewable Energy Directive for 2020, a goal of 20% renewable energy is set, and under this scenario, "Greece is projected to have an employment gain of roughly 1% and Spain of 0.6%, while Ireland only sees a negligibly small but still positive impact on employment," mostly caused by employment opportunities created by an energy transition. Finally, a majority of peripheral EU countries are net importers of energy, bringing in 2%-15% of their energy from foreign EU states. This lack of energy security is concerning to the authors, and could be solved by tapping into the potential of wind power, which is particularly prevalent on the northern periphery of the EU, in Ireland and Spain. In conclusion, the tangible and intangible effects of a massive changeover to renewable energy would be tremendous, including increased in EU GDP, employment and trade surpluses, and finally, trust. Creutzig *et al.* make a strong argument for tackling the recent European economic downturn and climate mitigation in one motion, and provide valuable models to prove the net positive effects of bringing climate change into the public consciousness permanently.

Creutzig, F., *et al.* (2014). "Catching two European birds with one renewable stone: Mitigating climate change and Eurozone crisis by an energy transition." Renewable and Sustainable Energy Reviews 38: 1015-1028.

Changing Consumer Actions and their Relation to Climate Change Worry
by Sam Peterson

Psychologists studying climate change have formulated many hypotheses concerning the inertia of public support behind the issue. One unforeseen obstacle that many studies have encountered is a public misunderstanding of "carbon footprints" and their relationships to greenhouse gas (GHG) emissions. Quantifying annual carbon consumption per capita is a relatively simple calculation, but the value produced is often challenging to place on a relative spectrum of carbon usage, in addition to complications stemming from the translation of carbon usage to GHG emissions. Sundblad *et al.* (2014) attempt to explain the relationship between "worry, in addition to personalized information about emissions of carbon dioxide" and "intentions to change consumption-related personal activities causing carbon-dioxide emissions," and by association, contributions to climate change, with the end goal of finding factors capable of motivating public change to carbon-producing activities. The study hypothesizes "people will form intentions to change activities that reduce CO2 emissions depending on how much they are worried about GCC [global climate change] consequences," implying a positive correlation between the variables of worry and intent to change.

The manner in which we react to climate change is generally dependent on our professions; journalists disseminate information concerning the subject, politicians legislate in accordance with their views, and the general public may change its habits based on its perception of risk stemming from carbon-consuming activities. A change in habits is generally a product of perceived risk, in this case defined as the probability of negative consequences (Slovic 1987, cited by Sundblad *et al.* 2014). According to several psychological hypotheses, "both cognitive risk assessments and anticipatory emotions are antecedents of intentions to reduce risk" (Loewenstein *et al.* 2001, cited by Sundblad *et al.* 2014). The study performed by Sundblad *et al.* involved 135 university students above the age of 24 years (to increase probability of financial independence) who were asked to calculate their personal carbon dioxide emissions, expressed in kilograms of carbon dioxide per year. The participants then read about GCC and were asked if they intended to change any of their carbon-producing activities in the following 12 months. Using several linear regressions to demonstrate the correlation between worry regarding GCC and intention to change, the data supported the original hypothesis of a positive correlation between the variables. This conclusion may be supported by the prospect of a "binding communication" in the calculation of annual GHG emissions, here defined as an "[implication] that a link has been established between persuasion and commitment" (Joule *et al.* 2007, Girandola 2007, cited by Sundblad *et al.* 2014). This correlation between worry and intention to change is promising, as it shows the public may be ready to alter their actions if they are forced to recognize this binding communication.

Sundblad, E.-L., *et al.* (2014). "Intention to change activities that reduce carbon dioxide emissions related to worry about global climate change consequences." Revue Européenne de Psychologie Appliquée/European Review of Applied Psychology 64(1): 13-17.

How Belief in Climate Change Affects Legislation and Personal Sacrifice

by Patrick Quarberg

Surveys from New Zealand have indicated that climate change skepticism is on the rise. Comparing surveys from the early 2000s and the 2010s, Chris G. Sibley and Tim Kurz (2013) have found that there is an increasing proportion of people attributing climate change to natural causes, or denying its existence altogether. This information alone is surprising and alarming, as the effects of climate change are becoming increasingly evident and the need to address climate change is growing. This is why Sibley and Kurz investigated the effect of increasing skepticism on voting habits and willingness to reduce personal consumption. Climate change deniers were identified through a forced-question survey and defined as people who attributed climate change to natural causes or who refused to accept its existence. Then, they tried to establish a correlation between these traits and support for climate-related legislation as well as personal efforts to reduce impact on the environment. After analyzing a survey from 2009 that covered a large variety of demographics in New Zealand, they found that there was a large correlation between support for public response to climate change and belief in climate change— as was expected. However, there was a weaker correlation between the strength of one's belief in climate change and the willingness to make personal sacrifices to protect the environment. This finding is surprising, as one would expect those who believe in climate change, and believe that it is caused by humans, would be more willing to make changes in their lives than someone who completely denies the existence of climate change. This points out a very important detail about the current fight against climate change, which is that even though many people are indeed aware of climate change's causes and effects, they are still not very willing to act against it. This issue in itself may hinder progress more than climate skepticism, and must be resolved if the fight against climate change is to gain any ground. However, Sibley and Kurz also found that just believing in climate change had a greater predictive effect on one's support of carbon reducing legislation, suggesting that it is perhaps more important to just focus on establishing climate change as real than it is to attribute it to human causes, at least for now.

Kurz, T, Sibley C. G. 2013. A Model of Climate Belief Profiles: How Much Does It Matter If People Question Human Causation? Analyses of Social Issues and Public Policy, Volume 13, pp. 245-261.

How Human Attitudes and Values affect Environmental Protection
by Patrick Quarberg

Human activity in general is known to accelerate climate change, but now it appears that perhaps human attitudes can mitigate it. A study conducted by Cheung *et al.* suggests that changes in attitudes towards other humans can influence one's attitude on environmental protection. People who view humanity positively exhibit more pro-social behaviors and have more humanitarian motives. Previously, it was observed that these tendencies could apply to environmental issues as well, but only issues that directly involved humanity. Cheung *et al.* hypothesized that those with a more positive view of humanity and lower self-transcendence values—the ability to see past oneself—would care less about the environment than those without those traits. Cheung *et al.* did two separate experiments to measure the effects of these variables. In the experiment, participants read a bogus article that either positively or negatively reflected on humanity, and were then asked how they felt about humanity. Their feelings were quantified by a scaled survey asking about feelings towards humans in general. It was found that the article's view greatly impacted respondents' views on humanity. From there, respondents' self-transcendence values were measured with another survey. As hypothesized, those who held self-transcendent values more strongly rejected the positive view of humans, and had a more ecocentric view of the world. That is, they placed more emphasis on the environment and protecting it. It was also found that the positive/negative article did not significantly influence the views of those who held self-transcendent values. A second experiment revealed that those who held self-transcendent values were more likely to have ecocentric behavior after viewing the pro-humanity article, whereas the opposite was found for those who did not have these values. Overall, the study showed that those who placed importance on the welfare of nature and of others were more likely to have strong motives to protect the environment. Considering the importance of the findings of this study, emphasizing the importance of self-transcendence could greatly increase the motivation to protect the environment among the general public, which is particularly important considering that apathy often cripples environmental movements involving both the public and the government.

Cheung, W.; Luke, M.; Maio, G. 2014. On Attitudes Towards Humanity and Climate Change: The Effects of Humanity Esteem and Self-transcendence Values on Environmental Concerns. European Journal of Social Psychology, Volume 44, pages 496-506.

Belief, Trust, and Perception—the Farmers' View of Climate Change
by Russell Salazar

What can motivate farmers to take action with regard to climate change? Several emissions reports and investigations have shown that the agricultural sector is a severe contributor to greenhouse gas emissions. However, such empirical evidence is not sufficient to encourage action from farmers and those in the agricultural sector. Arbuckle, Morton, and Hobbs (2013) zoom in on the relationship between belief, trust, and perceived risks of individuals and their likelihood to support climate change mitigation and adaption measures. Focusing on farmers in Iowa, the study shows that while adaption action is generally quite welcomed, perception of mitigation measures is more complicated.

Iowan farmers were chosen as the focus of the study for a few main reasons: first, agriculture accounts for a high proportion of the state's emissions; additionally, the effects of climate change, such as increased soil erosion, and planting and harvesting delays have been taking effect in the area. These characteristics put Iowan farmers in an appropriate context for the investigation on attitudes towards mitigation and adaptation action.

Data on trust of various institutions, belief in climate change and of its causes, and opinions on policies and actions were collected through surveying over a thousand Iowan farmers. The study found that while over half the responders believed in the occurrence of climate change, only a small percentage (10%) believed that it is mostly due to human activity. This finding goes hand in hand with the collected data showing a greater support for adaption action over mitigation measures; farmers acknowledge the potential risks of climate change and want to adapt and prepare, but do not believe in the human causes, therefore see lesser value in mitigation. Essentially, Arbuckle *et al.* have shown empirical evidence for quite a logical argument. Assuming Iowan farmers willingly support actions that supplement and develop the well being of their personal interests, such as the success and productivity of their farms, it follows that if the perceived risk of climate change, and belief in climate change due to natural change is high, the farmers are likely to support adaptive measures. Those who acknowledge the anthropogenic element of climate change go further to support mitigation measures, but this is a relatively small group.

The study also found that amongst farmers, environmental scientists were trusted much more than federal agencies and mainstream news media. This suggests there may be more effective means of communicating future policies and measures for implementation.

This study provides insight into methods for motivating farmers to modify their practices. Arbuckle *et al.* elegantly summarize the significance of their study: "By using outreach strategies that focus on adaptive practices that reduce risks and GHG emissions, the dual goals of adaptation and mitigation could be pursued while engaging the majority of farmers who do not believe in anthropogenic climate change."

Arbuckle, J., Morton, L., Hobbs, J. 2013. Understanding Farmer Perspectives on Climate Change Adaptation and Mitigation: The Roles of Trust in Sources of Climate Information, Climate Change Beliefs, and Perceived Risk. Environment and Behavior 47, 205-234. http://bit.ly/1FxJtYp

How Do We Decide What Fuels to Use?

by Russell Salazar

With average global temperatures on the rise, the American public has become increasingly aware of the significance of energy sources and production. What kinds of energy production should the country be pushing for? Ansolabehere and Konisky (2012) review multiple research papers regarding public opinion on energy production, focusing on two important attributes with which the public is concerned: economic cost and environmental harm. Through surveys and statistical analysis, they identify several interesting aspects of the American public's energy choices.

First, it is very clear that Americans place more value and weight on environmental wellbeing than on economic costs when evaluating their desired future use of different energy sources. Opinions on coal and nuclear power show a great disparity between the effects of perceived harm and perceived price on an American's energy choices. Essentially, higher perceived environmental harm would affect an individual's energy choices much more than higher perceived economic costs. In the case of nuclear power, this is most likely rooted in issues of the past with accidents at nuclear plants and the potential of meltdowns in the future.

Such a finding seems to bode well for active fighters of climate change; perhaps informing people of the harms of fossil fuels will be the more effective means of affecting future energy policies. Unfortunately, another study discussed by Ansolabehere and Konisky shows that there is a very weak correlation between concern for global warming and attitudes toward particular fuels. The concept of environmental harm is largely limited to local scales; individuals are more concerned with what they experience directly; things like smog in the air from gasoline, and fenced off areas for nuclear power plants.

Extending this to a global scale and considering the effects of particular fuels on the global climate, we find minimal effect on perceived harms and, hence, public opinion on different energy sources. Economic cost therefore seems like the more prominent 'swayer' of public opinion; a study showed that people would be more likely to support increases in fossil fuel usage over renewable energy usage when informed of the relative prices.

Ultimately, the summarized research points to a common thread: people see all fuels in a similar lens. Renewable energy and fossil fuels are not considered in those separate categories. Rather, costs and benefits are compared, and the most economically sound options gain the support.

Ansolabehere and Konisky suggest that given these findings, reducing the cost of clean energy is the best approach to a more sustainable future and a cleaner energy portfolio.

Ansolabehere, S., Konisky, D., 2012. The American Public's Energy Choice. Daedalus 141, 61-71.

Is the Government Accountable for Climate Change?
by Abby Schantz

In "Oregon teens sue state: Can local government be held accountable for climate change?" Samantha Laine tells the story of two teenagers who are attempting to sue the government for not protecting its people from climate change. Three years ago, Kelsey Juliana and Olivia Chernaik, at the ages of 14 and 11 respectively, filed a lawsuit in the Lane County Circuit Court. Juliana and Chernaik argued that the state of Oregon was violating the public trust doctrine by not working to mitigate climate change rapidly. House Bill 3542, which was introduced 8 years ago and set carbon emission reduction goals, was unaccomplished. The teens argued that just as the government protects forests, oceans, and other natural resources, it is the state's responsibility to protect the atmosphere. A nonprofit organization, Our Children Trust, has backed Juliana and Chernaik throughout the suit.

Kitty Piercy, mayor of the girls' hometown, Eugene, has also supported their plea, as has one of the world's leading climate scientists, James Hansen. On the other hand, many have criticized the case for reasons including Oregon's small impact on the amount of CO2 produced (0.01%) globally and what is viewed as the waste of a court's time and money. Judge Karsten Rasmussen dismissed the case on the grounds that a court lacks authority to require state officials to reduce greenhouse emissions because climate change is a political question. The girls appealed, and the Oregon Court of Appeals has sent the case back to the lower court for a trial on March 13th, 2015, which will address whether the atmosphere is considered a public trust.

Laine, S., 2015. Oregon teens sue state: Can local government be held accountable for climate change? Cristian Science Monitor, January 21st, 2015. http://bit.ly/1F4eIai

Sorry Business—not Climate Change—in The Kimberley

by Breanna Sewell

Author Sandy Toussaint uses her 2008 article, "Climate Change, Global Warming, and Too Much Sorry Business," to address the concern, or lack thereof, of a group of indigenous Australian people (specifically the Kimberley communities) with climate change and the reasoning behind this. Toussaint begins her article by defining the term "sorry business"—a phrase many indigenous Australians use to refer to death, mourning, and all of the emotional distress and familial responsibilities that are associated with the passing of a loved one. This time of grief and sorrow carries much weight in indigenous communities and has many rituals and traditional processes associated with it.

The author next explains that when she asks the Kimberley people questions about climate change, a common response is to ask her to remind them what climate change is. This serves to show the reader that issues of global warming and climate change are certainly not at the forefront of the concerns of the Kimberley people and other indigenous Australian communities like them. This is not to say that these people have no environmental concerns. They have large community involvement in environmentalist groups whose projects include the quality and control of their local Fitzroy River, awareness of the endangerment of the fragile local ecology, and the opposition of tourist practices that are detrimental to the local flora and fauna.

However, Toussaint shows that global climate change is not a primary concern of the Kimberley people (if it is thought of at all). She argues that this is because they are preoccupied with matters that are of far more import to them as a people—primarily the matter of "sorry business" because of the huge toll that "is taken on [their] social, emotional, and practical lives."

Toussaint realizes that it is not a straightforward choice between "sorry business" and climate change, but rather that people will continue to be more concerned with their daily lives and the matters of their community than the abstract concern of our planet's future.

Toussaint, S., 2008. Climate Change, Global Warming, and Too Much Sorry Business. Australian Journal of Anthropology.

Translating Climate Change into Marshallese
by Phoebe Shum

How do you effectively communicate the impending threat of climate change to those who don't even understand the concept due to lexical gaps? Peter Rudiak-Gould, currently an assistant Anthropology professor at University of Toronto, explains how much meaning is lost through translation between scholars to citizens, English to other languages, and even citizens to scholars when discussing climate change issues (2012). Rudiak-Gould spent almost two years in the Republic of the Marshall Islands researching local opinions on climate change. The Marshall Islands is especially endangered by rising sea levels, and information about the dangers have been relayed through various forms of media and government organizations, informing them that the 60,000 citizens will probably need to relocate in 80 years. However, since the word for 'climate' in Marshallese also refers to the environment and universe, citizens attribute climate change as a result of anything from solar eclipses to accelerating time. This has resulted in the Marshallese blaming everything on this omnipotent concept of climate change whenever something out of the ordinary happens.

Linguistic translation involves more than simply substituting phrases word for word, as different languages each have their own idiosyncrasies that reflect culture. For example, there are eleven Marshallese words for the stages of coconut growth, a word to describe the smell of an exposed reef (*ebbwilwodwod*), and a verb that describes the action of choking on a fishbone (*pal*). Translators must choose between what translation theorists call fidelity (faithful, literal translations that are less accessible to the general audience but more accurately convey information) and transparency (vernacular translations that sometimes misconstrue meaning) when conveying information about the time-sensitive issue of climate change. Usually, the more easily understandable a translation is, the less faithful that translation is to the original text.

While meanings lost in translation may be misleading and dangerous, Rudiak-Gould argues that we should treat these *mis*interpretations as *re*interpretations, ones that are capable of providing new opportunities. The Marshallese conflate climate and nature as one concept, which is actually a valid and more holistic outlook capable of inspiring new scientific thought stemmed from a humanistic point of view. Without these mistranslations, the climate change discussion would lie dormant and repetitive.

Rudiak-Gould P., 2012. Promiscuous corroboration and climate change translation: A case study from the Marshall Islands, Global Environmental Change, 46-54.

Skepticism Towards the Climate Change Skeptics
by Phoebe Shum

Justin Gillis (2015), apocalyptic climate activist and environmental reporter from The New York Times, presents the recent push from citizens to abandon the term "climate change skeptics" from the media. Physicist Mark B. Boslough started this movement late last year when he wrote a public letter on the issue on behalf of the Committee for Skeptical Inquiry. Many scientists including Bill Nye the Science Guy and Lawrence M. Krauss signed it, bringing it to the attention of a climate advocacy organization called Forecast the Facts. The organization turned the letter into a petition that eventually garnered the support of over 22,000 people. Boslough explains that skepticism is actually the foundation of the scientific method—climate scientists themselves critically scrutinize their findings and evidence throughout their research process. Some people who are rejecting climate change, however, are obviously not embracing the scientific method. Once the petition reaches 25,000 signatures, Forecast the Facts intends to formally present a request to all major news organizations to change their terminology. Some have suggested the alternative term "climate deniers," although the linkage to Holocaust denial is causing issues amongst those being referred to. Another option is "denialist," which evokes the same meaning, except without any Holocaust connotations.

Gillis explains that these denouncers of climate change are usually conservatives who perfectly well understand that climate change is caused by the excess of greenhouse emissions emitted from modern economic activity. However, in order to fend off government intervention in the free market, these "denialists" refuse to acknowledge the realities of climate change. For example, companies that profit from fossil fuels spend their money on publishing information that oppose climate science. Others deny carbon dioxide as a greenhouse gas, refuse to believe Earth's rising temperature, or simply reject human activities as a cause of climate change. Additionally, there is also a group of contrarian scientists who believe in "lukewarm" climate change, in which the Earth's temperature will rise so gradually that humans will successfully adapt to it. Contrarian scientists like these have been called "lukewarmers" by some. This debate over specific terms seems petty for now, but hopefully this discourse will benefit the climate debate in the long run.

Gillis, J. 2015. Verbal Warming: Labels in the Climate Debate. The New York Times.

Personal Beliefs in Reality of Global Climate Change
by Yijing Zhang

Teresa A. Myers (2012) suggests that perception processes shape people's belief in global warming. One perception process is experiential learning, in which one's experience strengthens his or her belief. The other process model by Myers is motivated reasoning, in which personal experience is significantly influenced by existing belief. According to a survey, cited by Myers, the majority of Americans have a low engagement in global warming issues. Hence, Myers hypnotizes that the motivated reasoning plays a main role in shaping people's attitude. One hypothesis is that both experiential processing and reasoning motivation affect people's belief in global warming. The second hypothesis is that people with personal experience engage more with the climate issue than those who do not have the experience.

Myers and fellow researchers conducted an experiment to testify the hypotheses. They constructed six models, testing relationships between Personal Experience (PE) and Belief Certainty (BC) combined with a time factor. By comparing these six models, they concluded that both hypotheses are correct, indicating that people with low engagement with an issue are more likely to be affected by personal experience while people with higher engagement level are more inclined to use prior knowledge about it to interpret their experience. The significance of this research is that there are more effective ways to enhance people's awareness of the climate issue than in use of present. Providing the public with more direct experience related to global warming may effectively raise their belief certainty. TV weathercasters could be more proactive in educating the audience; and public health officers could demonstrate consequences of warming climate in a community ; park interpreters could explain evidence of climate changes in situ. The gist of these technics is to give the public a direct sense and experience to connect these dots and form a general perception of global warming.

Myers, T. A., Maibach, Edward W., Roser-Renouf, Connie., Akerlof, Karen., Leiserowitz, Anthony A., 2012. "The relationship between personal experience and belief in the reality of global warming." Nature Climate Change 3: 343-347. http://bit.ly/1KtdVY3

Framing Messages of Climate Change
by Yijing Zhang

Nisbet (2009) suggests that the objective of framing news about climate change is to make the seemingly complicated policy debates understandable for the public and make them more of personal interest. In the past, people believed that merely increasing the number of quality news items could effectively raise the public's awareness. However, such a strategy is effective only for a small portion of audience, who is already engaged in the topic. There are a few findings from a third-party poll surveying the public's knowledge about climate issues. First, there is a dichotomy of opinions between Republicans, who tend to deny the urgent nature of climate change and Democrats, who are inclined to believing in scientists' concerns. One of the barriers to conveying the urgent nature of climate change is prioritization. Climate policy has always been at the bottom of the list when the public is asked to rank the policy issues that they are concerned about. Research explaining this result argues that climate change is essentially too complicated and its effect is neither immediate nor directly visible. Another barrier is the fragmented media system in the US, in which the public can choose the news they are interested in, further isolating climate issue from their top concerns.

To make matters worse, framing has reinforced perceptual differences between Republicans and Democrats. Republicans utilize frames of scientifically uncertain and economic consequence to give the public a false impression that scientists have little agreement about the cause of climate change. Therefore, they question the severity of the climate issue and whether the government should spend its budget on the environment. On the other hand, some politicians use specific climate impacts, such as a photo depicting a polar bear on the melting ice. But one of the consequences is that the over-dramatization may lead to an impression of exaggeration.

According to Nisbet, reframing is able to change the dire situation. To merge two views of groups of politicians, environmentalists suggest framing climate issues with economic development by extending the issue to developing energy technology and sustainable economic prosperity. Republicans, who focus more on economic growth and market opportunities, will be more interested in climate issues under such framing. Another way to frame is relating to morality and ethics. For instance, former US vice president Gore compared action on global warming with Civil Rights Movement and being an ally in World War II. In addition, a public health frame can emphasize some potential diseases that might be derived from the environment, given that public health issues have been not only of serious concern, but also one that the public has direct experience with.

Matthew C. Nisbet (2009) Communicating Climate Change: Why Frames Matter for Public Engagement, Environment: Science and Policy for Sustainable Development, 12-23, http://dx.doi.org/10.3200/ENVT.51.2.12-23

PSYCHOLOGY AND CLIMATE CHANGE

Climate Change—a Personal or a Global Issue?

by Brendan Busch

Popular psychology suspects that people have trouble relating broad, wide-scale issues to their own lives, and thus devalue their importance. Some climate change activists have taken this theory to heart and tried to avoid framing climate change as a global issue, instead pointing out the ways climate change will affect people's day-to-day lives. However, research presented by Patrick Devine-Wright, Jennifer Price, and Zoe Leviston in their article "My country or my planet? Exploring the influence of multiple place attachments and ideological beliefs upon climate change attitudes and opinions" suggests that this view of climate change perceptions may not be true. Devine-Wright (a human geography professor at the University of Exeter), Price (an environmental psychologist at CSIRO), and Leviston (a social scientist at CSIRO) examined the relationship between place identity and climate change support and found that people who feel a strong connection to the world as a whole have a much greater support for climate change than those who primarily identify with their country, state, town, or neighborhood.

Place identity, the central concept of the study, is a term that refers to the attachment people feel to a particular location or community. By conducting a survey of 1,147 Australians, Devine-Wright, Price, and Leviston were able to determine the correlation between place identity and climate change support. In the survey, the subjects were asked how strongly they identified with their neighborhood community, their city, their state, their country, and the global community, as well as how they felt about climate change. Surprisingly, people reported the strongest connections to their country and to the world, and not to their more local communities. Additionally, the degree to which an individual identified to the global community versus their own country was quite telling about their support for climate change action. A strong identification with the planet as a whole compared to identification with one's own country correlated with belief in climate change, while the reverse correlated with climate change denial. Furthermore, 53% of those who identified most strongly with the global community believed that a reduction of emissions would lead to an improved quality of life in the long term, compared to only 33% of those who identified most strongly with their country. These data suggest that a localization of climate change issues may not be the best course of action. Instead of shying away from addressing the large scale implications of climate change issues, perhaps fostering a stronger global community would be the best way to instigate climate change action.

Devine-Write, P., Price, J., Leviston Z. (2014). "My country or my planet? Exploring the influence of multiple place attachments and ideological beliefs upon climate change attitudes and opinions." Global Environmental Change, 30, 68-79.

Swedish Children's Coping Strategies for Climate Change
by Juana Granados

Although climate change is a growing issue, there is still no clear coping strategy evident for positive environmental participation. Ojala (2012) created a study focused on how children of late adolescence, specifically Swedish 12-year-olds, coped with climate change and how this coping related to their level of environmental engagement. In the past several years, research has shown that older children have started to grow an interest in the universal issues of today, including climate change. However, delicate issues like those of the environment have been found to cause anxiety associated with the constant negativity from the events. There is a coping theory developed by Lazarus that states that individuals have two ways of coping: emotion-focused and problem-solving. In emotion-focused coping, individuals ignore or distance themselves from problems to help their mental well-being, which actually starts to harm one's mental well-being. In problem-solving coping, people find ways to make the situation or problem better, ranging from simple informative research to the creation of large-scale initiatives. This results in a healthy well-being through time. Ojala took into account that coping was dependent on age, as well as different stressors. In her study, she analyzed how 12-year-old Swedish children coped with climate change through problem-focused coping, de-emphasizing the threat coping, and meaning-focused coping while also considering the effects the strategies had on each children's positive environmental engagement. It was concluded that problem-focused coping had a positive association with environmental engagement. That is, highly problem-focused children worried more about climate change. However, this worry was able to be effectively removed by optimism, purpose, and meaning-focused coping, which also resulted in a positive association with environmental engagement. The more meaning-focused coping the children used, the less they worried about climate change because they were well-informed on how to prevent it. The last strategy used was when the seriousness of climate change was de-emphasized. This resulted in a negative association with environmental engagement. It was clear that if something like climate change was not viewed with urgency, there was no worry as well as no motive for environmental engagement. The study concluded that different age groups might have different ways of coping because there are many possible coping strategies. Thus, according to Ojala a future study should either analyze more age groups or consider more coping strategies to get a more accurate association with environmental engagement.

Ojala, M. 2012. How do children cope with global climate change? Coping strategies, engagement, and well-being. Journal of Environmental Psychology 32, 225-233. http://bit.ly/1IXVGbj

Psychology of Climate Change

by Juana Granados

Many people are reluctant to change their ways of life to address climate change, even acts as simple as turning off a light, or taking shorter showers, because they cannot fully understand how an individual's action will contribute towards the massive change needed for climate mitigation. Aldhous (2009) reported strategies for convincing people to support mitigation for climate change with research collected from different studies. The American Psychological Association created a list of the common reasons people do not support climate change along with how to effectively convince individuals to disregard their beliefs and support mitigation. It is clear that everyone has a different way of perceiving what they hear. Thus, the appropriate methods must be considered for climate change advocacy. Particular demographics must be addressed in a specific manner, based on the interests and beliefs of the group. Instead of explaining the effects of climate change, it is more effective to stress the effects that revolve around the interests of the group. For example, instead of telling people to eat less meat for energy reduction, it is more effective to address the active, athletic young group of society and stress the health benefits. Another climate mitigation strategy is to compare people with others, creating competition, because people become embarrassed about standing out for the wrong reasons. No individual would want to be known as the neighbor who used the most electricity in the entire neighborhood. Data show that the usage of something as simple as smiley faces in an electricity bill made a difference in people's use of energy. Residents who used more electricity than their neighbors received a sad face and stopped using as much electricity. In comparison, those who received a happy face continued using the same amount because they knew they were already saving energy. It was concluded that the most effective way to engage public support for climate mitigation was by providing real numbers of energy usage and framing them in a way that reflected people's performance relative to others, along with clearly framing benefits on a short-term scale instead of long-term promises.

Aldhous, P. 2009. How psychology can curb climate change. New Scientist 203, 6-7.

Are Energy Efficiency Ratings Helping to Reduce Energy Consumption?
by JP Kiefer

The institute for Environmental Decisions in Zurich, Switzerland researched the effect that the energy efficiency ratings displayed on appliances in the European Union have on helping consumers to conserve energy. Since 2010, the European Union has standardized an energy label for more than 10 product categories, allowing each product to be rated with a letter ranging up to an A+++ and down to a D. While other information is displayed alongside the letter grade of each product, members of the Institute for Environmental Decisions feared that consumers did not know how to interpret the number of kWh used per year by a product, and that they instead focused only on the arbitrary letter grade. The institute describes an "energy efficiency fallacy" in which consumers assume that a high-energy efficiency rating automatically implies low energy consumption. This could be a problem if consumers unnecessarily buy larger versions of a product- say a large television- because it has the same energy rating as a smaller television, despite using substantially more energy. Consumers also might be more willing to leave appliances on when not in use if it is believed the electronics are energy efficient. Research suggests that while consumers are willing to pay more money for appliances with higher energy efficiency ratings, there is little correlation between a consumer's willingness to purchase an energy efficient appliance and their attitude towards other sustainable behavior.

The energy efficiency fallacy could contribute to the current trend towards larger products, which led to an increase in absolute energy consumption. A system that was designed to help reduce energy consumption might actually be increasing it by misleading consumers into thinking large products are okay. The Institute for Environmental Decisions calls for a redesign of the energy rating system that can help lead consumers towards sustainable purchase behavior and away from large appliances.

Waechter *et al.*, 2015. The misleading effect of energy efficiency information on perceived energy friendliness of electric goods. Journal of Cleaner Production xxx, 1-10 Science Direct http://bit.ly/1cVd4B8

Why Buy a Hybrid Car?
by JP Kiefer

With some experts expecting the transport sector to contribute to 50% of worldwide greenhouse gas emissions by 2030, hybrid cars may be a great alternative to reduce climate change resulting from increased vehicle use. Despite this, some consumers choose not to drive hybrid vehicles. Ritsuko (2011), claims that this is a result of a car being more than just a utilitarian means of transport, but also an item laden with cultural meaning and image such as identity and status. Ritsuko researched what makes a customer buy a hybrid vehicle in order to discover how to encourage them to do so.

Ritsuko did so by means of a survey with respondents from individuals who purchased a Toyota Prius three to four years previously. This survey was developed with help from four Toyota sales assistants who determined that the average Prius customer was middle-aged, well informed, and professional. Ritsuko developed a survey that divided reasons for buying a car into 5 factors that ended up accounting for 64.83% of the variance in reasons customers bought a Prius. The largest portion of this was the first factor, which was that people bought the Prius because driving it reduces the effects of climate change. This explained 22% of the variance. The second highest factor at 16% of the variance was that driving a Prius would provide a desirable image for the driver, followed by a desire to be considerate to others and being socially responsible at 13%. The fourth factor was that driving the Prius enabled the customer to gain independence from oil producers and provide access to free benefits to hybrid drivers, like specified parking spots at 8%. Finally, the lowest factor was that driving the Prius granted the customer government incentives and to spend less on fuel at 6%.

Overall, environmental friendliness seemed to be the primary motivator for an individual looking to buy a Prius, however this could be utilized better if advertisements highlighted more immediate or local environmental benefits than the global issue of climate change. Ritsuko also suggests that because the cost benefits of the Prius seemed to be of the least importance to consumers, government incentives should be aimed towards low-income families who would not be able to afford a hybrid otherwise.

Ritsuko, R., Sevastyanova, K., 2011. Going Hybrid: An Analysis of Consumer Purchase Motivations. Energy Policy 39, 2217-2227.

Can Advertisements Alter Environmental Behavior?
by JP Kiefer

With approximately 40% of the UK's emissions capable of being linked to actions undertaken by individuals, it is clear that public support is essential to counteracting climate change. The UK attempted to gain this support with its *Act on CO2* campaign, but it found that certain advertisements, such as those developed to elicit fear in its audience, were extremely ineffective. Adam Corner (2011) looks at the advertisements of the campaign in an attempt to systematically critique the social marketing approach to engaging the public on climate change.

Social marketing is the systematic application of marketing concepts and techniques to achieve specific behavioral goals relevant to the social good. It has been used to target issues like obesity and tobacco products, but never climate change. The first thing Corner noticed when attempting to apply social marketing to climate change is that information-based approaches were ineffective. This is due to the weak link between attitudes

125

and behavior. Information-based ads may have effectively changed the attitudes of their audience towards climate change, but did little to reduce greenhouse gas emissions. One factor that may make such advertisements less effective is that most other advertisements promote behavior that is not environmentally friendly. While not directly promoting that people should be wasteful with their greenhouse gas emissions, most advertisements promote self-enhancing values like materialism and personal ambition, which do not always go along with values of respecting the environment.

Corner states that no campaign will be successful in changing behavior if the behavior is widely acceptable, but that it is important to begin by targeting specific groups of people rather than the entire population. Advertisements directed towards a specific demographic will be able to strike a chord in an individual better than a general advertisement appealing to everyone. This is partly what makes social networks the most effective way to utilize social marketing. The fact that advertisements are able to target a group of people with common interests and that individuals are seeing the opinions of people who's opinions they trust and care about makes social networks very powerful. While no research has specifically tested whether social marketing on social networks can influence pro-environmental behavior, evidence about social networks and the diffusion of behavior in general suggests a promising course of action.

Corner, A., Randall, A., 2011. Selling climate change? The limitations of social marketing as a strategy for climate change public engagement. Global Environmental Change 21, 1005-1014.

Global Framing and the Production of Environmentally Conscious Citizens
by Margaret Loncki

One of the most obvious solutions to prevent further climate change is energy usage reductions, but with the increased magnitude of global energy consumption, these seem unlikely anytime soon. Spence *et al.* (2014) explore whether energy savings is most beneficial when presented in terms of financial cost, CO_2, or kilowatt-hours. In the United Kingdom, smart meters are used to measure the energy consumption of private residences. Although the government is pushing to have smart meters be standard in every home, only half of the population know what they are, and of those who do, only a quarter understand their purpose. Framing energy consumption in terms of cost is a very easy concept for consumers to understand but due to varying energy costs, the benefits of energy reduction are not often clear. Presenting energy consumption in terms of CO_2 release is not as easily understood as financial cost, but is thought to reduce the "psychological distance" of climate change. Spence *et al.* also found that environmental framing encourage behavioral spillover, the idea that changing one behavior for environmental reasons often leads to picking up other environmental behaviors as a result.

Two studies were conducted, both using samples of undergraduate students from the University of Nottingham. The first of the two studies found that when offered energy savings in terms of CO_2 output, students were more often motivated to save energy because of climate change, but when presented with energy consumption in terms of cost, students typically stated financial reasons for reducing energy consumptions. The second of the two studies suggested that environmental framing "increased climate change salience". Both studies supported the notion that environmental framing made climate change more accessible and increased desire to make a difference. This desire increased the likelihood of individuals developing other environmentally friendly practices.

Spence, A., Leygue, C., Bedwell, B., O'Malley, C., 2014, Engaging with energy reduction: Does a climate change fram have the potential for achiecing broader sustainable behavior?. Journal of Environment Psychology 38, 17-28.

Cognitive and Behavioral Challenges in Responding to Climate Change
by Sam Peterson

A serious increase in the rate of climate change began almost two centuries ago with the inception of fossil fuel combustion, and global warming became a focal point in media coverage more than twenty years ago, yet no industrialized or developing nation has sufficiently reduced greenhouse gas emissions (GHG), or adequately educated its populace to the dangers of rapidly fluctuating global temperatures. Norgaard examines worldwide response, or lack thereof, to climate change in a Development Economics background paper for the 2010 World Development Report for the World Bank and finds that citizens generally do care about climate change, but a systemic and systematic psychological routine of denial and widespread misinformation hinder the public response.

Climate change unequally affects the residents of Planet Earth. Public opinion in many industrialized nations centers around a belief that climate change is distant from daily life, while poorer nations already feel the burden of rising sea levels and increased severity of weather patterns (Norgaard 2006, Nisbet and Myers 2007, Brechin 2008, cited by Norgaard 2009). Compounding this problem are the disproportionate GHG emissions from developed countries in the northern hemisphere, as well as a widespread misunderstanding or general lack of knowledge regarding climate change (Watson *et al.* 1998, cited by Norgaard 2009). Multiple studies have found the public to be "poorly informed about global warming" (Dunlap 1998, cited by Norgaard 2009), and a widespread poor understanding of climate change (Bord, Fisher and O'Connor, 1998, cited by Norgaard 2009). Between 1991 and 2001, Brechin compiled public opinion surveys from 15 nations and reported in 2003 even as scientific consensus on climate change increases, "knowledge regarding causes of climate change by the public is minimal." In a 2001 survey, "citizens of Mexico knew the most about...climate change, but even here only one-quarter of respondents correctly identified burning fossil fuels as the primary cause of global warming." In the United States, only 15% of respondents correctly identified GHG emissions as the cause of global warming, slightly behind Cuba. According to a 2007 US Gallup poll, only 22% of respondents reported they understood the issue of global warming "very well."

This lack of understanding cannot be directly correlated with a lack of concern, but in a 1998 Gallup Health of the Planet poll, respondents from Canada, the US, Mexico, Brazil, Portugal and Russia reported they saw "global warming as a problem," but not nearly as important as ozone depletion or rainforest destruction. Additionally, very few respondents would voluntarily take steps to help alleviate effects of climate change, such as driving less. Gallup polls in America showed the percentage of people who "personally worry a great deal about global warming" dropped from 35% to 28% from 1989 to 2001, while the percentage that worry "not at all" rose from 12% to 17% during the same period (Saad, 2002).

There are several plausible theories regarding the lack of global response to what is considered the most important environmental issue of the 21st century. Norgaard identifies the following as reasons for public apathy:

"1) people don't know enough to realize the danger, 2) people don't care enough to take action, 3) there is hierarchy of needs and climate change is not an immediate need, 4) people trust that the government will fix the problem."

In 2006, Norgaard found people actually avoid acknowledging disturbing information, like climate change statistics, to avoid emotions of fear and guilt and follow cultural norms that help support positive feelings of national identity. This directly contributes to one of the most common problems with climate change response, which is the condition that public support hinges on the ability to solve an issue. Climate change, to a majority of citizens in developed countries, seems like an issue that has no solution, and therefore they employ psychological barriers to "resign themselves to their fate" (Hellevik 2002, Krosnic *et al.* 2006, cited by Norgaard 2009).

In order to understand the systematic apathy toward climate change, one must also examine the "social organization of climate denial." In Norgaard's previous research, she found that people generally knew about climate change, but failed to act on the information given to them in their everyday lives. Individuals "block out or distance themselves" for a variety of motives, including to maintain coherent meaning systems (Gecas and Burke 1995, cited by Norgaard 2009), and to stay in desirable emotional states (Rosenberg 1991, Meijndes *et al.* 2001, cited by Norgaard 2009). Climate change denial, used for the above reasons, can be placed in one of three categories described by British sociologist Stanley Cohen: literal, interpretive, or implicatory. Literal denial is the "assertion that something did not happen," and interpretive denial is the use of euphemisms to change meaning, so climate change apathy likely falls in implicatory denial, where "the psychological, political or moral implications that conventionally follow" information are denied (Cohen 2001, cited by Norgaard 2009).

Though there is widespread misinformation and lack of understanding regarding the causes and effects of climate change, it is evident that in recent years, a majority of people are concerned about global temperature increases, according to a 2008 Gallup poll. For the first time in history, this placed the citizens who were concerned about the state of climate change in a healthy majority, and signaled to policymakers that the public is prepared to move in the direction of reducing GHG emissions by governmental order, if not voluntarily. Norgaard recommends that policy be changed regarding the climate so that citizens do not feel powerless, but hopeful and prepared to actively participate in a group effort to halt climate change before it is too late.

Norgaard, K.M., 2009. Cognitive and behavioral challenges in responding to climate change. World Bank Policy Research Working Paper Series, Vol 4940.

Psychology Behind Climate-Related Inaction
by Emily Segal

Though many people agree that climate change is a pressing issue in today's world, very few of those people actually change their behavior to remedy this. In some cases there are structural factors limiting their ability to make decisions that would reduce their ecological footprint. For example, people on a low-income budget might not have the extra money to install solar panels. However, for those who are not restricted by structural factors, adaptation to a more sustainable lifestyle is not currently accepted on the scale it must be if those same people are serious about reducing climate change. Psychologist Robert Gifford suggests that there are three main reasons behind this inaction. Ignorance first will hinder people from altering their behavior because they are not aware of the problem at all. Secondly, once one becomes aware of the problem, various psychological processes may prohibit action. Lastly, after some action is taken, the person may think their action establishes they have done their part to reduce climate change when in reality they have not done enough, or they have done something that is counterproductive. To better understand this disconnect between awareness and lack of action, Gifford further divided the three main reasons behind inaction into seven psychological barriers preventing people from doing what they should in order to truly reduce climate change.

The first barrier is that as humans, we have limited cognition about the problem. The human brain has not evolved much since thousands of years ago when our primary concerns were short-term problems such as avoiding immediate danger. So, naturally, it is more difficult for humans to understand the danger climate change poses, which is thought of as more gradual and removed from our everyday lives.

Secondly, individuals' ideologies may prevent them from adopting new behaviors. When someone has integrated a belief system into their life that does not support climate change mitigation, it is unlikely they can

131

or will easily put the necessity of pro-environmental action above their commitment to their pre-existing beliefs.

The third barrier that inhibits the ability for people to change their actions (when they are aware that they should) is comparisons with other people. As social animals, people naturally compare their actions to those of the people around them and prefer conforming to social norms than changing their behavior and standing out from the crowd. So, unless a vast majority of individuals start investing in more sustainable lifestyles, the general public can validate their non-sustainable actions by arguing that they should not have to act responsibly to combat climate change since no one else around them is.

The fourth barrier is sunk costs. Once people have invested their money in something, even if it is harmful to the environment, it is difficult for them to part with whatever that is. Simply put, people do not like feeling as though they are loosing money, even if that is not necessarily the case. For example, economists have shown that over the long term, opting for public transportation or biking is more cost efficient than maintaining a fossil-fueled car. Yet, most people choose to hold on to their car, the sunk cost investment, because they cannot rationalize giving up something they had already spent money on. In addition, it can be difficult to convince people to change their habits once they are comfortable with them.

The fifth barrier, discredence, is based on the idea that individuals are less likely to follow advice from those they already perceive in a negative light. When people mistrust the scientists or government officials who are informing them about climate change, they can easily brush of their advice because they view the source of the information itself as faulty. Unfortunately, a result of combined mistrust and sunk costs is outright denial—that climate change is happening, that it is due to our actions as humans, or that any one person can help alter the course of climate change at all.

Perceived risks is the sixth barrier promoting inaction. As mentioned before, humans are comfortable with familiarity and are anxious about the uncertainty of changing their behavior. There are various different forms of perceived risk associated with living more sustainably such as functional risk (will my new electric car work?), physical risk (Will riding a bicycle increases the likelihood of accidents?), and social risk (Will others notice or judge me if I change my behavior?). Additionally, the financial risk of investing in sustainable products and the temporal risk that all efforts to reduce climate change may fail cause individuals to feel doubtful about changing their behavior at all.

Finally, the seventh barrier is limited behavior. People are more likely to do something that is easy to adopt, even if it only has a minor effect on climate change, rather than choose a more difficult option that would be much more effective. Additionally, once that one small action is taken, people feel as though they have already done their part in helping prevent climate change. They might even then do something that actually promotes climate change and not feel guilty about it because they have previously made an attempt to help reduce climate change.

Psychologists have come up with strategies that attempt to overcome these barriers. One such strategy includes studying specific barriers at the behavioral level, experimenting with intervention, and then analyzing the impact of that intervention. Another strategy would be to improve understanding of why people either support or oppose policies and technologies for limiting climate change and then use this new information to change the way climate change is addressed. Though it will not be easy, Gifford believes that it is possible for people to overcome the psychological barriers preventing them from acting to their full ability in terms of preventing climate change.

Gifford, R., 2011. The dragons of inaction: Psychological barriers that limit climate change mitigation and adaptation. American Psychologist 66, 290-302.

Psychological Effects of Climate Change
by Breanna Sewell

Global climate change adversely affects the Earth and its inhabitants in a multitude of ways. Perhaps one of the most noteworthy areas, although rarely noted, is the range of psychological effects that climate change can have on us. Susan Clayton and Thomas Doherty address this topic in their article "The Psychological Impacts of Global Climate Change."

The authors first discuss the potential causes of psychological effects that result from climate change. These include media representations of climate change and natural disasters, vulnerability versus resilience of individuals, and social and cognitive factors.

The article then discusses separately the indirect and direct effects of global climate change on the psychological state. The analysis of indirect psychological effects resulted in a wide spread of emotions describing the degree to which Americans feel concerned with the state of our planet. Ranging from "alarmed" to the belief that no action should be taken in regards to climate change, the majority of people fell in the "concerned" category. Those closer to this end of the spectrum are reportedly far more likely to experience sadness, anger, fear, etc. in response to climate change. A shocking 25% of Americans feel depressed or guilty about our environmental state. These emotions stem not from a single event that these people may have experienced, but rather, they are the general feelings associated with, and/or resulting from thought of our planet's deteriorating state.

Direct psychological effects on the other hand are far more straightforward and tend to be the result of a specific event such as a natural disaster. For example, common effects of experiencing a natural disaster include posttraumatic stress disorder, severe depression, and drug and alcohol abuse.

Clayton and Doherty conclude their article with a call to action, requesting an acknowledgement of the severity of psychological effects of climate change and pointing out the duty of psychologists to limit the damage done as a result of environmental issues.

Clayton, S., Doherty, T., 2011. The Psychological Impacts of Global Climate Change. American Psychologist 66, 265. http://bit.ly/1FJx84T

Climate Change and its Impacts on Mental Health

by Phoebe Shum

Francois Bourque and Ashlee Cunsolo Willox claim that besides its obvious environmental impacts, climate change is becoming one of the biggest threats not only to physical human health but mental human health as well (Bourque and Willox, 2014). Many have heard of seasonal depression in which cold weather affects our mood and energy levels, but scholars have only recently come across the much broader psychological impact climate change can have on our mental health. People previously diagnosed with mental health disorders are more likely to be affected, as well as those living in ecologically sensitive areas. The impacts can include psychological distress, depression, anxiety, increased addictions and higher suicide rates.

Bourque and Willox use examples from rural Australia to Northern Canada in order to illustrate the point that climate change can affect the mental health of various populations. For example, in Australia, researchers report that people who are constantly exposed to disruptions in agriculture and environmental degradation such as persistent drought and extreme weather disasters have higher levels of psychological distress and hopelessness. In the last decade, the chronic drought in Australia is believed to have caused suicides, distress, and anxiety. Additionally, older farmers, especially those who are economically disadvantaged and have limited access to mental health services, are most vulnerable to these outcomes, facing lower agricultural productivity and economic insecurity. Indigenous populations in Australia are also drastically affected through land degradation, as their cultural traditions may be simultaneously destroyed.

Similarly, Canada's Inuit population, who live close to the natural environment and rely on the land for food and cultural continuity, are facing immense health impacts due to the changing weather patterns of ice and snow. Activities like hunting, trapping and fishing are being disrupted. Suicide rates amongst the Inuit population are

11 times higher than the Canadian average, perhaps because of mental stress from climate change.

As climate change evolves into a globally accepted phenomenon, the authors suggest that people will be less inclined to take action due to the "diffusion of responsibility" theory. The research towards mental health sensitivity towards climate change will undoubtedly help to stimulate response and constructive steps toward climate mitigation.

Bourque, F., Cunsolo Willox, A., 2014. Climate change: The next challenge for public mental health? International Review of Psychiatry 26, 415-422.

Coping with Climate Change in Sweden
by Phoebe Shum

How does the young Swedish population cope with their climate change concerns? While many studies have focused on uncovering the emotions related to understanding climate change, Maria Ojala (2012), assistant professor in Sweden's Uppsala University, takes on the task of exploring how people of different ages cope with climate change. In order to encourage people to do something about climate change, people must first fathom its dire consequences on our Earth's future. Studying the different coping mechanisms that people have towards climate change can help to determine whether topics like ethical sensibility and action competence will cross their minds.

Ojala's study focused on groups of young Swedish children, ranging from late childhood/early adolescence, mid- to late-adolescence, and early adulthood. The study group was given a questionnaire that consisted of questions such as:

(1) Describe in your own words why you are not worried about climate change to any great degree.

(2) If a friend told you that he or she worries a lot about climate change, what would you say to make him or her not worry so much?

(3) In your own words, describe your main reasons for feeling hope concerning climate change; i.e., why are you hopeful?

Through thematic analysis, Ojala identified coping strategies such as: de-emphasizing the seriousness of climate change, distancing, hyperactivation, positive reappraisal, and existential hope. Overall, almost all of the strategies were used by all three groups, although each was used to different degrees. Ojala also aimed to identify the ways in which young people promote hope towards climate change. The youngest group tended to use distancing as opposed to the problem-focused coping that the older two groups used. Expectedly, the youngest group placed more trust in researchers and scientists than the others as younger children tend to accept facts given to them. University students, part of the third group, were more inclined to trust politicians and international agreements.

Ojala's study assists teachers in understanding how to approach climate change with children of all ages. While people don't usually think that distancing strategies are as productive as problem-focused strategies, children actually retain more information by disengaging themselves from their emotions. By understanding the cognitive and emotional reasons behind hope and cope, we can better accommodate the way we present our information to audiences and generate more effective conversation.

Ojala, M., 2012. Regulating Worry, Promoting Hope: How Do Children, Adolescents, and Young Adults Cope with Climate Change? International Journal of Environmental and Science Education 7, 537-561.

Relationship Between Values and Engagement with Climate Change
by Sarah Whitney

Adam Corner, Ezra Markowitz, and Nick Pidgeon (2014) analyze various works of research from philosophical, psychological, and anthropological fields to determine that those with self-transcendent values are most likely to actively engage with climate change related issues. This collection of research provides vital information for promoting sustainable practices successfully in campaigns and political policies. The authors first establish the difference between human values and the economic principle of valuation. A preference that can be influenced by the market, such as an incentive or discount, is one that is short-lived and does not influence long-term sustainable practices. The authors then state that values are a significant indication of engagement as they represent a relatively stable aspect of individuals' personalities, preferences and behavior. Values may change slightly over the course of a lifetime but are relatively engrained as opposed to the transparency of economic values. Shalom Schwartz's well established psychological theory divides values into four clusters: openness to change, conservative view of respecting tradition, self-transcendence, and self-enhancement. Self-transcendence is defined as focusing ones attention on others and being above one's own ego. This includes characteristics like altruism or charitable behavior, forgiveness and loyalty. On the other hand, self-enhancement includes ambition, hunger for power, and putting oneself before others. Schwartz concepts are used as a base in further writing of DeGroot and Steg who divide values into three categories of egoistic (self minded), biospheric (environmentally minded), and altruistic (others focused). Anthropologically these same values are divided between if they align with the needs of the greater community or self. Philosophically, values are a part of ethics, which are moral principles that help us make decisions. These values predetermine if one reacts positively or negatively to environmental issues. Specifically self-transcendent and altruistic values are associated with a positive reaction to mitigation methods regarding climate change. The values we hold filter the information we are exposed to about climate change which either lead or divert us from taking action.

The authors further state that association between values and public engagement with climate change determines political polarization. Political conservatism is often associated with skepticism towards climate change, and is correlated with the ambiguous relationship between traditional values and climate change engagement. In a recent study individuals with altruistic values found the issue of climate change more threatening than those with egoistic values. Individualistic communities sided with policies that supported free markets in regards to the matter of climate change. Political parties act as filter in which individuals divide themselves based upon their correlated values. The authors argue that it is crucial in politics to know the values of your audience to better advertise the significance of an issue like climate change. They also state that advertising climate change in regards to economics is not successful as the transparent value of money is only a short-term solution. Instead, the authors recommend touching on public health and the natural beauty of nature when promoting sustainable practices in the conservative party. The authors then continue to state that advertising directly to those with self-transcendent values rather than the opposition is the most influential strategy, as those with altruistic values are more likely to switch to sustainable long-term practices.

Corner, A., Markowitz, E., Pidgeon, A., 2014. Public engagement with climate change: the role of human values. WIREs Climate Change. 5:411–422

The Confusing Relationship between Consciousness, Culture, and Climate Change
by Sarah Whitney

The Memory Network (2014) conducts a discussion where Greg Garrard talks about the difficulties of cultural and individual comprehension of climate change.

As a society, we are perplexed by the idea of climate change, and how to approach and find solutions to its many effects. As individuals, humans are puzzled by the temporality, significant scale, and contributions they can make to mitigate climate change. Identifying and understanding these blockages may help formulate meaningful solutions and sustainable practices that can be easily enacted by the public.

Culturally, society is perplexed in the way we should currently perceive and act upon climate change. As a whole, society has formed the idea that humans have become a geological factor because of the massive effect we have on our climate. Our consciousness has organized climate change through scientification, where we blur all the facts together to form a specific outlook of global warming. Garrard uses "prolific mourning" to describe the current outlook on global climate change. This phrase describes the idea of looking to the future and then looking to the past, or otherwise thinking about the future predicament of the globe with climate change and what humans might have done differently if we had the chance. He then describes a factor of the ideology of "prolific mourning" called the predicament of "the ambiguous role of the child". When looking at the future, society views children as the reason to take current action to combat the effects of global warming as well as the hopeful solution to solve our problems. However society knows that a major driver of climate change is the fossil fuel consumption caused by the demand of goods by our increasing population. Therefore subconsciously, society has a dilemma between being hopeful in our children and considering not having them at all.

Garrard states that individually, humans have great difficulty in comprehending the scale and temporality of climate change. He uses an example of the final message of an "Inconvenient Truth" in which Al Gore wants brighten the spirits of the audience by saying that even turning off the lights contributes to mitigating the effects of global climate change. Garrard contributes lack of implementation of sustainable practices to the confusing relationship between the scale of the problem and the scale of the solution. He says that the vast issue of climate change is demoralizing to humans, as they believe they are helpless. Their actions, like turning off a few lights, seem completely insignificant when compared to issues like rising sea levels. Furthermore, the confusion of time scales confuses many individuals. Climate change is phrased as an urgent matter we need to attend to, yet some of its effects may not be seen for centuries. It is difficult for some individuals to plan ahead a few days let alone a decade or a century. Thus the problem of time becomes an issue when planning and implementing ways to combat global climate change as it is almost unfathomable to an individual. Finally, Greg Garrard discusses the "unbearable lightness of green". This example draws upon the psychological theory of diffusion of responsibility. As human population grows, so do the effects of global warming. The more people there are on earth, the less impact an individual has on fighting climate change. This exponential growth of the population diffuses the "heavy burden" of climate change and dilutes its urgency. Thus individuals feel insubstantial in any efforts to combat global warming and consequently this pressing issue seems "unbearably light".

Garrard, G. 2014. Climate Change and the Art of Memory: Greg Garrard. The Memory Network. http://bit.ly/1dsbAiL

POLITICS AND CLIMATE CHANGE

Florida Bans Terms Essential to the Climate Change Discussion
by Jordan Aronowitz

As the most low-lying and vulnerable region in the entire United States, Florida is at risk to be damaged by the most effects of global climate change. Many people in the coastal communities fear for their safety if a drastic increase in sea level were to occur. The destruction of beaches and coral reefs, and anxiety about farming have created a concerned population; however, according to an article by Tristram Korten (2015), the government has banned the terms "climate change" and "global warming" in official communication, sabotaging the fight to repair the environment. Their justification is that they will never support a theory without proof. Denial of climate change is not uncommon and can be discussed in a civilized manor, but the active practice of explicitly banning proper terms in order to hamper discussion is despicable and puts the state of Florida at a major risk of devastation.

Governor Scott has admitted that he is "not a scientist." On the rare occasions when he agrees to meet with local experts, little progress is made as the governor refuses to ask significant questions and tends to leave meetings early if no hard evidence is presented. The downward spiral began in 2011. Government officials already frowned upon the terms "climate change" and "global warming", but they took it one step further by firing employees who believed in climate change and global warming, mostly Everglade scientists, replacing them with consultants from big businesses. The government's reasoning was that they did not want employees contradicting their own opinion. Basically, they were fired because they believed in climate change.

The author of this article goes on to cite specific cases when the State of Florida mistreated local experts because they supported the idea of climate change and used prohibited terms. One thing is similar in all these cases: the scientists were fighting to maintain the fragile, yet unique, Florida ecosystem. The government is preventing them from accomplishing their goals.

Kortem, Tristram. 2015. In Florida, officials ban term 'climate change.' Miami Herald. Mar 8, 2015.

Does Ted Cruz's Ignorance Make Him 'Unfit' for the Presidency?
by Jordan Aronowitz

With the Obama administration in power for the past six years, the American people have become accustomed to a government that at least recognizes climate change. Even if the population does not directly see explicit progress, we know that there are people working hard to ensure the prolonged health of our earth. With the 2016 election quickly approaching, a drastic change in the administration's opinion towards climate change is possible. In an article by Shawn Thomas (2015), the opinions of one of the leading candidates in the upcoming presidential election, Ted Cruz, are analyzed. According to Thomas, Cruz's blatant denial of climate change make him unfit to lead our country in the 21st century.

Of course there will always be skeptics about whether or not climate change is a real threat to our survival; however, strictly following predetermined opinions and mocking experts in the field is extremely counter-productive. Cruz explains how in a recent visit to New Hampshire, an infamous swing state during election season, the abundance of snow completely discredits the opinions of scientists who are insisting that global warming and climate change are legitimate issues. He goes on to assert that the climate is always changing and the idea of global warming is a fad. These assertions would be fine if not for the fact that snowfall patterns

144

across the entire United States have never been more unpredictable, affecting the climate and the daily lives of people across the country. In this past winter, we have seen daily a temperature fluctuation from below freezing to above 60 degrees in the Northeast, a fraction of normal precipitation in Seattle, and snow long after snowfall usually occurs. Denial of climate change is not acceptable anymore.

We are in a period where the protection of our environment is imperative, so even if Ted Cruz is a practical option to be the next President of the United States, his opinions towards the future of our climate make him inept to lead.

Thomas, Shawn. 2015. Ted Cruz Climate Change Comments Make Him 'Unfit' For Presidency. CBS Local/Associated Press. Mar 24, 2015.

The Politicization of Climate Change
by Brendan Busch

In recent years, the debate over the proper response to climate change has become increasingly political rather than scientific. Noting this, Kerrie L. Unsworth, a professor and associate dean at the business school of the University of Western Australia, and Kelly S. Fielding, a Senior Research Fellow at the Institute for Social Science Research at the University of Queensland, set out to study the effects of an individual's political affiliation on their opinions about climate change. Before presenting their own research, Unsworth and Fielding point to a 2003 study by G.L. Cohen that demonstrated people's tendencies to follow their chosen political party unquestioningly, by showing that people were likely to support a welfare policy that was approved by leading members of their political party even if the policy went against their own personal beliefs or the core values of the party itself. Observing this study, Unsworth and Fielding wondered if they could produce a similar result with respect to climate change.

In order to test the degree to which political association affects climate change beliefs, Unsworth and Fielding surveyed two different groups of randomly selected Australians. One group was reminded of the major political parties' stances on global warming before being asked about their own opinions, thus reinforcing with their political identity (Unsworth and Fielding define this process as making the subjects' political identity "salient"). The other group, the control group, was not reminded of their party's position on climate change, and thus did not have their political identity made salient. After conducting their survey, Unsworth and Fielding found an important distinction between those who identified with the Liberal or National Parties (Australia's right-leaning parties) and those who identified with the Labor or Green Parties (Australia's left-leaning parties). While there was little difference between the opinions of the control group and the politically salient group for the leftist parties (who tend to support active response to climate change), there was a significant difference between the groups when it came to the rightist parties (who tend to deny the existence of climate change). In universities, 64.4% of the rightist control group believed that humans had a significant impact on climate change, while only 40.5% of the politically salient group expressed the same beliefs. A similar result was found for the general population of Australia, with a negligible difference between the leftist groups and a 44.7% to 36.0% split between the rightist control group and the politically salient rightist group respectively.

Seeing as the only difference between members of the control group and politically salient groups was their reminder of the parties' climate change stances prior to the survey, Unsworth and Fielding assert that simple affiliation with conservative parties (rather than an agreement with the parties' ideology) can have a significant effect on people's climate change beliefs. Although this survey was conducted only in Australia, Unsworth and Fielding believe that it has international repercussions, as Australia has a very similar political climate to both the United States and the United Kingdom. Although the study shows that political affiliation with the right currently propagates climate change denial, Unsworth and Fielding are optimistic about the survey's implications. Based on their research, they believe that if leaders of conservative political parties were to reverse their stances on climate change, it would cause a significant change in the beliefs of their followers as well.

Unsworth, K. L., & Fielding, K. S. 2014. It's political: How the salience of one's political identity changes climate change beliefs and policy support. Global Environmental Change, 27, 131-137. http://bit.ly/1Gxvq7o

Polarization of Climate Change—Scientific or Political?
by Brendan Busch

Due to the intense polarization of climate change in America, Congress has had very little success in addressing it. Noting this dilemma, Dana R. Fisher, an associate professor in the Department of Sociology at the University of Maryland, Joseph Waggle, a doctoral student studying sociology at the University of Maryland, and Philip Leifeld, a researcher at the Institute of Political Science at the University of Bern, set out to identify the characteristics and roots of the polarization of the climate change debate in American politics. After examining the records of several sessions of Congress, they found that, although the general public seems to be debating the science behind the existence of climate change, Congress has reached somewhat of a consensus on the scientific proof of climate change, and is instead considering the political ramifications of legislative actions against climate change.

Fisher, Waggle, and Leifeld first assessed the polarization of the climate change issue in the American public as a whole, and identified the media as one of its key driving factors. They asserted that, by allowing equal time for both mainstream climate change scientists and climate change deniers, the media is giving the public the idea that these are two equally supported and credible positions. This need to present two sides to the issue discredits the fact that the vast majority of scientists are in agreement about the existence of climate change, unduly strengthening the position of the countermovement against climate change science.

However, an entirely different type of polarization has emerged in Congress. By thoroughly examining the 109th (Republican-led) and 110th (Democratic-led) sessions of Congress, Fisher, Waggle, and Leifeld were able to determine the source of this polarization. Unlike the American public, most of Congress came to accept science behind climate change between its 109th and 110th sessions (the amount Congressional statements denying the existence of anthropogenic climate change dropped from 23% to 11% of total Congressional climate change statements). However, there was a stark disagreement in the effects climate change legislation would have on the nation's economy. Sixty-four percent of Congressional statements in the 109th session of Congress claimed that legislation limiting carbon dioxide emission would hurt the US economy, and this number dropped only to 42% in the 110th session. These statistics reveal the true characteristics of a debate that has been mischaracterized by public discourse; although it may seem that America's political elites are engaged in a scientific debate about the existence of climate change, they are really in a polarized disagreement about the political and economic consequences of climate change legislation.

Fisher, D. R., Waggle, J., & Leifeld, Phillip, L. 2013. Where Does Political Polarization Come From? Locating Polarization Within the US Climate Change Debate. American Behavioral Scientist, 57, 70-92.

Political Science Solutions to Climate Change
by Brendan Busch

While climate change has received a substantial amount of attention from scientists and economists, American political scientists have remained comparatively quiet on the issue. However, in a 2014 speech to the American Political Science Association, Robert O. Keohane, a professor of political affairs at Princeton University, advocated for the importance of considering climate change from a political science perspective. He believes that the current political framing of climate change (which is centered around mitigation) is critically flawed, mainly because of the free-rider dilemma: climate change mitigation will benefit the entire world regardless of who undertakes it, so people have no incentive to personally bear the cost of climate change mitigation. In his speech, Keohane outlines the strengths and weaknesses of several other political framings for climate change, and proposes a solution of his own.

The first alternative political framing that Keohane discusses is a focus on climate adaptation instead of mitigation. While this framing may be beneficial for wealthy nations, as it offers concrete, immediate solutions to citizens directly affected by global warming, adaptation is often not economically attainable for poor nations. Therefore, Keohane advises against this policy, as it will raise resentment and political tension between wealthy nations, that are the main contributors to climate change and the most able to adapt, and poor nations, that will be the most affected by climate change and the least able to adapt. Another political frame proposed by Keohane is the construction of new infrastructure to either remove CO_2 from the air or offer alternative sources of energy. He argues that this could be a better alternative to mitigation because it involves the construction of infrastructure, which is more politically appealing than enforcing regulations, and is therefore more likely to pass through Congress. However, he cautions that this policy would be extremely expensive and that not all of the necessary technology has been fully developed yet. A third political frame brought up by Keohane is the concept of using modern technology to reflect a small percentage of the sun's radiation, reducing some of the effects of global warming. Although this policy horrifies some scientists, Keohane believes that it is entirely possible that this option will be necessary in the future. Therefore, he recommends constructing some form of international governing body to make decisions about climate engineering now, while the need for such drastic action is still relatively low.

However, after examining all of these possible alternatives, Keohane believes that the best solution would be to reframe the current policy of mitigation. One way he proposes doing this is to impose a tax on carbon emission, but then redistribute the gains from this tax equally amongst the population. Therefore, people will be incentivized to reduce their carbon emissions, as people who use large amounts of carbon will not be fully compensated by the rebate, while those who use a moderate amount of carbon may be overly compensated and thus receive a profit from the policy. Keohane recognizes that this is not the only possible solution, but urges other political scientists to consider the issue and create incentive-based solutions to promote action on climate change issues.

Keohane, R.O., 2015. The Global Politics of Climate Change: Challenge for Political Science. PS: Political Science & Politics, 48, 19-26.

Pollution and Politics
by Jackson Cooney

Republican senator, Mitch McConnell, of Kentucky has been pushing states to ignore President Obama's global warming regulations. He argues that the administration's anti-coal initiative aims to destroy America's power generation under the pretense of protecting the climate. The EPA along with the President is requiring each state to submit a plan outlining how they are going to cut coal plant pollution. These plans will lead to the shutdown of hundreds of power plants in the Administration's attempt to rely more heavily on renewable energy sources. As of now, 12 states have filed lawsuits in protest of this plan. However Senator McConnell has advised that the best way to fight this initiative would be to refuse to submit state plans.

Democrats seem confused by McConnell's actions because, under the terms of the Clean Air Act, it is the job of the executive branch to deal with carbon pollution rules, not that of the legislative branch. Gina McCarthy, the administrator of the EPA, has been preparing a plan that could be applied to any state to deal with carbon pollution. This plan would be imposed on any state that fails to supply its own plan. This was the EPA's response to Senator McConnell's defiance. Because of this, the states that refuse to produce their own plan could be stuck with a stricter, generic plan created by the EPA.

As of now, it seems unlikely that Senator McConnell will be able to stop this process. If the Republicans in congress could pass legislation to weaken the rules required for each state, the President would veto. It is unlikely that the Republicans have two-thirds majority to override this veto. Because of this, the Obama administration is expecting a legal battle to ensue. The EPA has asked for $3.5 million dollars to pay for 20 lawyers to defend the regulations.

Davenport, C. (2015, March 4). McConnell Urges States to Defy US Plan to Cut Greenhouse Gas. Retrieved March 8, 2015, from http://nyti.ms/1FNLVNG

Obama's Take on Climate
by Jackson Cooney

On Wednesday April 20th, President Obama made a visit to the Florida Everglades (Shear, 2015), and gave a speech about the importance of wildlife conservation arguing that climate change should be a major issue in the 2016 elections. The fact that this speech was given in the backyard of the former Republican governor, Jeb Bush, and the Republican senator, Marco Rubio, shows that Obama believes this is a party issue. His trip to the everglades was intended to highlight the differences between the Republican and Democratic parties. This act could be construed as an attempt to give the Democrats a leg up in the upcoming election. This type of campaigning could be very effective, especially in a state like Florida, where the various effects of climate change are already appearing.

Obama refrained from mentioning the Republican governor and senator directly, however, it seemed clear that he intended to increase the pressure on those who would neglect climate issues. Mr. Bush and Mr. Rubio, both of whom have an opportunity to run for President, the latter having already announced his candidacy, will now be pressured to address climate change during their campaigns. Both of these candidates have showed that, to some extent, they doubt the relationship between human activities and the changing climate. Obama's remarks on Wednesday were also an attempt to bring support and attention to his climate change agenda. This summer, he is expected to reveal his final climate change agenda, which will involve a large cut in coal-fired energy sources. Republicans are calling this initiative the war on coal because it threatens to shut down hundreds of coal power plants.

This speech and the attention that it is being given show that climate issues should be addressed in politics; climate change has become a topic that will divide voters.

Shear, M. (2015, April 22). Obama Uses a Visit to the Everglades to Press His Climate Agenda. Retrieved April 26, 2015, from http://nyti.ms/1FxJStU

Public Participation and Trust in Chinese Nuclear Power Development
by Sam Peterson

Following the Fukushima Daiichi nuclear incident on Friday, March 11, 2011, Chinese citizens in the rural Shandong peninsula began stockpiling salt and consuming iodide tablets as precaution against radiation. Their government had provided little to no information regarding the immediate fallout of the Japanese nuclear event, and would continue to withhold information regarding the incident until several weeks later.

These levels of secrecy and privacy concerning nuclear information are common in China, where an "iron nuclear triangle," comprised of national Chinese government agencies, in particular the extremely powerful State Council, the National Development and Reform Commission (NDRC), and National Nuclear Safety Administration (NNSA), state-owned nuclear enterprises (SOEs) and scientific experts from universities and research institutes. There is a seemingly endless list of Chinese regulatory agencies with varying degrees of authority over nuclear power plant creation, safety, administration, and emergency preparedness. This bureaucracy presides over all nuclear activity, but there exists no "systematic legal system" with which to supervise the safety and development of Chinese nuclear ambitions. After the magnitude 9.0 earthquake and subsequent tsunami, which caused the Fukushima Daiichi plant disaster, a majority of OECD countries (Organisation for Economic Co-operation and Development) began thorough reviews of their respective nuclear programs. With every major nuclear incident, particularly those followed by massive radiation leaks, such as Three Miles Island, where a meltdown occurred March 28, 1979 outside Middletown, Pennsylvania, or Chernobyl, in the northern Kiev oblast of Ukraine, where an explosion occurred April 26, 1986, there have been serious social pressures against the continued expanse of nuclear power. Though there were massive protests in Hong Kong, involving 56 local groups and more than 1 million residents, following the Chernobyl disaster, the Chinese government has never shown any serious hesitations in their pursuit of nuclear energy.

This pattern of persistence has continued following the Fukushima incident, as evidenced by the 15 Chinese nuclear power plants currently in operation, and 26 undergoing construction as of 2013, a total which represents more 40% of global nuclear construction. The only change in nuclear policy the Chinese government has exhibited is a 79.8 billion RMB ($11 billion USD) investment in "nuclear power safety improvement, radiation pollution control, research and technology innovation, and emergency response."

While the opinions and objections of Chinese citizens are generally disregarded in the selection and construction process of nuclear facilities, a majority of citizens (80%) support the continued expansion of nuclear power in China, though less than 50% of the public supported a nuclear facility nearby their hometown. Governmental secrecy surrounding nuclear development in the new millennium has grown, exemplified by evidence showing a nuclear project in the Shandong province was unknown to 26% of nearby residents for nearly a decade. In a survey 96% of residents said they were not consulted before the Haiyang nuclear project in Shandong, and 93% of those same residents said they were not made aware of the risks associated with a nuclear power plant.

Though they are kept in the dark about the nuclear expansion in their country, citizens are generally trusting of their government (51% stated on a survey they trusted government information concerning a nuclear accident, and 77% said they trusted the capacity of the government to respond to a nuclear incident) and infrequently trust NGOs and international nuclear authorities. The importance of governmental trust cannot be overstated in continuing Chinese nuclear expansion, as the longevity of the delicate relationship between citizenry and nuclear power is contingent upon governmental prowess in dealing with any issues along the way.

He, G. Z., *et al.* (2013). "Public participation and trust in nuclear power development in China." Renewable & Sustainable Energy Reviews 23: 1-11.

Salience of Climate Change and Congressional Voting Records
by Sam Peterson

Resistance to acceptance of climate change is complex and can be attributed to several factors, including the collective action problem caused by mixing of greenhouse gas (GHG) emissions in the atmosphere and the inability of individuals to draw on "prior experience to guide their perceptions" of climate change effects. However, the primary contributing factor to defiance of climate change is most likely the difficulty individuals have observing the tangible effects of this phenomenon. To test the salience of climate change, Herrnstadt *et al.* (2014) used Google search intensity as a proxy for finding the importance of climate change to individuals by examining frequency of search queries such as "climate change" and "global warming" during periods of extreme weather in individual states. They find that searches for the above topics increase with unusually high temperatures or a noticeable lack of snow. They also examine US Congressional voting records from 2004 to 2011 and find voting members are "more likely to take a pro-environment stance on votes [regarding environmental bills] when their home state experiences unusual weather."

There is precedent for scrutinizing the extent to which short-term weather patterns determine individuals' beliefs regarding climate change. Researchers have used Gallup polls to show "short-term weather fluctuations do not affect individuals' beliefs, longer spells of unusually warm weather do have an impact," (Deryugina 2013, cited by Herrnstadt 2014), and have used independent polls to show that respondents are more likely to support "environmentally protective policy if their state experienced a heat wave or drought during the most recent summer" (Owen *et al.* (2012), cited by Herrnstadt 2014). The study produced is the first to use the weekly search intensity data provided by Google Trends to analyze individual responses to weather changes both with increased frequency and without location bias (former studies had limited geographic scope). The search intensity (monthly searches for queries relative to total monthly search volume per state) used in the study is an important characteristic, as it allows each state to be analyzed with respect to specific weather conditions (not every state receives every form of precipitation, etc.) The study used a 10-year baseline average temperature scale to determine the largest deviations from average temperature for different states using standard deviations from the mean temperature.

The study finds that search intensity for certain climate-related queries does respond to weather deviations. Unusually cold temperatures "have a large effect only in the fall and winter" while unusually warm weeks "are associated with increased search only in the winter and summer." There appears to be little relation between spring temperatures and search intensity. Though search intensity responds weakly to particularly dry weather, precipitation has a large coefficient of correlation to searches, as "coefficients on negative deviations in snowfall and snow depth are roughly four times larger than their counterparts". A week in which the average snow depth is lower than usual by 1 standard deviation— roughly 70 mm each day—is associated with an increase of 12.4% in the search intensity.

The temporal resolution of the study leads to several valuable findings, including the correlation between extreme weather and voting results of congressional members. Voting members, in particular Democrats, are more likely to vote for environmental protection bills if their state has recently experienced extreme weather. There is a stronger correlation between voting for environmental protection and extreme weather than "regulation unrelated to industrial or carbon policy and [the correlation is] absent for votes unrelated to environmental policy." The findings show that search activity may be a useful proxy for salience of some policy issues, and provides a useful connection between short-term reactions to weather changes and long-term beliefs about climate change.

Herrnstadt, E., & Muehlegger, E. (2014). Weather, salience of climate change and congressional voting. Journal of Environmental Economics and Management, 68(3), 435-448.

The Politics Surrounding Climate Science
by Patrick Quarberg

A 2008 study conducted by Riley Dunlap and Aaron McCright investigates the shifting views of Republicans and Democrats on climate change. Specifically, the study attempts to discover why environmental conservation, once thought of as an "issue that would unite the nation," has turned into an issue noticeably split along party lines. Comparing survey data ranging from the late 1990s to 2008, Dunlap and McCright observed a significant gap between the beliefs of Democrats and Republicans on the issue of global warming. Those surveyed were asked whether global warming was occurring, whether the media was exaggerating its effects, whether there was a scientific consensus on the existence of climate change, whether global warming was caused by humans, and whether global warming was a serious threat that would have effects within their lifetimes. It was observed that areas where the two parties seemed to be relatively in agreement in the 90s became areas in which the two parties were separated rather greatly today. The percentage of

Democrats and Republicans who believed that the effects of climate change were already happening in 1997 were 52% and 48%, respectively. In 2008, 76% of Democrats held this belief, whereas only 42% of Republicans did this. Dunlap and McCright found that party sorting greatly influenced those who claimed to not know much about global warming, so they just sided with whatever their party's stance on the issue was, but that still doesn't answer how the issue got so politicized in the first place. The study points out that the schism first happened during Ronald Reagan's presidency, when environmental protection was identified as a burden on the economy, and was henceforth no longer a spending priority. This shifted over time into what is now a culture of skepticism—and sometimes, outright denial—of climate science. The effect of this, as the study points out, is that both Democrats and Republicans who claim to not know much about climate change will just take the stance that their party takes—regardless of what that stance is or what it is based on.

Dunlap, R., McCright, A. 2008. A Widening Gap: Republican and Democratic Views on Climate Change. Environment: Science and Policy for Sustainable Development Volume 50, pages 26-35.

How Climate Change Influences Political Action
by Patrick Quarberg

A study by Hannah Knox (2014) examines climate change's ability to effect political change. She views this phenomenon from an anthropological perspective, considering both local movements and global interactions and processes. In Manchester, UK, the author considers climate change mitigation movements as political phenomena that "bring together substance, sociality, and numerical representation in a transformative mix of human and non-human co-becoming." This complex assertion can be broken down. Climate change mitigation unites multiple facets of society towards one goal that considers both humans and their surroundings. At a climate change talk, Knox found that many social theorists pointed out that new advances in scientific analyses of climate change have disturbed the boundaries between cultural and natural processes. That is, people are arguing that climate change is not simply a scaling up of local relationships between humans and their environments. Rather, the earth has entered an age where human interaction is the primary driver of planetary scale change. Humans are affecting the planet now more than ever. This change in relationship between the planet and humans has caused people to question the basis of assumptions that scientists have been making. Numbers calculated on the basis that the planet influenced humans more than the other way around could have produced bad estimates for the future. Knox relates this idea to the concept of biopolitics, where problems affecting individuals can be scaled up to the whole population using statistical analysis, methods which she claims are a central part of modern modes of power. In climate science, "the population" as a meaningful body does not really exist. Instead, Knox claims, "the population" in climate science has been constructed out of analyses of material processes, meaning that studies of the planet and its processes provide the "big picture" to climate change studies. Similarly, Knox states that society's contribution to climate change is meaningless until it is broken down into simpler parts. For example, which part of the population is responsible for the largest amount of emissions? This question is an essential one to answer if emissions are to be effectively reduced, and modern climate science frequently addresses it. Because climate change and climate science encompass a variety of fields and interests, Knox claims, it involves the whole governance system more than other contemporary issues, and brings about more political action as a result.

Knox, H. 2014. Footprints in the City: Models, Materiality, and the Cultural politics of Climate Change. Anthropological Quarterly, Volume 87, pages 405-430. http://muse.jhu.edu/journals/anthropological_quarterly/v087/87.2.knox.html

Environment and Politics: Alaskans Adapt to a Changing Climate

by Russell Salazar

While climate change *mitigation* must continue, societies are marching on into an inevitably warmer world. The ability for a community to *adapt* to a new environment will be a crucial characteristic in the coming century. Wilson (2013) presents a study of an Alaskan village to show how political and social changes are correlated with a community's vulnerability to the impacts of climate change. The paper focuses on the subsistence livelihoods of the Koyukon Athabascan people, describing major changes since the 1950s that altered their climate adaptability. These included an increased emphasis on formal education, a greater exposure to market economies, as well as the legislation and bureaucracy introduced by the government, all of which had a profound impact on the Koyukon Athabascan way of life. Wilson concludes by encouraging more cautious and deeper ethical considerations with regard to placing political constraints on communities.

Before the 1950s, the people of Ruby Village would move up to four times a year to follow the peaks of fishing season, and hunting and trapping season. Through observation, they would respond freely to changes in the population and behavior of the hunted animals, taking only what was necessary to sustain the community.

However, increased pressures on formal education came in with the second half of the century. The mobile community ceased the practice of travelling north during the winters, becoming a community focused around a central village area. Additionally, exposure to the market economy introduced the use of snowmobiles and gasoline, which allowed the now-settled people of Ruby Village greater hunting range and mobility. These seem like appropriate adaptations that support a continuation of the Ruby Village lifestyle. However, other effects were observed.

As a consequence of integration with the market economy, the community's dependency on gasoline increased, and hence a greater vulnerability to price changes. The greater problem arises when taking into account the effects of climate change: rising water levels and unfrozen patches made certain areas almost inaccessible. Greater gasoline consumption became inevitable, so that even minor changes in price could cause a devastating blow to the village's well being. The people of Ruby thus faced worrying travel limitations.

These limitations were amplified through the regulation of subsistence and hunting by state and federal agencies. Hunters had to abide by guidelines for area, timing, and intensity when hunting for game. No longer were the hunters of Ruby Village able to respond freely to personal observations of the animal populations. Unfortunately, the change in average temperature is said to have caused a change in the deer rutting season, and while conscious Alaskans felt the need for an extension of the hunting season, a great deal of bureaucracy stood in the way.

Ultimately, these changes to the socioeconomic scene of the Koyukon Athabascan people increased Ruby's vulnerability to climate change. Vulnerability to climate change is best kept at a low, and economics and politics must work toward that goal.

Wilson, N. J., 2013. The Politics of Adaptation: Subsistence Livelihoods and Vulnerability to Climate Change in the Koyukon Athabascan Village of Ruby, Alaska. Human Ecology 42(1), 87–101.

ECONOMIC BEHAVIOR AND CLIMATE CHANGE

Business Journals Lack Climate Change Discussions
by Jordan Aronowitz

Businesses are responsible for much of the greenhouse gas causing climate change, and are likely to be adversely affected by it. Nevertheless, Goodall (2008) found that even though there is talk about businesses going greener to protect their own futures, there is little written about climate change in business and management journals. Goodall noted that climate change is a science issue, and a typical business journal would not focus on the sciences, but the discussion about climate change started decades ago. Thirty years later, she thinks that these journals should have begun to include conversation about climate change.

To analyze the top 30 business and management journals, the keywords *global warming* and *climate change* were used as a base to determine if an article discusses climate change. Overall, only 9 out of the top 30 business and management journals included an article discussing climate change in the past 30 years, but 35 out of the 50 business and management journals ranked in or below the top 50 included an article discussing climate change in the past 30 years. This change starts an interesting dialogue. It could be inferred that the top-rated journals have an agenda to not include articles about climate change, while lesser-rated journals include articles about those topics. In order to maintain a large audience, the top-rated business journals may want to avoid writing about climate change as it could be seen as criticizing business practices and inciting unwanted change, upsetting readers.

For social science disciplines, such economics, sociology, and political science, Four times the number of the journals have had writing about climate change than business and management journals, suggesting that social science journals are more willing to criticize their readers and are less concerned with maintaining a conservative agenda. The author believed (in 2008) that business journals need to write more the dangers of industrialization and its effect on the climate. It will be interesting to look at more recent papers on this topic to see if anything has changed.

Goodall, A. H. (2008). Why Have the Leading Journals in Management (and Other Social Sciences) Failed to Respond to Climate Change? Journal of Management Inquiry, 20(10), 1-14.

Free Money—How Investing in Energy Can Save
by Jackson Cooney

A small organization called the Sustainable Endowments Institute (S.E.I) provides colleges and universities with help on the retrofitting issue. They set up "Green Revolution Funds", to encourage universities to save capital to invest in green projects. They also provide a software that enables institutions to track savings from these projects. The S.E.I has brought together $110 million to the G.R.F that can be used for green projects. Dension University and the University of New Hampshire are active partners in the S.I.E's billion-dollar Green Challenge, an initiative introduced in 2011 to build momentum for the G.R.F. The University of New Hampshire started with $600,000 in the fund and now has $1.3 million. As this example shows, investing in the G.R.F and using the money for energy efficiency can have significant effects on savings. Investing in energy efficiency is not only monetarily beneficial but will also lead to healthier environmental conditions.

The problem of emission of green house gases and climate change can be solved through investing in energy efficiency. There are few risks in doing this, and an opportunity for tremendous returns. According to a 2012 study, modifying buildings to be energy efficient in the US could save $1 trillion over 10 years, reduce greenhouse gas emissions by 10%, and increase American employment. People still seem wary, however. These facts seems to good to be true so people become skeptical, and the initial costs of increasing energy efficiency can be daunting, especially when budgets are being cut. However, with organizations like S.E.I., greenhouse gas emissions and climate change could be solved.

Bornstein, David. "Investing in Energy Efficiency Pays Off." Opinionator Investing in Energy Efficiency Pays Off Comments. New York Times, 06 Feb. 2015. Web. 08 Feb. 2015.

Pakistan's Developing Economy in a Warming World
by JP Kiefer

Despite contributing little to greenhouse gas emissions, the poorest countries and people will be negatively affected by climate change the earliest and most severely. This is due to an increased inability to adapt to changes in crop production, water resources, and human health. Akram and Hamid (2015) determined that Pakistan would be one of the countries hit hardest by climate change.

Temperature has been shown to have a negative and significant relationship with both Pakistan's GDP and its productivity in agriculture, manufacturing, and services sectors. Of these sectors, agriculture is hit the hardest. This is largely due to the industry's direct dependence on both temperature and precipitation. Just a 1°C temperature increase alone can reduce wheat yields by 1.74%. This does not include the effects that an increased frequency of heavy monsoons can have on farmlands, nor the negative effects that rising sea levels and floods can have by making soil saline. In the dry season rainfall has been reduced due to climate change, which can place severe strain on irrigation requirements. Livestock are also going to be impacted due to reduced feed and an increase in diseases and disease vectors. Overall, Pakistan's agricultural industry will be hurting if greenhouse gas emissions continue at their current rate.

Even sectors of Pakistan's economy that are somewhat removed from dependence on climates will be harmed by the impact of climate change on human health. It has been estimated that risk of diarrhea has increased to 10% due to climate change in certain regions of the nation. More significantly, studies in India have shown that the degree of global warming can increase incidence of malaria by around 10% as well. This would wreak havoc on Pakistan's workforce in its developing economy.

Pakistan began preparing for the negative effects of climate change when its "National Environment and Climate Change Policy" was formulated in 2005 to specifically focus on various climate change issues in Pakistan, specifically the increased variability of the monsoons, the rapid melting of Himalayan glaciers, and the increased siltation of dams. However, Akram and Hamid (2015) believe that in order for truly significant progress to be made, a joint and comprehensive policy should be adapted by the entire middle east to focus on both adaptation and mitigation measures that could cope with the impacts of climate change.

Akram and Hamid, 2015. Climate change: A threat to the economic growth of Pakistan. Progress in Development Studies, Jan 2015: 73-86.

Is Climate Change Tourism Ethical? Potentially Beneficial?

by JP Kiefer

The small archipelago nation of Tuvalu is home to 10,000 people likely to soon become climate refugees when their islands fall below sea level due to climate change. Tuvalu is attempting to take on an image of both victim and hero of climate change by becoming an extremely green chain of islands run by largely renewable sources of energy. It is able to take on this image with help from foreign aid and charities. Its people are also portrayed as model citizens without the issues of overconsumption and essentialized consumerism, though they fail in this in some ways. Tuvalu's tourist board attributes these failures to an invading and corruptive imperial force. Overconsumption and essentialized consumerism are tied hand in hand with climate change, so by rejecting these values Tuvalu hopes to show that man's carbon footprint truly can be reduced.

Farbotko (2010) notes that making Tuvalu an image of sustainable living has brought it media attention as a tourist site to "see while you can," as it is expected to be lost to the ocean forever in a few years. The idea of visiting a location because of the tragedy it has faced is not entirely new, but this climate change tourism is unique because the tragedy has not yet occurred. Tours of concentration camps like Auchwitz were the first form of this "dark tourism," but they did not begin until years after the Holocaust. Tour busses drove through neighborhoods recovering from Hurricane Katrina to watch the community rebuild, but even this occurred after the main disaster. According to Farbotko, climate change tourism is especially tragic and in some ways unethical.

Climate change tourism brings with it two major issues, the first being the irony of it. Transportation to the remote archipelago of Tuvalu is costly on the environment, suggesting that those travelling to the nation have little empathy for its people. Furthermore, this travel is costly and available only to wealthy people with no direct vulnerability to climate change. These tourists seem to treat Tuvaluan identities with a convenient childlike simplicity, which lessens their feelings of ethical involvement in the disappearing islands. The tourists seem more interested in the simple lifestyle of a beachside vacation than genuinely invested in understanding the likelihood of the inhabitants becoming climate refugees in the near future.

Overall, Tuvalu's tourist board views climate change tourism as a brilliant way to bring about empathy for the formerly faceless problems of emitting greenhouse gasses and of showing that sustainable living is possible. They do this while also promoting a simple beachside vacation that tourists can enjoy. Farbotko disagrees, instead believing that combining climate change tourism with a simple vacation desensitizes visitors, rather than enabling them to empathize with the locals.

Farbotko 2010. The global warming clock is ticking so see these places while you can': Voyeuristic tourism and model environmental citizens on Tuvalu's disappearing islands. Singapore Journal of Tropical Geography, 224-238.

Are Electric Vehicles Worth the Higher Costs?
by JP Kiefer

Electric vehicles, hybrid electric vehicles, plug-in hybrid electric vehicles, and fuel cell vehicles all offer promising alternatives to the conventional vehicle in reducing greenhouse gas emissions. These alternatives may not be as beneficial as they seem on first glance, however. While electric, hybrid-electric, and fuel cell vehicles all promise to minimize greenhouse gas emissions from their daily use, Gau and Winfield (2012) point out that each vehicle's life cycle assessment needs to be computed before jumping to the conclusion that hybrid vehicles minimize greenhouse gas emissions. The life cycle assessment analyzes the greenhouse gas emissions from two cycles: a vehicle life cycle that includes vehicle assembly, maintenance, dismantling, and recycling and a fuel life cycle that consists of fuel extraction, processing, distribution, storage, and use. These alternative vehicles are the products of a larger volume of greenhouse gas emission from the vehicle life cycle due to additional energy consumption involved with the batteries and other additional parts that go into the more advanced technologies. Electric, hybrid electric, and plug-in hybrid vehicles can also contribute to greenhouse gas emissions when the energy used to charge the batteries does not come from a clean energy source. Gau and Winfield calculate that alternative vehicles do consume less energy than conventional vehicles, which consume an estimated 3600kJ/km in their life time, compared to a mere 2250kJ/km by hybrid electric vehicles or 3000kJ/km by extended range electric vehicles.

After determining that alternative vehicles do appear to be more environmentally friendly than conventional vehicles, Gau and Winfield attempted to determine if such vehicles are also friendlier on the wallets of consumers. Alternative vehicles tend to come with larger price tags and the possibility of larger maintenance costs when compared to conventional vehicles, but their drivers will also save a considerable amount of money refueling as well. Electricity costs, which tend to remain relatively stable in the US, were estimated at $0.13/kWH, while the volatile price of gas was more difficult to estimate for the future. Results were computed for both a minimum of $2.00/gal and a maximum of $6.00/gal to show a range within which total costs of a vehicle over a lifetime might be. Gau and Winfield calculated that if gas prices are low, conventional vehicles might actually be cheaper than alternatives with a cost of just over $0.1/km. Hybrid electric vehicles were just slightly more expensive than this, but the remainder of alternative vehicles were significantly more expensive, especially if driven for many miles between charges. These alternative vehicles were estimated to cost between $0.15/km and $0.20/km.

If gas prices rose to their maximum projected cost of $6.00/gal, the alternative vehicles become more cost-efficient, especially when recharged frequently. Alternative vehicles hovered just above the price of $0.15/km, whereas conventional vehicles cost an estimated $0.20/km. Overall, Gau and Winfield did not declare a "best vehicle," but pointed out that the hybrid electric vehicle achieves the lowest energy consumption and emissions, but that it would not make economic sense if gas prices remain low.

Gao, L., Winfield, Z., 2012. Life Cycle Assessment of Environmental and Economic Impacts of Advanced Vehicles. Energies 5, 605-620.

Is Globalization Thwarted by Climate Change and Diminished Oil Supply?
by Margaret Loncki

Just how devastating are the potential effects of both global warming and peak oil on global trade? Fred Curtis, professor of economics and environmental studies at Drew University, explains that the effects are potentially disastrous. Curtis points out the four main characteristics of climate change are capable of undermining global trade: increased temperature, rising sea levels, increased precipitation, and increased hurricane severity. Curtis also explores how peak oil will play a role in global trade. Peak oil, a point at which maximum oil output is reached, will result in an increased gap between oil demand and oil supply leading to increased oil prices. Increased gas prices lead to less cost-effective shipping, and therefore, discouraged international trade. Curtis concludes that current climate change policy is too insignificant and will be unable to mitigate the effects of decreased international trade.

Increased temperature causes engine combustion to be less efficient causing all types of shipping to be less cost-effecting. Increased temperatures also decrease the amount of water in inland rivers resulting in the inability of large vessels to bring goods inland. Curtis suggests that rising sea levels threaten shipping infrastructure at low sea level such as ports and coastline airports. More frequent and intense precipitation as well as increased hurricane severity will most certainly result in more common flooding, slowing, or potentially temporarily stopping, shipping operations as well as transit speed. The impacts of global warming will most certainly increase the cost of freight-shipping, incentivizing manufacturers to produce products near the market in which they are to be sold. Importantly, this will decrease division of labor and increase the cost of production.

Increased fuel prices as a result of peak oil will similarly affect global trade. Increased fuel prices, as a result of high demand and low supply, will also increase the cost of global trade, making it no longer beneficial to produce products in distant locations. Infrastructure will have to be created near product markets in order to decrease shipping cost thwarting Globalization. Current climate change policy has been too insignificant to prevent the effects of global warming mentioned above. Although more policy needs to introduced in order to prevent further environmental decline, it appears that the peak of globalization will soon be behind us.

Curtis, F., 2009. Peak globalization: Climate change, oil depletion and global trade. Ecological Economics 69, 427–434.

How Much will Travelers Pay to Offset Carbon Releases from Fossil Fuels?

by Margaret Loncki

Tourism-related air travel has consistently been one of the fastest growing carbon releasing industries. Although, the industry has faced serious pressure to reduce their carbon output, it has struggled to find an efficient way to accomplish this. Choi and Ritchie (2014) aim to discover how much consumers are willing to pay to offset the CO_2 emissions released by their travel. Many airlines have carbon offsetting programs that allow passengers to pay a fee to help fund carbon reducing research and development programs as well as the production and support for new and existing clean energy programs and renewable energy sources. Although most travelers understand the implications of the carbon released by their flights, only a fraction of passengers have supported the carbon offsetting programs offered by airlines.

Passengers who have been willing to pay extra to support these programs have attributed it to the guilt and responsibility they feel for the size and implications of their carbon footprint. On the other hand, there are many reasons why people choose not to support these programs, the most significant being the lack of understanding of just how paying a little extra is going to reverse the negative impacts of the carbon emissions of their flight. Non-supporters also expressed concern that the carbon offset options are not placed in an important or visible place in the booking process and usually go unnoticed as they are located next to the hotel and car booking options. This location also contributes to the lack of trust in airlines and the disbelief that the fee will truly go to programs that will eventually result in reduced carbon footprints. Many consumers feel that airlines are often just trying to sell one more thing, and that this is another one of those things. The final reason for the lack of support of these programs is the increasing trip costs; the traveler may not be the one funding the trip, or simply does not have the financial ability to pay for carbon offsetting programs.

Choi and Ritchie found a significant willingness to pay for carbon reduction. The study also found that a strong belief in flight-caused climate change did not produce a higher willingness to pay than that of skeptical travelers. Travelers were also found to be more willing to pay to support programs that would eventually benefit the general public such as renewable energy programs as well as technological improvements and biofuels. Surprisingly, the study found no significant difference in willingness to pay between socio-demographic characteristics such as job, age, and income.

This study indicates that most travelers have a significantly higher willingness to pay for carbon reduction than indicated by the current lack of success of airline carbon offset programs indicate. With a few changes to the programs, they have the potential to become powerful tools in long-term climate change mitigation.

Choi, A., Ritchie, B., 2014. Willingness to pay for flying carbon neutral in Australia: an exploratory study of offsetter profiles. Journal of Sustainable Tourism 22, 1236-1256.

Economics of Nuclear Power and Climate Change Mitigation Policies
by Sam Peterson

The availability of nuclear power may be crucial in determining whether greenhouse gas (GHG) emissions can be reduced enough to reach the goal of limiting worldwide temperature increases to 2°C. The aforementioned goal, established during a 2009 United Nations climate change conference in Copenhagen, Denmark, appears contingent on the ability of nuclear power to generate electricity without GHG emissions (UNFCCC, 2009). In a 2012 study of the economics of nuclear power generation, Bauer *et al.* utilized a "long-term global multiregional model ReMIND-R" intertemporal model to analyze the effects of four differing paths for global nuclear policy following the 2011 Fukishima Daiichi meltdown in Japan. Early shutdown and removal of nuclear plants is shown to contribute to "discounted cumulative global GDP losses of 0.07% by 2020," and if policy dictates prohibition of investment in nuclear power, those losses will double. The study concluded that the discounted reduction in global GDP by 2035 would be significantly worse if global environmental policy shifts in the direction of a carbon budget of some kind, which would strongly suggest limits on and/or cap emissions from coal, natural gas and crude oil.

In 2010, before the Fukishima Daiichi incident, the Nuclear Energy Agency (NEA) estimated total nuclear capacity would increase between 37% and 110% by 2035, and the International Energy Agency (IEA) predicted nuclear-based electricity generation capacity would increase by 79% in the same time period (NEA, 2010; NEA & IAEA, 2010). Bauer *et al.* examined four scenarios concerning the future of nuclear power in the 21st century. The most severe policy constraints involved closing all existing nuclear plants and placed a complete moratorium on investment, known as the "Full Exit" scenario, reflecting "skeptical position regarding safety or public acceptability." In the "New Start" situation, all currently operating plants are shut down, but there is the possibility for future investment, working under the assumption that existing plants are unsafe. A more liberal approach is the "Phase Out" track, where existing plants operate until they are deemed unsafe, with no new plants constructed. In the most optimistic scenario, a nuclear "Renaissance" occurs, which functions under the present consensus on the relative safety of nuclear power.

The authors used a situation where no intertemporal carbon budget is implemented, representing the scenario with the least governmental intervention in the nuclear industry. The carbon budget, by general definition, is the quantity of carbon dioxide emissions humanity can emit while restricting global average temperature increases to 2°C. Over the course of the 21st century, "total primary energy consumption [will grow] by approximately 133%," but fossil fuels dominate production in the energy sector until 2050. In the reference scenario, nuclear power attains a 17.2% share of power creation in 2075, due to constraints of uranium production. Meanwhile, in the "Phase Out" scenario, a stringent carbon budget reduces use of "coal by 40%, gas by 18%, and oil by 13%" by 2020, at which point nuclear power begins to significantly contribute to power production. By 2050, this scenario leads to a discounted global GDP decrease of nearly 2.1%, or 2.3% if nuclear power is phased out compared to the baseline condition of no carbon budget and a nuclear phase-out.

Unsurprisingly, a majority of the global GDP loss occurs due to incorporation of a carbon budget as a component of climate policy. The authors conclude nuclear power is only of "moderate importance" for decreasing emissions in comparison to the carbon budget, though the budget allows for "flexible exhaustion." For example, natural gas utilized for electricity production can fulfill a significant portion of the shortfall caused by early shutdown of nuclear facilities, but this policy would be difficult to implement due to long-term commitments from international governments. In short, if public and scientific consensus remains unchanged regarding nuclear safety, a carbon budget would have less detrimental effects than currently estimated.

Bauer, N., *et al*. (2012). "Economics of nuclear power and climate change mitigation policies." Proceedings of the National Academy of Sciences of the United States of America 109(42): 16805-16810.

Potential for Tariffs as Climate Change Mitigation—Legal and Economic Analysis
by Sam Peterson

There exist many approaches to solving the problem of climate change, which generally can be delineated in one of two categories: adaptation and mitigation. Adaptive policies include efforts to change human behavior to be compatible with the evolving global climate. Mitigation techniques result from more stringent policies. Both carbon dioxide emission caps and legislation against use of fossil fuels are environmental approaches to mitigation policy. There also exist economic mitigation policies which, by their nature, utilize market forces to dissuade continued use of products harmful to the environment. Cottier (2014) examined the effects imposition of tariffs might have on decreased use of environmentally unfriendly goods and services. They conclude, through use of elasticity measurements, that multilateral action would be effective for pursuing tariff policy, which would lead to an "average 1.4% net reduction in carbon-intensive imports from a 5% increase in tariffs." The paper examines the World Trade Organization (WTO) legislation surrounding tariffs and concludes that countries can act unilaterally to increase tariffs or act as a group.

Tariffs, taxes on goods traded internationally, have long been used as a defense mechanism for growing and established economies to protect their industries from being undercut by their international counterparts who can produce goods at a lower cost. These protectionist policies are outlined by Cottier, who argues these tariffs "cannot be considered as a protectionist measure if the country is a member of an international climate change mitigation agreement." This is because while tariffs would protect domestic industries' goods, climate change is a legitimate environmental concern that must be acted upon multilaterally. Countries that are members of international climate change mitigation panels have reasonable cause and motivation to act as a group to raise prices on carbon-intensive goods.

A study examining most carbon intensive goods (paper, rubber, glass, plastics, iron & steel, cement, and basic chemicals) and the countries with the highest volumes of exports and imports (Australia, Canada, EU, Iceland, Japan, New Zealand, Norway, Switzerland, Argentina, Brazil, Chile, China, India, Indonesia, Israel, Mexico, the Philippines, Russia, South Africa, South Korea, Thailand, Turkey and the USA) indicates average tariffs on carbon-intensive goods are less than 1%. Using demand elasticity measures in these countries, the researchers conclude that raising tariffs by 5% on these carbon-intensive products would lead to a 1.4% reduction in use of these goods, a sizable decrease. This finding may prove extremely important if other mitigation strategies prove ineffective. Though many consumers may not participate in other mitigation strategies, when prices rise on imported goods, basic economic analysis tells us consumption of those goods will decrease, helping climate change in an economic way.

Cottier, T. (2014). "The Potential of Tariff Policy for Climate Change Mitigation: Legal and Economic Analysis." Journal of World Trade 48(5): 1007-1038.

Probability and Cost Estimates for Climate Change

by Sam Peterson

As the scientific consensus regarding the existence of climate change has grown, two separate, research communities have delineated differences in experimentation and modeling of climate change costs. The "integrated assessment community" has extensively examined the influence of "technological and socio-economic uncertainties on low-carbon scenarios," while the modeling community has focused on understanding the "geophysical response of the Earth system to emissions of greenhouse gases." Rogelj *et al.* (2013) unite these two seemingly mutually exclusive endeavors by generating "distributions of the costs associated with limiting transient global temperature increase to below specific values, [and] taking into account uncertainties in four factors: geophysical, technological, social and political." The study concludes that political choices that delay mitigation have the largest effect on the cost–risk distribution, closely followed by geophysical uncertainties.

In the study, the group generated cost distribution estimates by combining mitigation cost estimates with probable temperature projections, but did not account for avoided climate damages due to mitigation effects. In the absence of mitigation measures, the probability of limiting global average temperature increases to less than 2°C is "essentially zero," but with a carbon tax of $40 per metric ton of carbon dioxide equivalent emissions, that likelihood increases to 66%, denoted "likely" by the IPCC ($20 per ton of carbon dioxide equivalent emissions translates to 0.8%–1.3% of world GDP. The probability of staying below a given temperature limit is asymptotic for higher carbon taxes, as higher carbon prices help further reduce emissions later in the 21st century, but only affect temperatures after peaking. In the most pessimistic scenario, where carbon capture and storage (CCS) technologies are hypothesized as completely unavailable, the probability of staying within a 2°C margin is only 50%. CCS is the most important factor in keeping the temperature increases below 2°C, as without it, no level of carbon tax will be able to control usage. The sensitivity analysis does note that if mitigation action is delayed, governmental expenditures on the problem will have less effect due to the constrains of the model. The findings of the study conclude that for a hypothesized delaying strategy used by countries currently (offsetting the next climate change agreement until 2020) is only effective if there is continued use of demand-side (consumer side) limitations on carbon usage. This leads to the logical conclusion that political factors are the most important of the four posited in the study, as varying the timing of climate change political attacks has drastic effects on the viability of keeping global temperature increases below 2°C. In conclusion, continued stalling by governments for more than two decades will lead to a complete inability to reach the 2°C temperature goal.

Rogelj, J., *et al.* (2013). "Probabilistic cost estimates for climate change mitigation." Nature 493(7430): 79-83.

Willingness to Pay in Different Countries
by Patrick Quarberg

In an attempt to determine the consumer's willingness to pay for climate change mitigation, Carlson *et al.* (2012) conducted a survey in three countries in 2010: China, Sweden, and the United States. In general, they observed that the Swedes tended to be most informed and concerned about the effects of climate change, and thus had a higher willingness to pay (WTP). WTP values were found by asking respondents to pick a number from a matrix that identified the most they would be willing to pay to mitigate climate change. The survey asked respondents how much they would pay for different levels of CO_2 reduction, specifically 30%, 60%, and 85% reduction in CO_2 emissions. Additionally, if respondents stated that their WTP was higher than \$220, they were asked to fill in their actual WTP in an open-ended question. Even if respondents had a zero response at the 30% or 60% level, they were still asked about the next level of reduction. The survey also asked several questions about attitudes toward climate change, including whether climate change could be stopped, or just mitigated.

The results show that a large number of respondents from all three countries believe that global average temperature has risen in the past century, and that humans played some role in that increase. However, the Chinese and the Swedish are more likely to believe that their own country should be actively reducing emissions, even if other countries aren't. On the whole, Chinese and Swedish respondents were more in agreement about mitigation policy than Americans. An interesting finding is that a much smaller proportion of Americans, compared to the Swedes or Chinese, believe that climate change should be reduced in a place where it is cheapest to do so, rather than in their home country. Additionally, the proportion of climate change skeptics in America was markedly higher than in other countries. In America, as much as 27% of people believed that humans have not affected temperature increase, compared to 6% and 5% in Sweden and China, respectively. However, when it comes to WTP the Swedes have the greatest, and Americans just beat out the Chinese, which is interesting, considering the proportion of skeptics in America. Moving forward, investigations should look into the source of American skepticism to determine why it is so much higher in America than in other countries, as it seems that if more Americans simply believed in climate change, there would be a much greater mean WTP, which would be helpful in mitigating climate change.

Carlsson F., Kataria M., Krupnick, A., Lampi, E., Lofgren, A., Qin, P., Chung, S., Sterner, T. 2012. Paying for Mitigation: A Multiple Country Study. Land Economics. Volume 88, pp. 326-340.

The Learning Curve of Renewable Technology
by Patrick Quarberg

A 2007 study done by Patrik Soderholm and Thomas Sundqvist attempted to factor in "learning curve" expenses to renewable technology. They describe the "learning curve" expenses to be the increased cost of producing and installing a piece of equipment or technology while it is still a new product. As more of the product is implemented, implementation costs decrease. The study focuses on estimation methods for learning curve costs, and the importance of estimates in deploying technology like wind turbines and solar panels. Specifically, the study investigates issues regarding time as an important variable in learning rates, the interconnectedness of innovation and diffusion, and omission of other important variables in learning rate estimation. The reason for investigating time as an important factor, according to the researchers, is to find out whether costs are decreasing due to actual learning and innovation. The cost decreases should be explained by *cumulative capacity*—the implementation of additional units—not just time. This is indeed what was found in other studies, and was so included in Soderholm and Sundqvist's estimation equations.

They then examined the falling prices of wind turbines in four European countries: Denmark, Germany, Spain, and the United Kingdom. The observed trends were as expected. As more wind turbines were built, the individual investment cost decreased, though the actual cost differed from country to country due to several variables depending on the characteristics of the country, as well as the average size of windmill being built. Soderholm and Sundqvist then used these data to further refine their estimation equations. They came up with several variations of their elementary learning curve equation, each taking different variables into account. Interestingly, some models, which accounted for omitted-variable bias, found that the time factor did not affect the model's accuracy at all, so the learning-by-doing effect was completely isolated. After analyzing how each estimation equation performed, Soderhold and Sundqvist concluded that omitted-variable bias seriously affects the data, and must be accounted for in the equations. Additionally, they suggested that the relationship between innovation and diffusion—which they assumed to be dependent on each other—be tested in a later study, so as to confirm the validity of their estimates. They also noted that no matter what model is used, time will play some time of role in the trend observed, so steps must be taken to separate time and actual learning in order for estimates to be relevant.

Soderholm, P. Sundqvist T. 2007. Empirical Challenges in the Use of Assessing the Economic Prospects of Renewable Energy Technologies. Renewable Energy, Volume 32, pages 2559-2578.

Six Myths of Fossil Fuel Divestment
by Chloe Rodman

Across the nation and the world, colleges, universities, churches and other foundations and organizations are participating in the divestment movement by withdrawing their investments from companies that contribute to climate change through carbon emissions. Currently, 50 corporations have committed $50 billion in divestments. Surprisingly, the major oil company Rockefeller has committed $860 million to the cause. A representative from the company reported that they felt both morally and economically inclined to do so. Not only does the divestment help the fight to reduce carbon emissions, but Rockefeller also previously had a large portion of their money invested in reserves that are now to remain in the ground, untouched.

As opposed to Rockefeller, many oil companies are criticizing the idea of divestments. Another large oil company Exxon Mobil stated their point of view on the company website: "to not use fossil fuels is tantamount to not using energy at all, and that's not feasible." Harvard University is one of remaining institutions that is on the side of these corporations and continues to invest in fossil fuels. The University receives a $33 billion endowment. It is because of these statements against divestments that author Tim Dickinson addresses the six myths of divestment.

Myth 1: Divestment costs too much.

The opposition to divestment argues that getting rid of fossil fuel stocks means getting rid of profit for the investor. However, David Gould, who leads in the investment committee at Pitzer College recently guided the college to divest $125 million from fossil fuels and argues that there is a very low, if not beneficial, financial impact. Other foundations and corporations, such as McGraw Hill Financial have similar findings in their divestment process.

Myth 2: Fossil fuels are a safe investment.

Oil companies believe that they will be able to profit from the enormous quantities of oil reserves they have at their fingertips and therefore will remain a good investment. However, the International Energy Agency predicts that around $300 billion worth of oil reserves must remain in the ground to meet the reduction of carbon emissions determined to keep the temperature from rising above 2°C.

Myth 3: Divestment is too political.

The big oil and coal corporations do believe in climate change—they know the effect of carbon emissions. What they do not believe in is the strength of national governments to enforce low carbon emissions. They argue that what they are doing is strictly economics, and that they should not be involved in the political process. However, with such a great impact these emissions have on the environment, and therefore the lives of billions, this is not the case. Ellen Dorsey, Wallace Global Fund executive director says "If you own fossil fuels, you own climate change."

Myth 4: Fossil fuel divestment is harder than South Africa divestment.

Many people link the South African apartheid divestment with the current environmental divestment because they both are morally important. Fossil fuel promoters argue that limiting carbon emissions through environmental divestment will be much harder than ending apartheid but, in actuality, it's the opposite. During the South Africa divestment, 40% of companies did business with segregated South Africa. Currently, only 11% of companies invest in large fossil fuel companies.

Myth 5: The alternatives are too risky.

Some argue that the removal of all investments in coal, oil and other fossil fuel corporations is a bad idea because people are likely to take that money and invest it all in a green energy project. This is true—it is risky to take all your money and invest in one clean energy project. Instead, creating a low-risk and diverse investment plan is the smarter option and will be a safe alternative investment.

Myth 6: Divestment doesn't do anything.

The last myth focuses on the idea that if people sell their share of fossil fuel companies, other eager buyers will purchase them instead because many people don't believe in effective divesting. However, if we look at past divestments, such as the South Africa divestment, tobacco divestment and Darfur divestment, all these have succeeded. Divesting might not succeed if only a handful of corporations participate. However, universities in the United States, Europe and Australia have all begun divesting. California, the Church of Sweden, the World Bank, and the United Nations are all working on the divestment process as well.

Dickinson, T. 2015. The Logic of Divestment: Why We Have to Kiss Off Big Carbon Now. Rolling Stone. http://rol.st/1Ao7gv3

The Risky Business Project
by Chloe Rodman

Writing in the New York Times, Burt Helm (2015) discusses the roles of Tom Steyer, Henry Paulson Jr., and Michael Bloomberg in leading the new Risky Business Project. The Risky Business Project originated as a study called *Risky Business: The Economic Risks of Climate Change in the United States*, which was created to determine how American business will be affected by climate change and to determine the cost of carbon emission mitigation now, as opposed to the cost of waiting. While Risky Business comprises a wide variety of members who don't agree on much—democrats and republicans, billionaires, senators, and mayors—they do have one common goal: to show both Congress and corporations across America the impact climate change will have on the economy, a cost estimated at hundreds of billions of dollars.

The study found that if America continues to put off confronting climate change, crops will die and flooding will increase, causing problems for both the production and transpiration of food. A partner to Risky Business, the Rhodium Group, conducted further research. It found that Midwest crop yield will drop by 15% in 25 years, that the Northeast will have around $11.1–$15.8 billion of property damage due to an increase of storms, and that there will be an surge in demand for energy ranging from 3.4 to 9.2%.

Steyer's associate, Henry Cisneros, the former housing and urban development secretary under President Clinton, determined that real estate sales in both Florida and California will drastically decline due to an increase in storms and drought severity respectively.

The American public sees this information and knows that action must occur. A Pew and Gallup study shows that many Americans know that climate change is a big and urgent problem but according to a New York Times poll, 83 percent of people still rank it below jobs, health care, and the economy on a list of 'pressing issues.' It seems as if citizens, especially farmers, are more concerned with short-term gains than long-term outcomes. Farmers want incentives to cut carbon emissions because they are not willing to lose profit now for a future problem, especially since a large majority of farmers, according to a representative to the American Farm Bureau, don't believe that humans contribute to climate change.

Risky Business member Robert Rubin, the former secretary of the Treasury under President Clinton says that he used to believe that addressing climate change, especially regulating carbon emissions, would damage America's economy. However, looking at the facts presented by the Project, he has had a change of heart. Rubin says: "Once you see it as having catastrophic impact, any economic argument follows that, because you're not going to have an economy left...Climate change is the existential threat of our day."

Helm, B. 2015. Climate Change's Bottom Line. The New York Times. http://nyti.ms/1KtkTMM

Samsø Inspiration
by Chloe Rodman

New York Times' Diane Cardwell (2015) writes about the impact that Samsø, a 44 square-foot island off the coast of Denmark, has been making in regards to clean energy production. A majority of the island's 3,800 citizens decided that they no longer wanted to rely on foreign, costly fossil fuels. Rather, they made it their goal to become completely powered by green energy. This $80 million project has resulted in 10 wind turbines as well as solar, geothermal and plant- based energy systems. These four methods have allowed the island to thrive, producing more energy than it consumes. Samsø, which used to be primarily dependent on coal and diesel, has become a role model for many other islands around the globe, which are also striving to wean off of fossil fuels. The Samsø Energy Academy was created to educate others about new forms of green energy. Many individuals are sent to the academy to learn about the island's methods and return home to teach their own communities about the changes they can make.

One of the innovative steps Samsø has made is the burning of hay instead of oil to heat houses and water. The island is agriculture based, and the government is pushing for farmers to grow more elephant grass in addition to hay because it not only grows faster than hay, but also has higher energy content. These grasses are an eighth cheaper then the fossil fuels they had been using previously. The heat produced by the burned grass is transferred to households over the island in a central heating system using underground pipes. People who live on the outskirts of the island, too far away to be included in the central pipe system, receive government incentives to make their houses environmentally friendly by installing solar panels or heat pumps.

Using islands to test new green technologies that aren't thoroughly developed or cheap enough for mainland use has become a common trend. Soma, The Virgin Islands, The Caribbean Islands, and islands off the coast of Maine and Alaska have all been testing new ideas. For example, currently in the United States there are no offshore wind farms. However, Maine has set aside a portion of its lobster grounds as a test site. Similarly, Denmark, who's goal is to be fossil fuel-free by 2050, has taken wind turbine and central heating system technology from Samsø and incorporated it into many communities across the country. As of now, 40% of Denmark's electricity is from wind turbines and 60% of houses get their heat from a central green source.

Cardwell, Diane. 2015. Green-Energy Inspiration Off the Coast of Denmark. The New York Times. http://nyti.ms/1AsyL6o

Free Rider Problem Slowing Down Climate Change Progress
by Chloe Rodman

Yale University economist Robert Shiller (2015) explains how global warming can be slowed by a combination of idealism and economics in his article "How Idealism, Expressed in Concrete Steps, Can Fight Climate Change" for the *New York Times*. Little progress has been made regarding climate change and global warming. There have been many international conferences in the past few decades but they have been relatively unsuccessful in creating reasonable climate solutions or taking action. Economists have cited externalities as the cause for such large-scale inaction. People and governments have been unresponsive when asked to counter the negative externalities of climate change, such as pollution, by bicycling to work, turning off lights, creating regulation laws, or implementing other sustainable actions. However, in the rare occurrence that communities or people do decide to act, the positive externalities of these actions are consumed by free riders. The free-rider problem has been significant, where the benefits (cleaner air, for example) of sustainable actions are shared by every nation and every person, but the costs rest solely on the shoulders of people who decide to make a change in their daily lives. This free-rider problem reflects traditional economic theory, which states that most citizens and nations will decide not to make a change, because they believe that they can benefit from the change the few are making with no cost to themselves.

However, two individuals have questioned this portion of the theory recently. Harvard economistic, Martin Weitzman, and environmentalist, Gernot Wagner, created the Copenhagen Theory of Change, which elaborates on the idea that change will come from asking people to save the world through small actions. The theory is named for the phenomenon in Copenhagen, Denmark. Since the oil crisis of the 1970s, over half the city's population rides bicycles instead of driving cars. The citizens of this community believe that they have a social responsibility to limit pollution and bike to work. This social responsibility induces a social pressure to bike as well, as the majority of people participate in biking rather than driving. In fact, so many residents participate that they have eliminated the free-rider problem in the area.

Other tactics are being used to encourage more sustainable actions. Ethical investing is growing, where investors will not invest their money in companies who are not environmentally friendly. The president of the American Economic Association, William Nordhaus, proposed another idea: climate clubs. These climate clubs would consist of a group of nations that pledge to create incentives for their citizenry to cut back on greenhouse gas emissions in addition to raising tariffs on imports from countries that are not in one of these clubs. The clubs will grow as non-club participants see the advantages of membership. The Economic Theory of Clubs assumes that members in the clubs are completely self-interested but in this case, there must be an exception. These clubs will trigger a sense of global community and responsibility and will use these feelings to create a healthier world.

Shiller, R. 2015. How Idealism, Expressed in Concrete Steps, Can Fight Climate Change. The New York Times. http://nyti.ms/1Syai5z

Fossil Fuels Have Frightening Potential
by Chloe Rodman

    Michael Greenstone (2015) writes for the New York Times about the increase in temperature that would occur if we used all of our fossil fuels. Politicians around the world are working together in conferences trying to find a way to limit global warming, and they are on the cusp of creating a global carbon reduction agreement. In December 2015, at the Paris climate talks, the environmental world will showcase the United States' plan to cut back its emissions by 28% by 2025. The conference in Paris will promote goals like this one in hopes of achieving a global commitment of limiting the world to an increase of 3.6°F. Scientists have agreed that an increase in temperature greater than 3.6°F would cause environmental and global chaos. With this in mind, another large focus of the conference is to determine the quantity of fossil fuels that should remain in the ground.

    Michael Greenstone, economist and head of the Energy Policy Institute at the University of Chicago, has calculated both the projected warming from already harvested fossil fuels as well as the projected warming ability of the fossil fuels that are currently in the earth. Since the industrial revolution, the fossil fuels used have caused a 1.7°F increase in temperature. Greenstone determines that if all the cheap fossil fuel reserves were consumed, the Earth would warm by an additional 2.8°F. Using these reserves alone would cause a total global increase of 4.5°F, putting the earth over the safe maximum increase of 3.6°F. If the fossil fuel resources, those that are recoverable but are too expensive to recover currently, were used, they would further increase the global temperature approximately by 3.1°F. Lastly, Greenstone clumps the effects of coal into one group since the consequences are so large. The utilization of the world's coal alone would increase temperature by 8.6°F. All these fossil fuels, if used, would increase the world by 16.2°F. While this is the worst-case scenario, it is easy to see how quickly the world could slip past the limit of an increase of 3.6°F. Not only has the temperature already increased 1.7°F but also all of these fossil fuel resources are worth trillions of dollars—an amount that is very hard to resist.

Greenstone, M. 2015. If We Dig Out All Our Fossil Fuels, Here's How Hot We Can Expect It to Get. The New York Times. http://nyti.ms/1KfL6ev

Determinants of Technology Innovation in the Transportation Sector—Oil Endowments

by Russell Salazar

The development of energy-efficient technologies is becoming increasingly necessary in a warming world. How can countries encourage firms and individuals to innovate more eco-friendly technologies in an effective manner? Kim (2014) takes a closer look at the socio-economic motivators for the development of energy-efficient technologies, with a primary focus on the transportation sector. The study presents empirical evidence to support the claim that smaller oil endowments result in a greater incentive for the development of more eco-friendly vehicles and energy-efficient designs. These findings, combined with explanations from related economic theory, provide insight into potential sustainability schemes for policy makers around the world.

Kim closely examines the number of oil extraction patents and energy efficiency patents within countries of different crude oil endowments. The findings show quite clearly that given a large supply of crude oil, a country and its firms are much more inclined to engineer better oil extraction technologies, diverting attention away from energy efficiency. The study utilizes economic theory of complementary and substitute goods as a basis for explanation. Since crude oil and gasoline-fueled vehicles are complementary goods, an abundance of oil supply in a country–and hence lower relative oil prices–results in higher demand for gasoline-fueled vehicles. This, in turn, results in a proportionally lower demand for energy-efficient cars and thus a miniscule incentive to innovate green technologies.

The study also suggests social and cultural ties regarding innovation incentives. Given scarce oil resources, a fuel-saving and energy-conscious culture develops within the community. It follows, then, that the engineers and scientists living within this community face more day-to-day influence with regard to green living, and innovate to suit their needs and aspirations.

These findings extend to public policy by providing a potential focus: gasoline prices. Kim states, "an increased domestic gasoline price results in more innovation activities that move energy use away from fossil fuel," suggesting that using a tax–while politically controversial–could encourage technological growth. Furthermore, Kim suggests that such tax revenue could boost green innovation further through R&D funding and support.

Essentially, this study highlights a key stress point with regard to climate change mitigation. This kind of knowledge could lead to more effective policymaking strategies with regard to climate change mitigation in industry.

Kim, J. E., 2014. Energy security and climate change: How oil endowment influences alternative vehicle innovation. Energy Policy 66, 400–410.

A House Without an Energy Bill
by Abigail Schantz

In his article "Let There Be Light" in the January 2015 edition of the Economist, Edward Lucas uses the example of a particular energy-efficient house to illustrate his argument that forces affecting the energy market are currently pushing it in the direction of cleaner and more available energy. Coal, now the cheapest and most prominent fossil fuel, is also the dirtiest, and a major contributor of CO_2 emissions. Geopolitical events and price collusion make oil supplies unstable, and both natural gas and nuclear power spark intense political debates. The new phenomenon of hydraulic fracturing has made American a major oil producer, leading to a decrease in oil prices. Edward Lucas believes that the price of oil will keep falling but, rather than this undermining clean energy sources, the cost of clean energy will also fall. In the past five years, solar, wind, and other renewables have received an average of $260 billion a year of investment worldwide. The implementation of clean energy production that corresponds to the natural environment of different countries is starting to be utilized. In areas where the weather is hot, and access to most sources of power are expensive, such as in India, Africa, and Hawaii, solar energy has become a prominent solution. Additionally, with all of the new investment, the ability to produce and store solar energy efficiently is improving immensely. And these renewables are not the only alternatives. Clean coal, which involves capturing released CO_2 for storage or use, remains a viable option. The driving point: All of the technology for reducing emissions and resorting to cleaner energy is already available and improving rapidly. Implementing it has large upfront costs but also immense longterm savings. Lucas uses Michael Liebreich's energy efficient house in London to demonstrate the possibilities. The house runs on solar panels and a 1.5 kW fuel cell which is powered by gas with over 90% efficiency. A heat pump provides heating, low energy appliances reduce demand, and a water tank stores any excess heat. Extra electricity goes back into the grid. Although the house was expensive to construct, Mr. Liebreich expects to make money from it, receiving a net payment for the excess electricity he produces while not having to spend anything on an electricity bill himself. A standard house of similar size would cost at least $5,500 a year to run.

Lucas, Edward, 2015 Let there be light. The Economist. January 17th, 2015. http://econ.st/1Q5gSfV

Would You Pay to Reduce Climate Change?
by Abigail Schantz

In the article "Actions and intentions to pay for climate change mitigation: Environmental concern and the role of economic factors," Christian Dienes (2014) studies the correlation between individuals' concern for the environment and their willingness to pay or act for change, and how these correlations are affected by financial circumstances. Dienes reviewed previous studies and used one survey to analyze his own results. He took the responses from the Life in Transition Survey (2010) by the European Bank for Reconstruction and Development and the World Bank. In this survey, which included 35 countries, 37% of respondents expressed intent to pay to reduce climate change and 11% were unsure, but 45% responded that they had the highest concern level (five out of five on the survey) for climate change. This showed a discrepancy between people who are deeply concerned with climate change and those willing to pay for improvements. Dienes took into account other variables such as age and gender in order to minimize bias. Additionally, he looked at how peoples' responses changed depending on the effect of the financial crisis on their families. The results suggested, first, that those with a high concern for climate change were more likely to pay to reduce it. Second, those greatly affected by the financial crisis were less likely to be willing to pay for climate mitigation. The data also confirmed that those who believe that climate change is being exaggerated are less likely to pay to reduce its effects. Finally, in countries with lower GNI per capita, people were less motivated to reduce climate change because they were more vulnerable to economic downturns and therefore unable to prioritize the climate change issue. Ultimately, the study found a weak correlation between peoples' concern for climate change and their willingness to pay to reduce it. A much higher correlation was found between people with high concern and willingness to take personal action to reduce its affects.

Dienes, C. 2014. Actions and Intentions to Pay for Climate Change Mitigation: Environmental Concern and the Role of Economic Factors. Elsevier. Volume 109. DOI:10.1016/j.ecolecon.2014.11.012

The Auto Industry and Climate Change in the US

by Abigail Schantz

The history of the automobile industry, in many respects, illustrates the progression of society's perception and response to climate change. Caetano C.R. Penna and Frank W. Geels compare the progression of climate change from 1979 to 2012 using the Dialectic Issue LifeCycle

(DILC) model in *Climate change and the slow reorientation of the American car industry (1979–2012): An application and extension of the Dialectic Issue LifeCycle (DILC) model.* The DILC classifies the progression of an issue into five major stages. In the first stage, the problem emerges, generally due to activist groups, and the affected industry rejects the issue and downplays its importance. During this stage, there is little progression in changing technologies. In the second stage, public concern begins to increase as activists generate social movements. Public agendas address the issue and policymakers create committees to study it, although this action is mainly symbolic. In the third stage, rising public concern spurs political debates, leading to formal hearings and investigations. The industry argues for voluntary implementation of solutions and attempts to show that the costs and technical complexity of rapid change make radical solutions impossible. Meanwhile, firms in the industry often take defensive measures, privately exploring solutions in laboratories. In the fourth stage, policies begin to be implemented through legislation. Suppliers and others that support the industry begin to develop technology while the industry itself actively argues against the new policies. At the same time, industry firms begin to invest in alternative technologies and embrace them more publicly in order to maintain the company image. This often leads to an innovation race. Finally, in the fifth phase, a new market emerges due to changes in mainstream consumer preferences and/or because regulators impose taxes or incentives, or other legislation causes a shift in economic conditions. To bolster the public image of the company, most address the problem in the company's beliefs and mission.

Penna and Geels compare the phases that actually occurred for the auto industry to those predicted by the DILC. To do so, they looked at four major quantifiable factors. First, they searched major news sources including *New York Times, USA Today, Wall Street Journal*, and *Washington Post* for articles on climate change, in order to get a sense of public attention towards the issue. Next, consideration by Congress and the Executive Branch was explored through entries in the *Congressional Record* and the *Federal Register*. The American edition of *Automotive News* was used to quantify the attention American automakers were giving to climate change. Finally, the USPTO database was searched for records of patents related to certain technologies in order to see developmental trends in the auto industry. The selected timeframe was broken into the five anticipated stages based on the level of public concern about climate change: 1. 1979–1988 (very little public attention to climate change), 2. 1988–1997 (low-moderate public attention), 3. 1997–2005 (moderate public attention), 4. 2005–2009 (very high public attention) and 5. 2009–2012 (high but decreasing attention). Pemma and Geels found that in the first phase (1979-1988), new scientific evidence on climate change became available and the topic started to be discussed at scientific meetings and conferences. Due to the oil crises of 1973 and 1979, the federal government already had fuel economy regulations in place. Additionally, the auto industry was working on beneficial improvements in cars, such as the three-way catalytic converter, to reduce air pollution. At the same time, the automobile market was shifting towards larger size vehicles like minivans and SUVs. In 1986, Senator Al Gore and others declared concern about climate change and called for political action, putting the issue more on the public radar.

By the second phase (1988–1997), public attention was increasing in part due to natural changes noticed in environment, such as unusually hot summers and the prevalence of droughts. In this stage, there was a Senate hearing on the climate change and, in both 1990 and 1996, reports were released by the newly created Intergovernmental Panel on Climate Change (IPCC), helping to distribute information about the problem. Both President Bush (Senior) and President Clinton took collaborative and voluntary approaches to addressing the issue, prompting development of technologies without imposing regulations. California, on the other hand, created the 1990 'Zero-Emissions Vehicle' (ZEV) mandate. By 1994, other states were considering adopting similar mandates, which led the "Big Three" (GM, Ford, and Chrysler) to begin major lobbying campaigns. Before long, attempts at stronger regulation regulations began to decrease.

Stage Three (1997–2005) became increasingly international. In the Kyoto Protocol (1997), many countries pledged to reduce green-house-gas emissions 5% below 1990s levels by 2012. The US did not sign the protocol, but international car brands with major sales in the US began to adopt new technologies. Both Toyota and Honda released hybrid cars, the *Prius* and the *Insight* respectively. By 2007, the *Prius* was the eighth best selling car in the US Although the US government was not doing much in the way of regulations due to fear about energy security, the government invested heavily in the technological development of alternative energies, mostly fuel cells.

Social changes were largely the driving force of the increase in pubic sensitivity to climate change during the fourth stage (2005–2009). At the 2005 G8 meeting, Tony Blair announced climate change as a top priority. The same year, Hollywood released *Day after Tomorrow*, a movie drastically overdramatizing sudden effects of climate change. In 2007, both IPCC's *Fourth Assessment Report* and Al Gore's *An Inconvenient Truth*, helped broaden public understanding of the issue and increase prevention efforts, winning IPCC and Al Gore the Nobel Peace Prize. Meanwhile, Toyota had taken the lead in HEV but many new entrants emerged in the market, including Tesla.

The fifth stage (2009–2012) saw an unexpected decrease in public concern due to the financial crisis, which caused people to focus on the faltering economy. Climate change skeptics took the opportunity to attack the scientific basis of climate change, creating doubt within the population. Newly elected President Obama did impose some new regulations and mandates, but overall the movement dwindled.

Comparing the five phases of attention to climate change to the five phases predicted through the DILC model allowed Penna and Geels to identify plausible inconsistencies that would result in the climate change movement not following a typical pattern. They classified both stages four and five as equivalent to phase 3 1/2 in the DILC model. The authors predict that in order to shift to stage 4 from stage 3, there must be one dominant solution to the problem. But the plausible solutions for improving the environmental footprint of cars are too numerous for companies to be able to commit to a single solution, and the risk of choosing the wrong one is too high. Also, the DILC model predicts radical changes to start occurring no earlier than stage 3, while in the auto industry, because of firms acting with strong political agendas, changes were occurring long before phase 3 was reached. Finally, the correlation between changes in the auto industry and other concerns, such as air pollution, rising oil prices, energy security, and the financial downturn, cause each stage of the lifecycle to be influenced by factors aside from climate change.

Penna, C.R. C., Geels, W. F. 2014. Climate change and the slow reorientation of the American car industry (1979–2012): An application and extension of the Dialectic Issue LifeCycle (DILC) model. Research Policy.

Divesting Universities of Fossil Fuel Investments
by Abby Schantz

That some universities are divesting of fossil fuels, as James Lawrence Powell points out in his article, "Universities Fail on Climate Change", is inevitable because fossil fuel companies (FFCs) produce products known to increase the probability of climate change, and many students take issue with investing in them. There is precedent for divestment as a means to encourage changes in corporate behavior. For example, Harvard and Brown Universities divested from companies in the tobacco industry, although they did so for the symbolic purpose of opposing a harmful product and did not expect to actually effect change in the industry. In addition, the data make it clear that divestment is not a bad financial decision in the climate change context. Powell points out that if ten years ago an investment of $1 billion went into a portfolio with no FFCs, today it would be worth approximately $2.26 billion, as compared to a portfolio with FFCs being worth $2.14 billion. Furthermore, it is highly unlikely that FFC stock will gain value due to the nature of the product. Because FFCs rely on reserves, they are highly susceptible to government regulation, competition from other energy sources, legality issues, and scarcity of the resources. Despite all of the information supporting divestment, including a statement from Brown's Advisory Committee on Corporate Responsibility in Investment Policies that, due to the social harm caused by FFCs, the university could not profit from them without violating its values and principles, both Brown's and Harvard's presidents rejected divestment. Considering previous divestment campaigns such as South Africa, in which students, parents, and major donors had no self-involvement with the issue but still strongly urged divestment, Powell argues that because climate change directly impacts each individual, a university president can put off divestment, but will eventually have to succumb to it. Furthermore, he argues that mitigating climate change to its greatest ability is for the benefit of the entire university, as it is impossible for a university to succeed in its mission with the full potential effects of climate change occurring. Powell views climate change as the greatest threat in human history and believes that divestment is a means for universities to change the course of history while there is still a chance.

Powell, J., 2014. Universities Fail on Climate. The Nation, Vol. 298, Issue 7, February 17th, 2014.

Entrepreneurial Social Networking can Aid Environmental Protection
by Emily Segal

Decreasing investments in sustainable energy startup firms in the Silicon Valley, one of the world's largest centers for technology innovation, can partially be attributed to the Valley's creation of new markets rather than working within existing ones. In the early 2000s, investors were extremely interested in "clean tech."

However, once they saw that energy technologies required overall larger investments and had longer development cycles, the dynamics of investing in the Valley shifted. Increasing competition from Chinese competitors who brought their own solar panels to the market added to already changing investment patterns. A substantial amount of the money that might otherwise have been invested in environmental startups instead was invested in social networking, software, and Internet investments. In light of California's severe drought, this focus on software and social interactions is relevant now more than ever. Innovators in the Silicon Valley who might otherwise be working on water conservation projects are instead focusing on these other areas.

However, social media may prove valuable in this context as well. WaterSmart, a startup from San Francisco, utilizes the Internet's ability to reach many people in order to inform individuals about conservation needs and attempt to change consumer behavior. WaterSmart customers are given Home Water Reports that inform them about their water usage and provide examples of similar households' water usage to compare theirs to. A customer's Home Water Report also provides suggestions for saving water customized to their living situation. Each WaterSmart customer has an online Portal where they can find more details about incorporating water conservation into their lifestyle. Other services provided though WaterSmart include long-term trend tracking of water usage, estimates of savings, information about local programs and events, real-time leak alerts, and data analytics tools among others. The company recently announced a new $7 million investment. Steve Westly, an early investor in the company, is aware that the Valley seems to be disinterested in the water shortage, but he sees this as advantageous for WaterSmart. Westly points out that water conservation is not an issue unique to California, but rather is a global issue and therefore will continue to effect people all around the world.

Markoff, J, 2015. Silicon Valley's Water Conservation Conundrum. The New York Times 21 Apr. 2015, New York ed., D2 sec. 20 Apr. 2015. Web. 25 Apr. 2015. http://nyti.ms/1G1py1B.

Capitalism or a Stabile Climate—Can You have Both?

by Breanna Sewell

Hans Baer uses his 2008 article, "Global Warming as a By-Product of the Capitalist Treadmill of Production and Consumption—The Need for an Alternative Global System," to address the causes and effects of climate change and the severity of it all. Baer classifies climate change as "one of the most important issues of the 21st century" along with the growing socioeconomic gap between the rich and the poor, which, he argues, are both caused by our capitalist society.

The author covers many of the effects of climate change that are currently taking place as well as the ones that may take place in the future if the global temperature increases by three degrees Celsius as is expected. The effects include increased flooding, droughts, and hurricanes; loss of ice caps and increased sea level; and the less well-known effect, disease. Baer states that global warming "has been implicated in the resurgence of a number of epidemics" such as malaria and cholera.

When turning to the causes of global climate change, the author places the blame on humans because of carbon emissions. Specifically, he points out that it is the capitalist system that is to blame for the situation our planet is in. This is because even after we have come to the conclusion that climate change is our doing, it is very unlikely that changes such as carbon taxes or carbon sequestration will be made. Why? He argues that our global capitalist system will not allow it. According to the author, we are far too concerned with production, consumption, and of, course profit.

Baer advocates for an alternative global system, one that will place more emphasis on protecting our planet and less on profit. He also calls for an increase in emphasis on a collaborative study of the impact of global warming on humanity between climate scientists, social scientists, and other specialists in order to fix what we have done to our planet.

Baer, H., 2008. Global Warming as a By-product of the Capitalist Treadmill of Production and Consumption—The Need for an Alternative Global System. The Australian Journal of Anthropology 19, 58-62.http://bit.ly/1ayrBSB

Greening Capitalism
by Breanna Sewell

Andrew Sayer questions whether global warming is an indirect effect of capitalism or an inherent part of its global relations in his 2008 article, "Geography and Global Warming: Can Capitalism Be Greened?" Sayer begins his article by acknowledging the disastrous effects of global warming and the deterioration of our climate. He also points out some unfortunate integral aspects of capitalism. The first being the capitalist system's perpetual thirst for profit; it's "pleonexia" (insatiable acquisitiveness) and lack of acknowledgement of "environmental constraints or concept of environmental well-being." The second issue is a result of the first: in a capitalist society we are never content with what we have; we always need more.

The potential climate change solution he offers up is the development and use of carbon-neutral technologies. However, he believes that this solution is unlikely to ever fit in with the profit-minded capitalist system. As of now, any carbon-efficient technology we have would result in a decrease in efficiency, which means a decrease in profit. Sayer points out that any attempt in reducing green-house gas emissions means making a trade off with our pleonexia.

The thirst for profit and material objects is not the only obstacle we face as a result of capitalism when trying to remedy global climate change says the author. We must also work around the undeniable inequalities between the rich and the poor. The lower end of the socioeconomic ladder lives a more eco-friendly life yet suffers far more from the negative environmental effects of global warming. The upper and middle class could not expect to keep living the way they are when it comes to their carbon footprint, however, Sayer acknowledges, an entitlement to their wealth, profit, and way of life is an undeniable feature of capitalism.

Based on these observations, the author makes his claim that the odds of capitalism "being greened" are slim.

Sayer, A., 2009. Geography and global warming: can capitalism be greened? Area 41, 350-353.http://bit.ly/1HeurGH

Soy Sauce or Water? China's Soil Contamination and Water Supply

by Phoebe Shum

For many Americans, the term "local" food usually coincides with sustainability, farmer's markets, and everything environmental. This is not the case in modern day China. In fact, it is the very opposite. He-Guangwei, investigative reporter for *The Times Weekly*, explains that China's rapid modernization has brought about severe stress on the agricultural soil quality. The contamination in soil has brought about a myriad of other problems such as water quality degradation due to heavy metal pollution and cancer-caused deaths. In particular, Lake Tai, the third largest freshwater lake in China that supplies drinking water to more than 30 million people, has become so polluted as a result of factory run-off. The water has even been described to resemble soy sauce. It's devastating to see that the once crystal-clear waters of Lake Tai now have the ability to turn people's sweat into a color resembling mud. Farmers around the Lake Tai area refuse to eat the very crops they grow, fully aware that their produce is planted in cadmium, lead and mercury infused soil. The government remains unresponsive to the scale of the issue, wary of attracting negative media and international attention.

While the country's recent economic development has brought about increased wealth and better living conditions for a small percentage of it's citizens, China's decision to pursue short-term economic growth at the expense of the environment for the past three decades has finally caught up to them. In the 1990s, government officials were solely concerned about GDP, and didn't mind building factories and chemical plants near areas of civilization as long as there was economic profit involved.

As a result, 19% of China's farmland is now contaminated, and more than 3 million hectares of arable land is classified as moderately polluted.

The Ministry of Environmental Protection has promised an action plan that will use economic incentives to promote soil restoration. But it won't be easy to counteract the heavy damages that contaminated soil has caused. China will have to pay the price for the soil that has afflicted villages with cancer, reduced harvest cycles, and caused much of Chinese food to be viewed as unsafe for consumption.

This is the first of three articles that Guangwei featured on soil pollution in China. It is a joint project between Yale Environment 360 and Chinadialogue. Hopefully this is the beginning of many.

Guangwei, He. 2014. China's Dirty Pollution Secret: The Boom Poisoned Its Soil and Crops. Yale Environment 360. June 30 2014 http://bit.ly/1dsea8q

Crying Over Spilled Milk: Australia's Diminishing Dairy Production
by Phoebe Shum

Due to climate variability, Australian dairy production may face challenges in the coming years. Authors Kevin Hanslow, Don Gunasekera, Brendan Cullen and David Newth (2012) outline the economic effects of climate change on pasture-based dairy production in Australia. Climate change undoubtedly affects agriculture in general, but pasture-based dairy production, which is heavily reliant on climate, experiences difficulty in efficiently converting pasture to milk when the temperature is not right. The drastic climatic changes will force farmers to alter their grazing systems. Hanslow *et al.* focus on the south-eastern regions of Australia, *i.e.* Victoria, Tasmania and South Australia, which produce 80% of Australia's milk. Since climate change will reduce the supply and reliability of water supplies, dairy herds that rely on rain-fed pasture will not be able to survive as easily. Their results prove that the regions with drastic changes in climate will experience the greatest loss of dairy output. Additionally, shifts in temperature can also cause stress-related illnesses such as heat stress in cattle, resulting in reduced cattle productivity. Stress-related pests such as cattle ticks can also occur. Surprisingly, Tasmanian dairy production experienced a relatively low amount of decline in dairy productivity when compared to other states for reasons unstated.

There is a relatively inelastic demand for dairy products, and high substitutability between dairy products from different states. Warmer temperatures will mean that there will be an increase in water requirements for dairy production. But this demand will coincide with the decreasing water availability. The warm and dry climate of southeastern Australia will be most affected by the temperature shifts. To sustain the production quantity, solutions such as increasing the amount of food (grain, dietary oils) for cattle or changing the grass to deep-rooted and heat-tolerant varieties may help to alleviate production difficulties.

The article also covers effects on international dairy production. The similarly pasture-based dairy industry in New Zealand will experience a 2.8 to 4.3% decrease in production due to climate change. Reduced rainfall in Central Europe will cause their dairy systems to suffer. The United States will experience higher temperatures in the coming years, causing a significant negative impact on dairy production. By 2050, the analysis indicates that dairy production will have dramatically decreased.

Hanslow, K., Gunasekera D., Cullen B., Newth D., 2012. Economic impacts of climate change on the Australian dairy sector. Australian Journal of Agricultural and Resource Economics, 58, pp. 60–77.

Economic Effects of California Drought
by Sarah Whitney

In an article in Forbes magazine, Tom Zeller Jr. relayed the information that on April 1st, 2015, governor Jerry Brown announced that the state of California would now be subject to unprecedented water usage restrictions. California is currently in its fourth year of severe drought with record low levels of snowpack, only 5% of normal levels. Lack of precipitation and snowpack has prevented recharge of reservoirs and aquifers. In addition, over the 21st century, drought conditions are projected to intensify as the average number of days above 95°F will double or even triple, and the days below freezing will decrease by 60 to 90%. Furthermore, the intensity of heat will cause a greater number of wildfires, affecting the air quality and safety of Californians.

Zeller notes that if mitigation methods to global warming are not put in place to live more sustainably, California's situation will only worsen with time, reaching a tens-of-billions-of-dollars problem. A study by the Risky Business Project states that California will experience significant and multiple economic risks due to climate change. One major effect is a great decline in the amount of agricultural products the state can produce. Without adaptations, farmers will be unable to produce heat sensitive commodity crops like corn and cotton. The south-inland region of California is likely to experience economic losses of nearly $38 million per year by the end of the century. Other effects of climate change like rising sea levels could cost the state billions of dollars in property and infrastructure loss. This estimate includes $8 to $10 billion of property that would be underwater and $6 to $10 billion would be threatened by high tides by the middle of the century. Overall by 2100, a total of $20 billion of property would be under water.

Weeks before the announcement of these restrictions in California, Governor Jerry Brown said that not acknowledging global climate change and climate science "borders on immoral." He describes the Senate Majority Leader Mitch McConnell's actions to protect coal interests as risking "the health and well-being of America". Clearly Brown is passionate about global warming and the impacts that it has upon his state. Even if skeptics like Mitch McConnell who attributes the drought to a natural flux of Mother Nature were correct, human-induced global warming would nevertheless intensify its effects and timescale, and thus, according to Zeller, action must be taken.

Zeller, T., 2015. Drought, Climate Change and California's Multibillion-Dollar Problem. Forbes. Energy. http://onforb.es/1JNZtsz

Haze Pollution and its Impact on Tourism
by Yijing Zhang

Aiping Zhang (2015) tried to study how the haze pollution in China can influence the tourism industry via a survey on potential tourists. As the motivation of tourism is to release accumulated pressure, the environmental quality must be included as a factor of determining a destination. On the other hand, the air condition in Southeast Asia is not very optimistic. The number of haze days, indicated by the value of PM2.5, has reached 189 in Beijing in 2013. This number shows that over half of a year, Beijing was covered by probably toxic haze that also decreases people's vision.

Zhang conducted a survey of potential tourists, who want to travel to Beijing, from two provinces close to Beijing. In the questionnaire, questions were asked to find out people's intention to travel, awareness of haze, impacts of haze pollution on travel, attitudes towards of impacts of haze and the following consequences of different attitudes.

There were several findings overall. Even though people lack a clear image of what haze is, the vast majority of people agree that haze is harmful to health. With respect to different purposes of travelling, people value haze pollution differently. People who travel to Beijing for sightseeing and leisure tend to weigh haze as having a greater impact on their travel. But people traveling for business or visiting friends and relatives are more restricted by their own travel purpose, so they tend to value haze less seriously. Also, the results indicate that among all the impacts of haze pollution, its impact on safety, including traffic as well as health safety is the most significant.

However, haze pollution might not be the priority factor when people consider a travel destination, because the traditional factors like travel expense, availability of spare time, and companion's influence still paly a role. Also, the external factors like national holidays in May and October become the most popular travel time. Therefore, haze pollution becomes the secondary factor. The significance of the study is that to minimize the harm of haze on public, the tourism authority can broadcast timely information on haze. More importantly, the environmental office should put more effort on fixing air pollution.

Zhang, A., Zhong, L., Xu, Y., Wang, H., Dang, L., 2015. Tourists' Perception of Haze Pollution and the Potential Impacts on Travel: Reshaping the Features of Tourism Seasonality in Beijing, China. Sustainability 7, 2397-2414. http://www.mdpi.com/2071-1050/7/3/2397

SOCIETY AND CLIMATE CHANGE

Nepalese Sherpas Affected by Climate Change
by Jordan Aronowitz

Cut-off from the rest of the world, the Sherpas of Nepal spend their lives in the Himalayas. Overall climate change, mainly the average increase in global temperature, has negatively affected the Himalayas, but according to a recent paper (Sherpa, 2014), the Sherpas are ill informed about these changes, and can barely define "global warming." NGOs have strived to inform this population about the imminent dangers of climate change, but cultural barriers, such as sexism and disdain for western culture, prevent success. The Sherpas are not causing climate change, but the NGOs want to inform them about possible dangers they may face in the future, saving lives, cultures, and livelihoods.

Glacial lake outburst floods, also known as GLOFs have become increasingly common in Nepal. These floods occur when glacial melts overpower glacial dams and overflow the glacier. The rush of melted glacier water can flow for miles, and the lack of technology prevents proper warning systems from being successful. They can destroy the poorly structured buildings common in this part of the world, and most natives are not adequately informed to prepare their homes and business.

Due to Everest's rise in tourism over the last few decades, the lives of Sherpas have become connected to the western world, but the only individuals to have frequent contact are hotel owners. Besides them, it is hard to find people to teach the dangers that climate change may have on their society. For example, when the NGOs encourage women to help, they respond with "..women are not good for these things; ask only the men to speak. We don't know anything." This clear lack of confidence worries outsiders.

These organizations are desperately trying to save the lives of the Sherpas, but most have no idea that average global temperatures are increasing, their own mountains are melting, and that Himalayan glaciers are causing deadly GLOFs, placing uninformed Sherpas in danger.

Sherpa, P.Y. (2014). Climate Change, Perceptions, and Social Heterogeneity in Pharak, Mount Everest Region of Nepal. Human Organization, 73(2), 153-161.

No Clear Policy for Climate Change "Refugees"
by Jordan Aronowitz

Individuals who are forced to leave their country to escape persecution are referred to as refugees. In situations of war, most first world governments will accept refugees; however, the definition of refugee is evolving. The Brookings Institution's Elizabeth Ferris (2015) examined how gradual global warming is creating a new type of migrant. The "Climate Change Refugee" is defined as an individual who must seek asylum in another country because climate change has made it unsafe to remain in their current country. This opens the debate as to whether countries can, and should, accept evacuees with this reasoning. According to Ferris, clear guidelines need to be set, because in the future, we do not know how many individuals there will be seeking refuge.

The number of people displaced by climate change who must find a new country that will provide them with a safe place to live is increasing. Due to refugee laws often that only support asylum from war or imminent persecution, many countries cannot guarantee shelter to those displaced by climate change. For example, a native from the island of Tuvalu, who could no longer remain there due to the rising sea level, was denied refuge by a New Zealand court because the laws did not apply to his situation. It is not clear how many people will be forced to migrate by the climate in the next few decades, but policy preparation is imperative.

Initiatives are attempting to create a uniform policy by filling a gap in international law that leaves victims with nowhere to live. They believe the best and most efficient solution would be to build an agenda that directly addresses the worries of the victims of climate change displacement.

Ferris, E. (2015). Who Will Welcome Climate Change Migrants? Newsweek. Apr 24, 2015.

Could Climate Change Cause Famines?
by Caroline Chmiel

More than ever, the rapid growth of the world population is causing a heightened demand for food. Making this struggle infinitely worse is climate change. Per decade, food demand rises by 14%. Climate change reduces wheat yields by 2% compared to the amount without climate change, and corn yields by 1%. The demand for food causes worry and stress, so the idea that climate change worsens an already critical situation makes the fight to feed billions even harder. This is the bleak picture painted by Eduardo Porter writing in the New York Times. Food price spikes because of increased demand strongly correlate with urban unrest. From temperature changes due to global warming, production of crops can change. Less than expected production often causes producers to ban exports and importers to try to hoard the crop. Overall, commodity markets experience chaos and strain further than just feeding people. The culmination of climate change, increased population and demand for food leads to a serious question about the possibility of famine. More likely, though, is a volatile world full of wars over substances. The most highly affected population will be the poor, unable to afford increased food prices.

An example of the repercussions of these food price spikes occurred in 2007. Prices rose, leading big producers like India and Vietnam to ban exports to protect themselves domestically, while importers like Bangladesh, Nigeria, and Iran entered the markets planning to hoard as much grain as possible. This disorder took the focus away from efficiently allocating food during high price periods, revealing the potential for alarmingly selfish actions.

One certain way to improve this situation lies in saving food that is currently wasted. Humanity wastes one quarter of food produced. Poor storage and transport infrastructure lead food to be unusable, while wasteful consumers in wealthier areas get rid of valuable food. Limiting this waste is crucial in efficiently dispersing food as to feed the growing population. In addition, patterns show that humanity has the capacity to invent ways around constraints, and will act efficiently when necessary. Specific suggested adaptations are farmers breeding new crops to better resist heat and drought, new techniques for water harvesting that will hold off evaporation for longer, and improving yields of crops through rotation.

Porter, Eduardo. "Old Forecast of Famine May Yet Come True." The New York Times Web. 1 April. 2014

Arctic Communities in Alaska See Climate Change as Akin to Social Changes
by Caroline Chmiel

Ecosystems in the Arctic have been undergoing rapid changes as a result of global climate change. This has significant implications for the livelihoods of Arctic peoples. In the past twenty to thirty years, the impact of environmental changes on subsistence-based lifestyles has been observed. The difficulty in figuring out how Arctic communities experience and respond to climate change comes from the inseparability of environmental, social, economic, cultural, and political realms for community residents. It is hard to distinguish the response to climate because many informants live based on various incomes from subsistence harvesting of fish and game. Many factors go into practicing subsistence livelihoods, so the perception and experience of climate change is altered among these factors.

The dramatic socioeconomic cultural transitions taking place in northwest Alaska communities take precedence over climate change in impacting sustainability of subsistence practices. Scientists believe that understanding how environmental changes impact subsistence practice and culture in Arctic communities

208

will help gain a better sense of how global change affects our survival and adaptation methods.

Specific changes in the Arctic include less numerous and changing size of fish populations. This change is attributed to many factors. Some are increasing beaver activity, shallower river levels, warmer water temperatures in the summer that create unfavorable spawning conditions, and melting permafrost that leads to increased sedimentation in the spawning beds of the Dolly Varden, decreasing egg survival. Additionally, changing water levels and fish movement patterns make challenges for local harvesters to meet their subsistence needs. Water levels also affect transportation in that boats commonly get stuck or hit rocks while traveling. This causes expensive damage and difficulty for families traveling to fish camps in the spring and fall in search of whitefish. Also, the faster spring movement of fish makes fisherman often miss the optimal time to catch them. The warmer weather during spring also lowers the quality of fish.

Interestingly, the village residents do not perceive these environmental changes separately from other social changes in local fishing practices, but view conditions and interacting drivers of change together. Indigenous people of the Artic recognize environmental and social spheres in unity. Older peoples also see changes as a difference in contemporary living, not from environmental and climate-related changes. Not realizing these detrimental changes come from climate change will prevent Arctic people from realizing they shouldn't simply accept the changes, but advocate for fighting climate change.

Moerlein, Katie J., and Courtney Carothers. "Total Environment of Change: Impacts of Climate Change and Social Transitions on Subsistence Fisheries in Northwest Alaska." Ecology and Society (2012). Web. 26 Apr. 2015.

Effect of Climate Change on the Tourism Industry
by Tyler Dean

Tourism is a climate-dependent industry because many destinations owe their popularity to their pleasant climates during traditional holiday seasons. Amelung,

Nicholls and Viner assessed the potential climate change impact on the tourism industry. The authors focused on the "potential implications of projected climate change on international and regional tourism flows throughout the coming century" and "the implications of projected climate change on tourism seasonality in the summer European market." A large portion of tourism is due to leisure travel centered on the expectation of relatively pleasant climatic conditions and scenery. It is also based on the scheduling and occurrences of holidays and school vacation periods. Climate change threatens to change of both the timing and conditions. It threatens the aesthetic appeal of numerous natural attractions, makes certain tourist destinations unattractive or unbearable and disturbs the alignment of the holidays and peak travel times. At the very least, this can cut revenues and increase expenses in the industry by forcing it to market destinations more, or validate the value of traveling to the destinations at different times of the year. Ultimately this could change the landscape of the industry as a whole, and may be difficult to reverse. So far several industry leaders have increased marketing, increased spending on support of climate preservation and began to lobby to have school holidays change with the climate. The results are unknown and only time will tell whether or not climate change proves to be detrimental to the tourism industry.

Amelung B., Nicholls S., Viner D. 2015. Implications of Global Climate Change for Tourism Flows and Seasonality . Journal of Travel Research 45. 286-296.

Effects of Extreme Weather on Homeless People

by Tyler Dean

Climate change has proven to increase the severity and frequency of extreme weather and temperature conditions. When people experiencing homelessness are exposed to high or low temperature extremes they are more vulnerable than those who are not. For people experiencing homelessness, such exposer can sometimes be fatal. In addition, homeless people are more likely to have chronic, comorbid illnesses such as respiratory infections, gastrointestinal problems, musculoskeletal problems and poor dental health than the general population. They also reduce the priority of health needs due to their consistent struggle for shelter and food. Cusak and Kralick (2013) conducted a five-phased qualitative interpretive study to identify the extreme weather-related health needs of homeless people and the response by homeless service providers in Adelaide, South Australia.

Phase one involved identifying the needs of homeless people during extreme weather events. Phase two involved identifying government and nongovernment organizations providing services to the homeless in the inner city area of Adelaide. In phase three organizations were approached to participate in a telephone interview to explore the level of planning they undertook for extreme weather events and the types of services they offered to the homeless during these times. Phase four involved the research team undertaking a gap analysis of findings. Phase five involved dissemination and discussion of the research report and recommendations with homeless service providers and Adelaide local government.

The study concluded that urban heat in the built environment raised the ambient temperature, increased the risk of heat stress to those who were unable to move into cooler conditions. Even the nighttime temperatures remained very high, providing no relief from the heat. Heat-related health issues include an increase in allergies and related conditions such as asthma, exacerbation of psychosocial health issues, increases in sunburn, dehydration, heat stress and a rise in insect bites led to increased skin and vector-borne infections.

The study also concluded that during the winter months those living in cold and wet weather with little opportunity to dry out and warm up, experience more health issues, such as respiratory and foot infections, and exacerbation of their chronic medical conditions. Ultimately health suffered more from cold weather than hot weather.

Cusack L., Loon A., Kralik D. 2013. Extreme Weather-Related Health Needs of People Who Are Homeless . Australian Journal of Primary Health 19. 250-255.

Gender Mainstreaming and Climate Change
by Juana Granados

The implementation of gender mainstreaming is important in climate change mitigation because responses to climate change have ignored the impacts on women. Gender mainstreaming is defined as the process of assessing the implications for both genders when making policies while ultimately creating gender equality. Alston (2014) argues for the overall incorporation of gender mainstreaming in climate change responses and women's empowerment in society because global mainstreaming has not resulted in advances for women.

Failure to consider gender inequalities in post-disaster reconstruction efforts can be attributed to the fact that bureaucratic processes are conservative and traditionally associated with patriarchal values, where males make up a large portion of the government. Thus, male privilege is founded on traditional superiority. In order to address the local implementation of gender mainstreaming, several barriers must be considered: a lack of understanding of each gender because it makes the goals of gender mainstreaming unclear, acknowledging that radical policies originated from patriarchal support, and terminating poor treatment and ignorance of women in organizations aimed at addressing climate change.

Research has continuously shown that women are more vulnerable to climate change disasters. Thus, in order to most effectively rebuild resilience in communities that have undergone environmental disasters, policies need to reconsider gender norms. Assumptions regarding gender norms should not play any role in policy making because there is often a technocratic assessment, where men are given more attention than women in the government because throughout time, men have consistently been in powerful roles than women, such as in the government. There is a reluctance to give up on gender mainstreaming in climate change policies because women's traditional practices and local knowledge can enhance climate change technologies. They, like men, are full of knowledge that can address climate change, but in many places are still not acknowledged in policy making because of existing gender relations and female subordination to men. For this reason, the only way gender mainstream can fail is if there is the continuous lack of feminist consideration in politics.

Alston, M., 2014. Gender mainstreaming and climate change. Women's Studies International Forum 47, 287-294. http://bit.ly/1GxyRLh

Climate Change—a Possible Peacemaker
by Brina Jablonski

Erik Garzke examines the unusual and atypical idea that climate change could result in peace rather than violence, as most people believe. To prove his claim, Garzke studied the effect of climate change on international conflict after the era of European industrialization. The results show that with an increase in climate change there has been some increase in warfare in some areas and a decrease in others, thus proving that there is no consistent conclusion that climate change negatively affects political violence.

Garzke understands that global warming may result in increased civil and even interstate warfare because groups will compete for water, soil, or oil. However, he makes a point of saying how industrialization leads to economic development and democracy. Both economic development and democracy are usually correlated with peace. Prosperity also supports international institutions and stabilizing global and regional hierarchies. This supports the idea that global warming can correspond with peace. However, no studies have proved that global warming is actually capable of preventing warfare yet. In contrast to the idea of peace, if efforts to fight climate change cause nations to decay economically, then the world may start to crumble into a state of turmoil. In other words, the fear that climate change could induce political conflict could come true.

Garzke concludes that although climate change poses a number of critical challenges for citizens and policymakers, it does not need to be looked at fundamentally as a security issue. The changing patterns in economic prosperity will lead to an increase in average international income and thus an increase in world peace. He also makes a point of saying how middle-income states are the most prone to conflict in todays' world. This implies that efforts to stop or prevent climate change should focus on these middle-income areas in order to prevent the increase of conflict.

Gartzke, E. 2012. Could Climate Change Precipitate Peace?. Journal of Peace Research, 49 (1), 177-192. http://bit.ly/1GxySPu

Impacts of Climate Change on Senior Kenyan Women
by Brina Jablonski

Women in rural Africa produce sixty to eighty percent of the total food supplies through rain-fed farming. These women also contribute to the management of natural resources such as forests, land, and water along with the job of farming. Examples of these interactions include herding cattle, collecting fuel wood, and other forms of small-scale farming. Because women are so involved with the environment they have not only witnessed the effects of climate change but are now also suffering from the effects as well.

In Chebarus, in Nandi East District, Kenya, women are currently fighting the problems that come with changes in the weather. High rainfall increases landslides and soil erosion due to unsustainable farming practices and deforestation. Most of the population is already poor so the combination of changing weather conditions along with the lack of markets and infrastructure forces social change among the people of Chebarus. In order to prove that climate change is indeed impacting the people of Kenya, Linda Chebichii gathered verbal narratives from both young and senior women asking them about their views, observations, and experiences, of the changing climatic, economic, and environmental situation as well as the changing social exchanges.

Paulina Bett, a sixty-five year-old woman living in Kapinder village described how the land around her village is changed and how the rainy season has become erratic and unpredictable. Along with these physical changes the children in her village are now more disrespectful towards their elders. Anna Chepkurgat, a resident of Kipkimba Village mentioned how children of the village are now more rebellious and no longer listen to nor obey the wishes of their female elders. Esther Choge of Cheboin Village explained how the deforestation and the lack of rainfall have affected the young people of her village negatively. She expanded on how the young no longer listen to the advice given by the elders of the community and have adopted immoral behaviors as well as substance abuse.

These live reports go to show that climate change is no longer just a force affecting us physically, but also mentally and emotionally as human beings.

Chebichii, L. 2010. Impact of Senior Women in Small Rural Community Farming in Kenya. Climate Change, Globalisation and Changing Social Relations. Women & Environments International Magazine. 84/85, 20-22. http://bit.ly/1AswWXj

Climate Change and its Effects on Alaskan Inuit Populations
by Margaret Loncki

Ford *et al.* (2008) explore the vulnerability of two populations of Alaskan Inuits to climate change. The authors begin by explaining the cultural importance of the "procurement, sharing, and consumption" of traditional food. Global climate change plays a very important role in these Alaskan Inuit's ability to efficiently and successfully harvests viable food sources. As a result, Climate change has the potential to bring about social, cultural, and economic change.

Alaskan Inuit populations have observed increasingly abnormal weather conditions since the 1990s. These changes have made hunting far lass predictable. Variable winds make it more difficult to determine whether or not ice is thick and stable enough to travel on. Similarly, climate change has brought about shorter ice seasons as a result of delayed ice freeze-up. This has shortened the caribou season by nearly a month, forcing hunters to harvest when weather and ice conditions are less than ideal, making the hunt far more dangerous. For the Inuits, fishing season is typically ended only because of ocean freeze-up and the inability to reach successful fishing spots. Shorter Caribou hunting seasons increases the fishing season, a characteristic of climate change that the Inuit's tend to welcome. Rapidly changing weather conditions also make the hunting knowledge that has been passed from generation to generation less reliable, and as a result, making hunting a more dangerous task. Increased use of technology such as GPS and snowmobile has seriously changed the ways these Inuit populations hunt. Although snowmobiles allow hunters to travel farther and faster than ever before and GPS makes tracking and navigation obsolete, this new technology results in hunters taking more risks than hunters of previous generations. As reliable hunting skills deteriorate from generation to generation, hunting has become a more and more dangerous task.

The importance of sharing and social connection has been found to increase the Inuit's ability to adapt to changing climate conditions. Food and supplies are often brought to those who do not have the resources to hunt on their own, although the importance of this practice has decreased from generation to generation. Inuit populations have slowly shifted to a more western lifestyle, more often relying on foreign markets for resources and full time jobs for financial support. Increased use of money detracts from the giving and sharing culture of Inuit communities and decreases reliance on one and other for support. Similarly, government imposition of education requirements has reduced the ability of younger generations to learn the hunting strategies and techniques of previous generations. Although hunting has been the only way of life for generations of Alaskan Inuits, it is uncertain that they will be able to maintain this way of life. In the past, they have proven to be very capable of adapting to changing weather conditions, but this soon may not longer be the case.

Ford, J., Smit, B., Wandel, J., Allurut, M., Shappa, K., Ittusarjuat, H., Qrunnut, K., 2008. Climate change in the Arctic: current and future vulnerability in two Inuit communities in Canada. The Geographical Journal 174, 45-62.

Increasing Vulnerability of Island Communities to Climate Change

by Margaret Loncki

With the current trajectory of global Climate change, Island communities will be the first to be noticeably affected. Heather Lazrus describes the vulnerabilities of island communities as well as their ability to adapt to environmental changes brought about by climate change. Along with altered precipitation and storm patterns, and rising global temperatures, island communities face land loss due to the rise of sea levels and may soon face forced migration as a result. Lazrus also explains that many societies have portrayed small island communities as helpless victims of large developed nations' irresponsibility and the climate changes that this irresponsibility has brought about. Lazrus makes the point that small island communities are not beyond saving and if climate change is correctly handled, migration will become unnecessary.

Island communities are typically thought of as "small, isolated, and dependent communities" adding to the perception of island communities being helpless against changing weather conditions. Lazrus points out that the interconnectedness between many island communities allows them to be far more resilient than many believe. Through the Alliance of small Island States (ASIS), Small island communities have been able to be heard at the United Nation's Conferences. Lazrus also commonly refers to traditional environmental knowledge and its importance in island communities' ability to adapt to changing climate. Because it is believed that every person has a right to "retain their homelands", every carbon producer around the worst is in some way obligated to prevent further climate change in order to maintain the homelands of the world's island communities. If nothing can be done to mitigate global climate change before island communities are forced from their homelands, they well have no choice other than to migrate. For island communities, migration has historically been a way of adaptation to climate change, but in modern times, would be considered failure to adapt. Migration of island communities poses many problems such as citizenship and sovereignty.

Lazrus, Heather., 2012, Sea Chance: Island Communities and Climate Change. The Annual Review of Anthropology 41. 285-301.

Will the Combination of Overfishing and Climate Change be Too Much For Coastal Fishing Communities?
by Margaret Loncki

Around the world, small fishing communities have been struggling to maintain their fishing industry under the extreme pressure of overfishing. Many small coastal communities have relied on their fishing industry for economic stability and prosperity for generations. Van Putten *et al.* (2014) attempted to determine the extent to which the additional pressure placed on these communities by climate change will further exacerbate this crisis.

Many coastal fishing communities have been forced into new marine sectors resulting in overall job loss. For a large percentage of individuals in coastal fishing communities, the fishing industry is all they know. Van Putten *et al.* found that this specialized industry knowledge results in the inability to migrate into other industries. High entry costs in the fishing industry also prevent the younger generation from entering the market. Van Putten *et al.* also reported that many individuals in the fishing community are driven by a love for the sea as well as financial needs. Someone in another community may not be phased by moving from a desk job in another industry, but individuals in the fishing industry are far less willing to move to a more stable industry due to their love for the fishing way of life.

Reductions in the fishing industry also results in significant effects on other industries in the community. Because the majority of businesses in these communities are very small, typically employing less than five community members, they are greatly affected by a significant change of demand in the market. Climate change continues to exacerbate the decline of costal fishing communities, and therefore the decline of the entire fishing community.

Van Putten, I., Metcalf, S., Frusher, S., Marshall, N., Tull, M., 2014. Transformation of coastal communities: Where is the marine sector heading. Australian Journal of Regional Studies 20, 286-324.

Climate Change Effects More Visible in Women and the Poverty-Stricken
by Patrick Quarberg

Writing about the societal effects of climate change in 2002, Fatma Denton posited that women are more likely to be exposed to poverty in developing countries than men are, climate change will affect men and women differently. This is based on the idea that people in poverty do not have the willingness or means to address or cope with climate change. Denton thinks that social changes brought by climate change will increase gender welfare disparities, introducing a swath of new social issues. Therefore, it is wise to prepare to preemptively counteract these changes, so that a larger section of the population is able to deal with climate change.

Since climate change will increase income disparities while at the same time decreasing the amount of usable resources, it will become increasing challenging to mitigate income disparity. People in poverty need access to "reproductive resources", which include fertile land and clean water. As CO_2 levels rise, both of these will become scarcer. This creates a sort of self-feeding cycle in which the people living in poverty are not only excluded from policy-making decisions related to climate change, but are also incapable of even dealing with mitigating climate change. This furthers the severity of climate change, which could in turn force more women and poorer people into poverty. This cycle could be cut off, or at least heavily slowed down by educating and providing for women living in poor countries. In many less developed countries, resources are not divided evenly among men and women, which is why this issue is especially pertinent to women. While this is certainly an issue regardless of the effects of climate change, it will be made even more severe once the effects of global climate change are factored in. For this reason, preemptively fighting this issue, before climate change has a major effect, is extremely important.

Denton, F. 2002. Climate Change Vulnerability, Impacts, and Adaptation: Why Does Gender Matter? Gender and Development Volume 10, pp. 10-20

How Climate Change Is Causing Global Conflict

by Patrick Quarberg

People in less-developed countries are more likely to move out of climate change-affected areas and cause conflict, a study by Rafael Reuveny (2007) finds. Developing countries face serious threats due to climate change, such as severe scarcity in the food and water supply. These fundamental issues cause larger numbers of people to leave the country. Reuveny analyzes this from an economic perspective. That is, when the net benefit of staying in a place is overshadowed by the net cost, people—especially in developing countries—are inclined to leave that area or country. The displacement of many people leads to greater conflicts in a few ways. Increased competition for resources in the receiving country lead to increased tension and conflict. If displaced people are of a different ethnicity than the people of the receiving country, this effect is amplified. If the trend of migration continues for long enough, the host country's citizens develop a tradition of distrust for anyone from that country, prolonging the struggle of the migrants and providing an opportunity for conflicts in the future. A final contributing agent to conflict is when migrants move on so-called "fault lines", which can be any sort of large change in way life. For example, migrants who move to an urban area from a rural area experience greater tension and conflict due to the transition.

The widespread effects of climate change on lesser-developed countries is especially concerning because it places additional stress on countries that are also struggling to handle its own citizens. Increasing tensions due to climate change could destabilize entire regions, since so many people will need to migrate away from their homes, due to the net cost exceeding the net benefit. Mitigating the effects of climate change is very important for the whole world, but alleviating existing tensions and social issues will also be incredibly beneficial for-lesser developed countries.

Reuveny, R. 2007. Climate change-induced migration and violent conflict Science Direct, Volume 26, Pages 656-673

Climate Change Brings About Activist Culture
by Patrick Quarberg

Climate produces a culture of environmental activism, a study by Linda H. Connor of the University of Sydney finds. Climate change gives way to a culture in which active citizen participation in protecting the environment is the norm. Arising initially out of necessity, the culture of protecting the environment could likely thrive until it is no longer required to exist. Environmentalism as we know it now will die out soon, and is different from the culture that Connor claims will develop. She states that modern environmentalism is too disconnected from the everyday operations of the average citizen, and runs against the consumption society present in many places. Thus true environmentalism, in the modern sense, is nearly impossible to practice. Furthermore, Connor points out that current governments cannot perform the role of active citizens when it comes to the environment, as evidenced by the global hesitation on making carbon-reducing policies. Connor studied The Hunter Valley in New South Wales, Australia, an area with abundant black coal and seam gas. For this reason, the Hunter Valley is exposed to a lot of the effects of burning coal. It is also very susceptible to the effects of climate change, like rising sea levels and drought. Since the area stands to lose so much by standing by and allowing coal to be burned, it is a great place to encourage activist culture, Connor finds. As a result, people turn to local action groups, which they later say are part of their identity. One action group in the Hunter Valley area, Rising Tide, is very ambitious and active. It aims to find sustainable solutions to the current environmental crisis. Members of the action group cite environmental conservation as a major part of their self-identity, a change which has come about since joining the group. This passion among the members could certainly lead to the movement being very effective and long-lasting Connor also goes into detail on several other groups in the area to provide evidence for how widespread the effort is. In short, it seems that the activist culture formed out of necessity could certainly persist until the effects of climate change are mitigated—if they don't destroy the earth first.

Connor, L. H. 2012. Experimental Publics: Activist Culture and Political Intelligibility of Climate Change Action in the Hunter Valley, Southeast Australia. Oceania. 82 volume 3 pp. 228-249.

The Greatest Threat to National Security
by Patrick Quarberg

Climate change has many adverse effects on the environment and society, among which is the threat it presents to national and individual security. A paper by Jon Barnett (2003) explores how climate change threatens security. In the paper, he defines security as the condition of being protected from, or not exposed to danger, in general. More specifically, security is the assurance that people will be able to continue to enjoy the comforts they currently enjoy. Using this definition, it is evident that climate change poses a threat to security. Island nation-states are severely threatened by rising water levels, Inuit communities are threatened by inconsistent ice shelves, which affect hunting, and countless places are endangered by malaria-carrying insects that come as a result of changing temperature and rainfall.

The span of climate change places it at the level of thermonuclear war, when it comes to threats to security. Because climate change is a *global* issue, it presents a global threat, much like global nuclear war does. Both climate change and nuclear war affect the whole world, and have potentially devastating effects. When it comes to national security, climate change has various effects. Increased levels of CO_2 in the atmosphere could lead to conflicts and wars over uncontaminated air or other scarce resources. Another potential (and very real) effect is rising sea levels, which affect different countries very differently. For example, a 45 cm rise in sea level would result in a 10.9% inundation of Bangladesh's landmass, which would force millions of people to relocate.

Scarcity in resources caused by climate change could destabilize developing countries, which are often reliant on consistent access to resources within their own territory. Mass migration from one country to another can bring about additional unrest, especially in areas already stricken by conflict, like the Middle East and some parts of Africa. This presents a severe threat to the security of many developing countries, but is not too much of an immediate concern to developed countries. This is a threat in itself, since developing countries are likely to be the first to be struck by the effects of climate change. This can cause unrest and conflict between states, making climate change a threat to political stability and personal security across the world.

Barnett, J. 2003. Security and Climate Change. Global Environmental Change, Volume 13, pages 7-17. http://bit.ly/1JNVjAJ

National Security Threatened by a Warming World
by *Chloe Rodman*

Jeff Goodell (2015) writes in Rolling Stone Magazine that 30 of the United States' domestic military bases are in jeopardy due to climate change and rising sea levels. These stations either must be relocated in the near future or put out of commission because not only are they sinking into the ocean, but the compounds become flooded with each storm, making work almost impossible. Because of these recent trends, the Pentagon, as well as President Obama, believe that "…climate change poses immediate risks to our national security." While many powerful and important members of the military and government believe action must be taken regarding climate change, some members of congress do not agree. These congress members, some of whom happen to be on various military committees, castigate those who believe in climate change or those who liken it to other global disasters such as terrorism or infectious disease.

The climate-denying politicians, predominantly Republicans, strive to diminish the link between national security and climate change. Recently an amendment passed in the House forbids the Pentagon from spending any money related to climate change. In 2009, the CIA, headed by Leon Panetta created the Center of Climate Change and National Security. This group was backed by the National Academy of Science, and its goal was to collect information on the global and domestic impact of climate change. When the report was completed, the press conference that planned to release the findings was canceled by some unknown hand, and lost in a pigeonhole—out of sight, out of mind.

However, Donald Rumsfield, secretary of Defense for George W. Bush, did manage to publish 'An Abrupt Climate Change Scenario and Its Implications for United States National Security.' This document found that climate change was a greater menace to not only to the United States, but also to the world, than terrorism.

The cost of trying to counter the impact climate change will have on the United States military is enormous. Since it is predicted that 28 million acres of land and 555,000 bases, on both East and West coasts, will be affected, the project would cost hundreds of billions of dollars. The cost will not only be monetary, but the United States will also lose many invaluable station vantage points all over the globe—island bases that will soon be under water due to the melting Arctic permafrost.

Problems have already arisen from climate change. Droughts and food shortages due to a warming world are partially responsible for the start of the Egyptian Arab Spring, the Syrian civil war and the terrorist attacks in Nigeria. Now, tensions are high in between United States and Russia once again. Resources are being uncovered due to the melting permafrost in the Arctic. Russia recently placed one of its flags in the uncovered seabed, unofficially claiming the territory. Normally, this wouldn't concern the Pentagon but the new Russian midrange nuclear missile, the Bulava, can travel from this Arctic region to any East Coast city, such as New York City or Boston.

The United States is not equipped to work in the Arctic however, even if it wanted to. We do not have the resources that Russia has. The United States Navy weather forecasting ability, satellite communications, and lack of seabed surveillance in the area leaves them relatively blind in the freezing conditions. In addition, representatives on the committee that supervises Coast Guard Affairs argue that if a country wants to be successful in dealing with the Arctic conditions, they must have Icebreakers—equipment made specifically for freezing conditions. Russia has 43 Icebreakers, and the United States has one—which happens to be 40 years old.

The United States Navy is the most competent sea force in the world, however, as the climate warms and sea levels rise, chaos will also increase with natural disasters and political and social upheavals. With this increase in disorder, the Navy will be expected to intervene more often, to both aid and rescue other countries. The problem is, however, with the number of climate deniers in congress and their strategic locations in congressional committees, it does not appear that they will have enough resources to do so.

Goodell, Jeff. 2015. The Pentagon & Climate Change: How Deniers Put National Security at Risk. Rolling Stone. http://rol.st/1Ao5ES1

The Syrian Civil War—A Result of Climate Change?
by Chloe Rodman

Kelley *et al.* (2015) writing in The Proceedings of the National Academy of Sciences linked the Syrian Civil War to climate change. The Fertile Crescent, more specifically Syria, has experienced a severe prolonged drought since 2006. In a country dominated by agriculture, the drought killed enormous amounts of livestock and crops. To make matters worse, before this dry spell began, former Syrian President Hafez al-Assad implemented policies to increase agricultural production, despite a shortage in water. These policies made Syria particularly defenseless when the drought began.

While two-thirds of farms relied on rainfall as their primary water source, the remainder relied on groundwater and irrigation systems from nearby rivers such as the Tigris and the Euphrates. Turkish dams control these rivers but the Turkish government has been generous enough to supply Syria with water during their multiple long-term droughts. These three sources of water are unreliable however. The amount of rainfall on a year-to-year basis is unpredictable and has been decreasing in the winter, groundwater is now scarce due to both the previous agriculture policies as well as the drought, and it is predicted that the rivers in the Fertile Crescent area will continue to dry up. To try to counter the lack of water, a law was passed in 2005 that required well diggers to get a license, but it was not enforced and therefore ineffective.

While Syria has experienced droughts throughout history, they have become more severe recently, with the winter of 2007 and 2008 being the driest in instrumentally recorded history. The lack of groundwater has been one of the main contributors to the severity of the drought because Syria previously relied on it when precipitation was scarce. Satellite data has found that the downward trend in rainfall correlates with shrinking vegetation and groundwater due to a rising surface temperature in the Fertile Crescent area.

These long-term trends of increasing temperature and evaporation as well as the decrease of precipitation line up with the human-caused climate change timeline. Therefore, not only do scientists believe that the severity of these droughts are caused by the increase of greenhouse gases, it is also predicted that with the little counteraction to climate change in progress, the frequency of these severe, long-term droughts will increase.

Since climate is shown to have a large influence on the frequency and severity of the droughts in the Fertile Crescent region, especially Syria, it can be linked to the cause of the Syrian Civil War. Due to the increasing lack of rainfall and groundwater, farms were no longer producing what they once had. In 2003, 25% of Syria's gross domestic product was from agriculture. Five years later in 2008, it had dropped to 17%. Not only were farmers no longer making a profit, but President Bashar al-Assad also eliminated subsidies on food and fuel, causing even further distress to farming families. Approximately 1.5 million men, women, and starving children were forced to move from rural farm areas to the outskirts of urban centers. This shift in population, paralleled with 1.5 million Iraqi war refugees migrating into Syria, created a ghastly result. The increase from 8.9 million people in 2002 to 13.8 million people in 2010 put a huge strain on resources and caused high rates of unemployment, overcrowding, and crime in cities. Assad's government ignored the situation and, paired with the severity of the drought, the situation turned into national chaos.

Kelley, C., Mohtadi, S., Cane, M., Seager, R., & Kushnir, Y. (2015) Climate change in the Fertile Crescent and implications of the recent Syrian drought. http://bit.ly/1Ao5H0g

Pressures of a Changing Climate on Women of Rural Mexico
by Russell Salazar

Subsistence agriculture is a difficult practice in a world of uncertainty in temperatures and rainfall, and food security in some areas is a primary concern. A study by Bee (2014) looks at potential effects of the changing climate on the lives of women in rural Mexico, and gains insight into the choices they make given their "socio-political, economic and environmental contexts". Eighty-eight percent of the female interviewees claimed to be engaged in "unpaid domestic work", which includes the provision of daily food for the household through crop farming, namely maize and beans. Bearing the burden of household food security against unfavorable climates, these women act as teachers and decision-makers. They have learned to adapt to the weather, gaining knowledge about food sources and cultivation and passing that knowledge on to their children.

The main crops, maize and beans, are deeply ingrained in the Mexican culture, and many interviewees showed a clear need for the staples. Crop cultivation is, however, susceptible to annual weather conditions. Currently, the women of La Colorada and La Cuadrilla have developed practices to maintain food security during hard times. One method of keeping a steady inflow of food involves the gathering of *quelites*, or edible wild plants, while weeding. This provides the household with sustenance without sacrificing money or other produce. Unfortunately, the situation is complicated with the changing climate and its potential threat to the subsistence agriculture lifestyle. It may be the case that genetically modified crops must be introduced in order to continue the steady consumption of maize and beans in less predictable climates, which is a program sponsored by the Municipal government of La Colorada. Participants of the study have expressed skepticism and discontent for the introduction of GM seeds that may threaten the land quality, and that produce crop of different taste and texture. The women's lifestyle informs and defines the decisions they make.

Ultimately, Bee argues that regardless of the situation, women play a crucial role in the rural Mexican household. They are "active agents in knowledge production and decision-making in the context of uncertainty", and it is the study of their behavior that can give insight into potential adaptive strategies and public policy with regard to climate change in rural areas.

Bee, B. A., 2014. "Si no comemos tortilla, no vivimos:" women, climate change, and food security in central Mexico. Agriculture and Human Values 31, 607–620. http://bit.ly/1Ao5I4d

Where Climate Change Meets Social Inequality
by Breanna Sewell

Author Phoebe Godfrey uses her paper, "Race, Gender & Class, and Climate Change" (2012) to address the potential sociological outcomes of global climate change, specifically in regard to the intersection and overlapping effects of the social constructs, race, gender, and class.

She begins her article by denying the validity of the argument that global climate change may or may not exist and diverts the reader's attention to the sociological effects of climate change; first admitting that, regrettably, environmental sociologists have only in recent years turned their attention to climate change, and then asserting her opinion that the "complementary and contradictory intersections" of race, gender, and class are present everywhere and their importance is underestimated.

Godfrey mentions an article with a similar subject in order to call attention to the specifics of her debate. The second author makes a call to action, requesting that "we" realize the importance of sociological inequalities in correspondence with global climate change. This "we" is what is in question by Godfrey. She asserts that correctly defining "we" is crucial to understanding the complicated relationship between the intersection of sociology and climate change.

In the first scenario, if "we" is meant to mean the world's entire human population, then, Godfrey argues, fate will be in the hands of the "white elite of the Global North." There will be a great divide in the lifestyle of those of different classes, and living in a green utopia will be entirely dependent upon your social privilege, or lack thereof.

The second scenario, if "we" is meant to mean those who are ready to live sustainably and take action against global climate change, Godfrey argues, that there is no "we" until more of us are ready to address the overlap of environmentalism with sociology.

Godfrey does not see a positive future in regards to global climate change until social inequalities are addressed, due to their inextricable connection to both how we see ourselves in relation to other people and also the causes and effects of global climate change.

Godfrey, P., 2012. Introduction: Race, Gender & Class and Climate Change. Race, Gender & Class. http://bit.ly/1KthZrp

How Will Future Generations Deal with Climate Change

by Breanna Sewell

Rob White writes his 2011 article, "Climate Change, Uncertain Futures and the Sociology of Youth," in order to call attention to the environmental problems that the future generations face, and to address the relationship between these issues and the sociology of youth. The author begins by giving a general overview of the disastrous effects of climate change, and the future state of our planet, both environmentally and socially. White states that "social inequality and environmental injustice will undoubtedly be the drivers of continuous conflict for many years to come," due to the fact that those at the bottom of the socioeconomic ladder are currently and will continue to suffer the brunt of the climate change blow, even though they are, typically, the ones that contribute to the problem the least. He predicts increasing amounts of social conflict centered on our environmental issues, namely water and food shortages.

White discusses youth identity in relation to global warming, questioning how future generations will categorize themselves based on all that is going on in the world due to climate change. For example, will some be labeled as "the privileged" and others "the victims"?

White also addresses the concept of survivalism, a frightening thought when food and water shortages loom in the distance. If survivalism becomes a societal reality, White points out that reversing or even mitigating the effects of climate change may be pushed by the wayside in order to address the more pressing concerns like getting enough food and water. If it gets to the point where survival is a common concern, no time or energy would go into fixing the planet.

The author calls for action in the sociology of youth and hopes to have our priorities regarding the planet altered. White leaves the reader with the ominous words, "we ignore [the issues of global warming and climate change] at our peril."

White, R., 2011. Climate Change, Uncertain Futures, and the Sociology of Youth. Youth Studies Australia. http://bit.ly/1eoKQju

Climate-Induced Migration
by Breanna Sewell

"Casualties of Climate Change," a 2011 article by Alex de Sherbinin, Koko Warner, and Charles Ehrhart addresses the issue of forced migration due to climate change as an introduction to their research on forced migration due to climate change. The authors first point out that throughout history, "climate-forced migrations have reshaped civilization," giving examples such as the drought and famine in Canaan four thousand years ago, a prolonged dry-period in Central Asia one thousand years ago, and the American Dust Bowl in the 1900s. The authors argue that our current state of climate change is another example of this, just with a new twist. This time, we have brought the climate change upon ourselves through our excessive greenhouse gas emissions, and we are seeing the disastrous effects of it including greater frequency of natural disasters, sea-level rise, ocean acidification and higher rainfall variability.

The article provides the reader with some shocking facts regarding climate change, such as: "in India alone, 40 million people would be displaced with a one-meter sea-level rise." Statements like this are a reminder of the severity of the situation. In the opinion of the authors, the next great humanitarian challenge that our international community will face is the forced migration and displacement prompted by climate change. With their studies, de Sherbinin, Warner, and Ehrhart hope to spread awareness regarding the future state of climate-induced migration as well as determine the locations of and solutions for the migrations that are likely to occur.

de Sherbinin, A., Warner, Ehrhart, 2011. Casualties of Climate Change. Scientific American. http://bit.ly/1zZHVll

How Climate Change Affects Women in Ghana
by Phoebe Shum

Who knew that gender bias could exist even in a topic such as climate change?

According to the UN, women are most vulnerable to climate change due to their role in food production. After all, 70% of the world's farmers are women, and these women produce 60-80% of the world's food crops. Trish Glazebrook (2011), Philosophy Professor from Dalhousie University in Nova Scotia, explains how climate change particularly affects women subsistence farmers in areas of poverty. In northeast Ghana, the successful growing of crops is highly dependent on the rainy season due to the lack of irrigation technology. The rainy season is the only growing cycle per year, and when anthropogenic climate change causes extreme and abnormal weather conditions like droughts and floods, farming patterns are altered and the women are not able to provide subsistence for their families. Land degradation, desertification and soil erosion heavily affect the women, and the many people they provide for. On average, one woman can be responsible for 6 to 17 people, from children to the elderly to the sick to the handicapped. Their survival heavily depends on natural resources.

Glazebrook emphatically pushes for the inclusion of women in climate change adaptation policy. She makes it clear that women subsistence farmers in Ghana have vast knowledge in using sustainable farming practices. They use methods like intercropping and crop rotation. They know which crops are best for their fields and use natural alternatives to the insecticides and fertilizers they cannot afford, like ash and animal dung. Through her research efforts, Glazebrook hopes to spread awareness of the growing vulnerability of women in developing countries as climate change continues to take its toll on our environment. These women have valuable insight towards adapting to climate change, and the faster their voices are heard in adaptation efforts, the better off we will be.

Glazebrook, T. (2011) Women and Climate Change: A Case-Study from Northeast Ghana. Hypatia vol. 26, no. 4, 762-782.

Climate Change and Aging Populations
by Yijing Zhang

According to Adapting To Global Change: Aging, Urbanization and Resilience by Francesca Birks and Katherine Prater, the demography has shifted towards an aging population across the entire world. The authors point out that as a relatively vulnerable group, the elderly deserve more help from the society, especially more from the government. Although the vulnerability of this population may not be apparent on daily basis, it will be exposed under extreme conditions, such as natural disasters like hurricanes and earthquakes. With the lack of medical materials and weak evacuation instructions, the vast majority of fatalities caused by Hurricane Sandy were the population over 45. When the heat wave hit Moscow, the outcome of the forest fire was the poor air quality. Among the entire population, the elderly are the most susceptible to these consequences. Therefore, Birks and Prater suggest the importance of design solutions to address this problem.

According to Birks and Prater, providing easily accessible infrastructure in the residential areas is one solution. This should be a governmental duty. Probably, the simplest and most efficient solution would be posting clear signage in public spaces such as metro stations, because signs convey direct information to the elderly via pictures and prints. Further support could be offered to municipalities via transportation systems. Public transportation should be affordable, accessible and reliable in a crisis. They also point out that in order to respond to emergency situations, public alert information should be delivered through various means, including radio and television.

To build a resilient city, social structures and communal spaces are very important, because this might be the place where the older population spends most of their time. Larger spaces, circulation routes, mail service and amenities are indispensable elements of a good community. Particularly in megacities, the aging population can be easily overlooked. Yet, New York is an exemplary model of an age-friendly society. They cite the renovation of pedestrian streets, taxi programs specifically designed for the elderly and 59 initiatives created under the program Age Friendly NYC as examples. As for the elderly, social isolation has increasingly become a huge concern. Their participation in community activities is also one of the considerations of this journal. Locating senior housing in the central area might help senior citizens interact and communicate with people. Birks and Prater recommend such a housing model because people share common financial responsibilities. In all, the objective of these design solutions is to prepare against emergency situations while making a better living condition for the elderly.

As I read the article, I felt that the authors focused more on the problem solving part than on how exactly climate changes can significantly affect the aging population. But I appreciate the weight in the solution because it is more pragmatic.

Birks., F. and K. Prater. (2014). "Adapting to Global Change: Ageing, Urbanisation and Resilience." Architectural Design 84: 28-35. http://bit.ly/1LvaFZt

Anthropology in Climate Change
by Yijing Zhang

Barnes (2013) strongly suggests that natural scientists cannot solve the climate issue alone even if they have understood every scientific aspect of it. Therefore, anthropologists can further enrich the study of climate change in three ways, particularly when the climate debate involves social, cultural and political topics.

The first way to improve the climate study is to apply ethnographic insights. Instead of focusing on one specific community, Barnes argues that the climate change requires a broader perspective. Extending subjects from local places to international environments, and from science departments to companies and non-profit organizations, Barnes suggests that anthropology research is able to study how pure scientific knowledge could be incorporated into policies. By studying the language used in communication and debate, anthropologists can analyze how scientific knowledge is conveyed to the public.

The Intergovernmental Panel on Climate Change is a typical example of how scientific knowledge is interpreted. Research, which focused on how decisions were made and how presentation affects the debate in the panel, finds that anthropological elements help participants in the debate to think more broadly and help them to include cultural and social factors.

The second perspective that anthropology can offer is historical. As climate change is studied in a very long time scale, anthropologists suggest that the debate topics in environment and climate are not new. Since the time of Hippocrates, people have pondered whether humans can control environmental change. In addition, when scientists are talking about impacts of climate change on susceptible groups, they are, in fact, talking about uneven development processes in different countries, which has been a frequently discussed topic over the years. Hence, Barnes argues that discussions on past topics can effectively improve present mitigation or adaptation strategies.

The last way that anthropology can help is offering a holistic view. In contrast to solely emphasizing on the big picture, Barnes suggests that it is better to think about how new policies can influence people's livelihood. Though people's living quality, determined by politic environment and cultural influence is difficult to quantify, it is still important to address these issues, and anthropological approach helps to prevent an overemphasis on climate change data, bringing social responses into the picture.

Barnes, J., *et al.* (2013). "Contribution of anthropology to the study of climate change." Nature Climate Change 3: 541-544. http://bit.ly/1PGaRvt

Climate Change Impacts on Urban Communities

by Yijing Zhang

In a review of climate change impacts on the built environment, Wilby (2007) begins by pointing out evidence of global climate change. Extreme events like heat waves and intense precipitation have put us in great risk. In urban regions, the heat islands effect has caused 5–6°C warmer than rural areas. The rising temperature decreases the cooling potential of natural ventilation and increases people's demand for energy. The energy is used for mostly air-conditioning, cooking, and industrial processes. The UHI effect also causes air pollution concentration to rise, due to the correlation between temperature and photochemical smog.

An early climate change impact study by LCCP showed that with respect to built environment, the potential risk would be building subsidence on clay soils and increased ground shift in winter, affecting pipes and underground infrastructure. Therefore, it is important to integrate resilience in the design stage, which significantly reduces the long-term cost.

Urban drainage is closely associated with flood risk. The UK is estimated to have 80,000 properties at risk from flooding caused by intense precipitation, although there is a great uncertainty. In addition, coasted cities around the world are facing flood risks from sea level rise.

Climate change can affect fresh water resources in various ways. Rising temperature can lower river volumes leaving higher nutrient concentration that can cause eutrophication. The effect is not limited to the environment. People tend to use more water for garden watering when summer is hotter, while industry processes become less efficient since water-cooling is less effective.

One critical solution to flood risk and the urban heat island effect (UHI) is green space. Urban vegetation can help reduce the UHI effect, and the public enjoys outdoors spaces. But the vegetation should be carefully chosen so that these species would not cause unwanted consequences, like exacerbating air pollution and drying local soils.

Wilby, Robert L. 2007. "A review of climate change impacts on the built environment." Built Environment 33.1: 31-45. http://bit.ly/1lTFysP

CLIMATE CHANGE PROBLEMS
AND ADAPTATIONS

Ecosystems Altered by Strengthened Winds
by Jordan Aronowitz

Over the years, industrialization and urbanization have increased the amount of carbon dioxide and greenhouse gases present in our atmosphere. Obviously, these changes have affected the environment by increasing average temperatures and overall sea level, but surprisingly, climate change is also affecting wind levels. Over the past 25 years, many researchers have sought to determine whether these changes in wind speed positively or negatively effect related ecosystems. A 1990 hypothesis proposed that these winds are increasing and will positively affect the neighboring ecosystems. A synthesis of the data from experiments analyzing these patterns is the best way to see if the changes in these essential wind patterns have helped or harmed the ocean ecosystems under them. It was determined that these winds have been increasing overall, but further data must be collected to see their effects on the prosperity of the ocean ecosystems.

Three out of the five upwelling ecosystems analyzed had clearly intensified winds in recent years. Year-round wind intensification was present in the California system (northern Pacific) and the Humboldt system (off the coast of Chile). Wind intensification was present when reanalyzing quantitative model-data of past wind patterns and comparing the findings to present examinations in the Benguela system (southern Atlantic). Wind intensification was present when analyzing original data obtained through observation from the primaries studied by the writers in the Canary system (off the eastern coast of the United States). On the contrary, in the Iberian System (off the coast of western Africa), the data found went against the hypothesis, as contemporary winds were weaker than the originally observed wind patterns.

The wind intensification in the California, Benguela, and Humboldt ecosystems will ultimately benefit marine life. If there is a lack of nutrients, these winds can provide sustenance to the water, a refreshingly positive result of climate change. However, if the winds are too intense, they can end up harming the ecosystems connected to them by disrupting plankton migration or increasing the presence of acid in the waters. In addition, more harshly intensified winds were found at higher latitudes, leading to more severe effects on colder ecosystems. The changes can either help or harm fisheries, showing that climate change will have unpredictable effects on the ecosystems affected by these upwelling winds. Fisheries may be constrained if the winds prove to be harmful, increasing the price of fish and damaging ecosystems in the long-term. Over time forecasting of these changes will become easier and the consequences will be determined. Fortunately, the effects are not entirely negative, providing some hope for individuals concerned with the effect of excess carbon dioxide production on the worlds' oceans.

W. J. Sydeman, García-Reyes, M., Schoeman, D. S., Rykaczewski, R. R. (2014). Climate change and wind intensification in coastal upwelling ecosystems. Science, 345, 77-80.

Biodiversity in Danger from Climate Change
by Jordan Aronowitz

Biodiversity is a vital aspect of the earth's ecosystems. Without biodiversity, disease and disaster can wipe out essential flora and fauna, permanently damaging the fragile biomes supporting the planet. A recent study by Céline Bellard at the University of Paris-Sud (2012) examines the effect that climate change has had on biodiversity. Unfortunately, the outlook is grim. Over the 4.5 billion years the earth has existed, there have been five mass extinctions. If we continue on the current track of climate change, a sixth mass extinction is a serious possibility, but this will be the first one partially due to harmful actions by humans. Unless we can take actions to reverse climate change there will be massive, irreversible effects to the earth's biomes by means of a decrease in biodiversity.

The researchers examined three characteristics of biodiversity to determine future predictions: spatial, temporal, and self. For space, if a species is unable to live in its current space, it will have to move. Temporally, a species will adapt and change the timing of life cycle events. For self, a species will change its traits to adjust to new climatic conditions. By shifting one to three of these traits, the species might be able to adjust, but in the process may decrease biodiversity due to limited resources and variation in environments through climate change.

Biodiversity is present everywhere, from individual to biome. The reason climate change may decrease diversity is due to environments and evolution. For example, if climate change drastically changes an environment, such as rising sea levels altering marine habitats, organisms present will have to adapt in order to survive in the new conditions. Rising sea levels would be a gradual change caused by increased temperatures over a long period of time, giving the ecosystem more time to adapt, and may not necessarily be caused by humans; however, sudden changes, such as deforestation, a change directly caused by humans, would completely delete habitats, without proper time to adapt. The concept that climate change is cyclical may not be verified, but one thing can be agreed upon: the actions taken by humans to damage the planet are definitely not helping. A decrease in biodiversity would cause catastrophic damage to the world of agriculture, and in effect, mass extinction of organisms. It is another factor in a list of possible dangers occurring due to climate change.

Bellard, C., Bertelsmeier, C., Leadley, P., Thiuller, W., Courchamp, F., (2012). Impacts of climate change on the future of biodiversity. Ecology Letters, 15, 365-377.

Future of China's Agriculture in Danger
by Jordan Aronowitz

Popularly characterized as one of the most industrial countries in the world, China has been blamed for much of the increase in carbon dioxide and greenhouse gases in the atmosphere. With the increase in average overall temperature, the prevalence of droughts has increased, adversely affecting production agriculture production and water supply. When the rain finally does arrive, it arrives with monsoon-like conditions, creating too much runoff, as the dry land can't contain the rain. Many independent projects have traveled to China in order to inform the population about climate change. Urban areas need to become greener, while rural areas need to be aware of dangers they face. The negative trends in China's agriculture and water resources can be corrected, but without proper support from the population and the rest of the world they will not be successful.

Warming trends indicate that average winter temperatures have increased by 0.04°C per year while average summer temperatures have increased by 0.01°C per year, with future trends indicating a further increase of 1-5°C over the next few decades. Rain trends have remained nearly constant nationwide, but regions in drier northeast China are receiving less rainfall during summer and autumn, while regions in wetter southern China are receiving more.

China always seems to take the blame for overall global changes such as increases in temperature, increases in sea level, and decreases in the amount of ice on the planet. Even if the accusations are true, and China has been rightfully charged for causing these vicissitudes, the press, western and eastern, does a poor job reporting on stories that show devastating events, such as frequent floods, destroying rural China. With this proof, the writers determined that China's agriculture and water supply are in danger, and that their own over-industrialization may be the cause. The coming changes in agriculture may be the most drastic.

Shilong, P., Ciais, P., Huang, Y., *et al.* (2010). The impacts of climate change on water resources and agriculture in China. Nature, 467, 43-51.

Sub-Saharan Africa Hurt by Food Production Struggles

by Jordan Aronowitz

The movie *Interstellar* introduces the idea of food scarcity due to climate change as a valid fear. A modern dust bowl prevents farmers from cultivating essential, staple crops. Famine has become more common around the world in recent years, but areas with advanced infrastructure are more adept at handling tough conditions. In Sub-Saharan Africa, one of the least developed areas of the world, changes in aggregate production will put residents in danger. A recent paper by Wolfram Schlenker (2010) looked to see if the current state of African agriculture is as deprived as predicted. The researchers discovered that the environment in Sub-Saharan Africa is becoming worse every year. Without the proper care, it will become harder to produce copious crops, if any.

Maize, sorghum, millet, groundnuts, and cassava were the five crops analyzed since they are important sources of calories, protein, and fat compared to other crops in Sub-Saharan Africa. In addition, these crops are rarely irrigated, making them quintessential indicators for how the climate affects crop production. The researchers collected the data by comparing country-level yields to four different temperature and precipitation statistics over the course of four decades, and used these data to predict crop yields in 2065. All crops will experience severe decreases in yields, with the largest decrease seen in maize. When investigating Sub-Saharan countries individually, of course they will all see decreases in production, but the most severe damages will be seen in South Africa and Zimbabwe.

With a top ten lowest life expectancy, Zimbabwe can't afford decreases in domestic crop yields, and it is hard to negotiate trade between Sub-Saharan countries due to the constant conflicts found in this region. In order for these countries to prosper one of two things must happen: either the world must work to maintain the fragile environment here to ensure that crop production will be able to support human life, or the countries must band together to maximize distribution of the few resources available. The future is grim, but avoiding a complete shutdown of agriculture, leading to the catastrophic events in *Interstellar*, is possible with proper support.

Schlenker, W., & Lobell, D. B. (2010). Robust negative impacts of climate change on African agriculture. Environmental Research Letters, 5, 1-8.

Rural Tanzania Needs a Shift in Agriculture
by Jordan Aronowitz

Rural populations are the most likely to sustain damage from a decrease in agriculture production. An anthropology paper by Jen Shaffer (2014) examines the harsh effects that climate change has when a community is ill prepared to deal with crop shortages. For centuries, the farmers of Tanzania depended on nature to provide a bountiful harvest, enabling them to live without serious worries of food production. In recent years, studies have shown that climate change is slowly damaging Tanzanian farmers' ability to produce. Possible solutions are being examined as ways to aid the current situation, but one necessity is to keep traditional ecological knowledge (TEK) in mind when considering new techniques. The Tanzanian farmers need to modernize their farming practices, but require dependence on their customary practices.

Because 80% of Tanzania's population lives in rural areas, basically the whole country is affected by climate change, notably a mean daily increase in temperatures by 3-5°C and a further increase in the variability of precipitation. A team of researchers sent to Tanzania is striving to combine modern farming practices with the TEK. As expected, many of the inhabitants were perplexed about the recent climate changes. A Mlingotini elder states: "...now [the bird] calls but nothing happens or the rain comes at the wrong time." Their lack of knowledge is dangerous when considering the future of food production in Tanzania. Using co-production, the idea that Western ideas can be combined with TEK, these teams hope to improve Tanzanian agriculture.

The unpredictable nature of 21st century agriculture in this area of the world is leaving these populations starving. After reading detailed charts explaining the patterns that Tanzanian communities look for when predicting weather, it is clear that they are significantly out of touch with modern techniques. These methods used to work well, but climate change has made them useless and unreliable. A gradual combination of traditional ecological knowledge and modern farming practices will enable them to balance climate change and bountiful production.

Shaffer, L. J. (2014). Making Sense of Local Climate Change in Rural Tanzania Through Knowledge Co-Production. Journal of Ethnobiology, 34(3).

More Benefits of Reversing Deforestation than Meet the Eye
by Caroline Chmiel

A seemingly simplistic method to battling rising temperatures may be one of the most effective. Saving tropical forests, largely through natural growth, has proven an immensely important and promising strategy to limit climate change impacts. Saving the forests that are left and allowing new ones to grow, or regrow, will impact our planet in many positive ways. Forests play a huge role in the carbon cycle of Earth because trees pull main greenhouse gases, CO_2, out of the air and lock carbon away in wood and in soil beneath them. When forests are destroyed, typically through burning, CO_2 is pumped back into the air, substantially contributing to raising temperatures and climate change. Burning of coal, oil and natural gas moves carbon out of the ground and into the active carbon cycle causing the globe to warm more rapidly now than in any similar period. Research displays a hopeful method for the control of CO_2 cycle: if forests around the globe are reclaimed and burning comes to a halt, forests will evermore naturally help pull dangerous emissions from the air, preventing quick, out of control, temperature growth.

Examples of countries implementing these methods, whether rapidly successful or slowly executing change, include Costa Rica, Brazil and Indonesia. At the forefront of reversing deforestation are the undertakings of Costa Rica. Policies pushing regrowth, and the fall of beef market lead farmers and the government to allow forests to reclaim land, began 45 years ago. Now, more than half of the country is covered in forests. Better than countries spending billions on carbon capture programs is simply allowing and helping the natural growth of trees.

In comparison, Brazil's progress in environmental soundness began only about a decade ago, controlling rampant deforestation. The Brazilian government took control by cutting the rate of forest loss by 83%. The CO_2 kept out of the air in Brazil far exceeded anything any other country has done to slow global warming. The impressive and inspiring status of Brazil has ignited hope for Indonesia's forest state. Deforestation remains a pressing issue, with the production of vegetable oil from palm trees a profitable business opportunity. The economic incentive here provides difficulty in attempting to stop deforestation with government intervention, as profiteers will simply go elsewhere. Aiding our globe in reversing to its natural state continues to prove successful in at least slowing climate change.

Gillis, Justin (2014, December 23). Restored Forests Breathe Life Into Efforts Against Climate Change New York Times. http://nyti.ms/1GVUbbx

More than Simply Divesting in Fossil Fuels
by Caroline Chmiel

The New School in Manhattan takes an unusual move in the current trend of divesting fossil fuel investments. As other institutions and groups try to divest in fuel, the New School has added elements in addition to eliminating all of its fossil fuel investments, the New School plans to reshape its entire curriculum, bringing climate change and sustainability to the forefront of the school's mission and values. The New School focuses primarily on the field of design, so there is an immense opportunity to emphasize designing for the future with an eye toward climate change. Some examples of potential actions are: minimizing waste in clothes making, minimizing transportation of medium and aligning urban environmental planning with weather patterns. Outside of teaching these methods, the school itself plans to reduce its own carbon footprint by reducing energy use, paper use, and waste. It also wants to search for small-scale local food suppliers.

The directors of the school plan to completely reposition the school's values far beyond divestment. The school plans to primarily use divestment as a teaching tool. Economics students study companies and practice adding environmental awareness to their decisions on keeping or selling stocks. Their end goal is to create an environment where all 14,000 students, faculty and staff serve the climate needs of a changing world while aware of the impacts of every action taken.

One difficulty in executing this vision lies in studies of students not in traditional public policy or environmental courses. Drama students, for example, will be encouraged to change the messages of their work in speaking on climate issues. Battling climate change and salvaging our future will require creativity, just maybe the creativity the New School fosters.

Schwartz, John. "The New School Divests Fossil Fuel Stock and Refocuses on Climate Change." The New York Times Web. 6 Feb. 2015

Severe Health Consequences from Climate Change
by Caroline Chmiel

Haynes *et al.* (2014) discuss the impending health risks to humanity if climate change persists at a rapid rate. They argue that if fossil fuel burning remains unconstrained, global average warming in the long term may be 12°C and by 2100 this heat could cause a 40% reduction in global labor capacity. During especially hot months, the temperatures would create hostile environments for laborers in many areas of the country. As population increases, this decrease in productivity would be especially detrimental to maintaining economic levels. Additionally, temperatures of extreme heat may cross the "afterlife" threshold. This occurs when the effect the temperature would have on humanity is so large that there is a "discontinuity in the long-term progression of humanity". New and extreme health risks are crucial aspects of crossing the "afterlife" threshold.

One example of a human life health risk is preparedness for the effects of a catastrophic flood with short return time. Another could range all the way to saltwater entering freshwater in small islands, so the water quality could force people of the island to have forced migration. These effects stem from rapid climate change and alterations over time. This small island example leads to the specific vulnerability of low-income countries to health issues arising from climate change. These types of countries will be less prepared for helping their citizens overcome changing health dangers. Crucial relationships between low-income and high-income countries must be made. These equitable partnerships will mitigate extreme hardships.

Interestingly, the vulnerability to climate change is often inversely related to historical greenhouse gas emissions. The impoverished areas are affected based more on their group and susceptibility of adaptation than on direct impact on climate change. The authors suggest that the global health community needs to take a long-term look at climate change because of the potentially catastrophic affects on human health.

Haines, Andy, Kristie L. Ebi, Kirk R. Smith, and Alistair Woodward. "Health Risks of Climate Change: Act Now or Pay Later." The Lancet 384.9948 (2014): 1073-075. Web.

When Mitigating Climate Change Health Consequences Backfires
by Caroline Chmiel

An often-unmentioned effect of climate change for our future will be increased need for population movement and relocation in coming decades. The growing concept of "environmental refugees" embodies a trend that many analysts fear. Health impacts in current living areas will arise from heat waves and other extreme weather events. Especially people in underdeveloped and economically instable areas, the need for relocation will be immense. The largest issue, though, will be the location of migration. Forced displacement may further increase risks of adverse health outcomes for vulnerable groups. These groups may include children, women, the elderly and ill people. Moving from one dire situation to a potentially worse one also may cause mental health issues. The overarching image of our changing world is that environmental alterations may lead to relocation into similarly desperate health situations.

Particularly in urban areas, the already poor water and sanitation facilities will be made worse by the expansion of slums or vulnerable situations. In addition, mental health issues from transitions between extremely gloomy living conditions may arise. The reduced access to health care and loss of social networks and assets comes as a shock to many. In our day-to-day lives we truly rely on strong networks to share goods and services. Being transplanted to an unknown area eliminates this stability. Though climate change may cause migration to be unavoidable, the way in which it happens could make or break its success. Complexities and individual states of migration must be assessed in order to avoid greater health risks than pre-migration. Policy makers, overall, have responsibility to cautiously contribute ideas and solutions. It is estimated that tens of millions to 250 million people will move in the coming decades because of climate change. Migration is an adaptive response, but may be dangerous to exercise, and end up being maladaptive.

McMichael C, Barnett J, McMichael AJ. 2012. An Ill Wind? Climate Change, Migration, and Health. Environ Health Perspect, 120:646-654.

The Unexpected Power of Solar Energy to Empower Developing Countries
by Caroline Chmiel

Solar energy is an expensive carbon mitigation alternative, but in developing countries it proves to not only combat climate change but also promote economic and social development. Jacobson *et al.* (2007) focuses on rural electrification with solar energy in Kenya. Not only are the economic benefits helpful in this country, but the educational opportunities and connective power of television, radio and telephone charging help elevate peoples' knowledge about and relationship with the outer world. In rural communities, especially, the electrical power increases connection to urban areas, which aids in poverty alleviation and sustainable development.

Attaining this solar power in developing areas may be costly, but a recent increase in donor support has come from solar policy makers and advocates who use a "basic needs" type argument to justify international support for solar electrification. Specifically, Solar Photovoltaics (PV) is a small-scale technology that helps get decentralized electrical service to homes or businesses and would work well in the types of markets in need. The combination of support for solar electrification in the technology movement and neo-liberalism around the environment provide a result of altering world capitalism while also emphasizing mainstream thinking on this market service and expanding global capitalist markets.

Kenya provides an example of leadership in renewable energy technology. Not only in spreading solar PV systems amongst rural households, but also in terms of policy, Kenya has developed the system with minimal direct government support and small help from international aid. Over-the-counter cash purchases of household solar systems drive solar sales. This market-based approach shows the opportunity and feasibility of succeeding in rural energy service. The important aspect of household use is how the rural middle class is able to see national and international ideas from television, radio, and cell phones. Additionally, social activities like evening studying for children are made possible with electric light. Since there are small amounts of the PV energy, most of it tends to be used for TV viewing. Overall, all aspects of this energy create a potential for further education and development of the middle class in Kenya and other developing countries. The immense power of this energy coupled with its sustainable environmental aspect makes it a revolutionary tactic for growing countries.

Jacobson, A. "Connective Power: Solar Electrification And Social Change In Kenya." World Development 35.12 (2007): 144-62. Print.

The Risk Climate Change Poses to the Electricity Supply
by Caroline Chmiel

US and European electricity supply is increasingly defenseless to climate changes. 91% and 78% of the total electricity in the US and Europe, respectively, is produced by thermoelectric power plants, which are nuclear and fossil-fueled. These plants and the processes to get electricity rely on the availability and temperature of water resources for cooling. The changing climate directly affects temperature and water resources, so the heavy reliance on these factors in electricity is at high risk. Freshwater withdrawals for cooling coal, gas and nuclear-fuelled power plants are highest in North America. Next highest worldwide is Europe.

Specifically, dry summers in 2003, 2006 and 2009 revealed the direct affects of warming climate on thermoelectric power plants in Europe when these plants were forced to lower production. The supply of electricity was limited and production costs increases, so rises in electricity prices rose. This also created an adverse economic effect, originating from climate. The US had similar events in 2007–2008 from a lack of surface water for cooling, causing shut down or reduced production of plants. Power plants are highly regulated on water withdrawals and temperature of water. So, conflicts between environmental benchmarks of receiving waters and economic consequences of reducing production have to be quelled and balanced.

This paper predicts future low river flows and increases in water temperature. This combination is especially problematic for cooling-water use. This will be prevalent especially in summer and thermoelectric power plants in southern and southeastern Europe, and southeastern US will be the most affected. Alternatives may be dry cooling systems or non-freshwater sources for cooling, but this may be limited by availability. Therefore, adaption options for electricity plants should be a priority in todays planning to meet the growing demand for electricity. Electricity not only receives impacts of climate change, but also producing emissions adding to climate change.

van Vliet, Michelle T. H., John R. Yearsley, Fulco Ludwig, Stefan Vogele, Dennis P. Lettenmaier, and Pavel Kabat. "Vulnerability of US and European electricity supply to climate change." Nature Climate Change (2012): 676-681. Web. 24 Apr. 2012.

The Decline of American Aspen Forests
by Jackson Cooney

One of the biggest crises that we are faced with regarding climate change is the increase in global temperature as well as the punishing droughts that affect some areas of the world (Gillis 2015). Aspen trees are vulnerable to climate change because they require a lot of water. They have very shallow root systems, which limit their ability to absorb water that isn't near the surface and because of this; these conditions have had a huge effect on aspen forests in the American West. If this trend of increasing temperature with the lack of rainfall becomes common throughout the US, then the aspen tree will likely suffer great losses. Recently a drought in Colorado killed off millions of aspens, further illustration the danger that massive droughts could have on the aspen population as a whole.

Research has been conducted to discover the exact way in which these changing conditions affects the trees. Dr. Andereg found that when the trees are left without water, air bubbles appear in the xylem and phloem. These bubbles block water and nutrients from passing through these tubes essentially suffocating the tree of all its vital nutrients. He has also devised a computer model to predict the trajectory of tree loss if the current climate parameters remain. He has discovered that there are likely to be many more mass die offs of aspens just like the one that occurred in Colorado.

Many people believe that aspens are an indicator species; meaning that their disappearance is an indication the problems with the environment and that these conditions will likely lead the disappearance of many more species. These droughts could have a huge affect on other types of trees as well as our ability to produce food. As exemplified in California, where food production has suffered due to the fourth continuous year of drought. These droughts could definitely be reduced is we take control of our carbon emissions today.

Gillis, J. (2015, March 30). Climate Change Threatens to Kill Off More Aspen Forests by 2050s, Scientists Say. Retrieved April 6, 2015, from http://nyti.ms/1Hr8tPi

Implications of Geoengineering
by Jackson Cooney

A government-sponsored panel, assembled by NASA and other federal agencies, was assembled on February 10, 2015 to discuss the implications of using geoengineering as a way to fight climate change and greenhouse gas emissions. Henry Fountain, writing in The New York Times summarizes as follows: geoengineering falls into two categories. One method captures and stores CO_2 that has already been emitted. The other involves reflecting the sun's rays back into the atmosphere so that less heat would enter the Earth. The first option has minimal risks, however it would be expensive and take time to see any noticeable effects. There would also be a need for more research in order to find a way to successfully store the CO_2. The second option, solar radiation management, is more controversial. This involves dispersing sulfates into the atmosphere to reflect the sun's rays away from Earth. This method is inexpensive and the effects are seen quickly, however it would have to be repeated many times. It would also do nothing to solve global problems related to CO_2 like Ocean Acidification.

Opponents argue that pursuing geoengineering would create a moral hazard because it would distract from the need to reduce greenhouse emissions. However, the panel believes that we have reached a point where the benefits of geoengineering outweigh the risks. They still don't think that anything drastic needs to happen today, however it would be prudent to research geoengineering so that if there is a crisis, a solution could be provided. Some say that researching for geoengineering could have unintentional consequences. For example, research could set society on a full deployment of the technologies. However, the National Academy of Sciences panel believes that this process could pose no immediate risks if it is developed properly.

The panel said that the best way to mitigate the effects of a warming planet to reduce the emissions of CO_2 and other greenhouse gases. Saying this, the panel still believes that geoengineering could have positive effects on this warming.

Fountain, Henry. "Panel Urges Research on Geoengineering as a Tool Against Climate Change." The New York Times. The New York Times, 10 Feb. 2015. Web. 14 Feb. 2015.

Biofuels and their Implications

by Jackson Cooney

In an effort to reduce the use of gasoline and diesel many governments have pushed to increase the use of bioenergy, but today, biofuel makes up only 2.5% of the worlds transportation fuels. The European Union estimates that their dependence on biofuel will increase to 10% by 2020, and, the US also is expecting a large increase. The International Energy Agency foresees biofuel as accounting for 27% of the world's transportation fuel by midcentury. Other renewable energy options seem more limited because, with the current technologies, it would be impossible to supply the entire world's energy needs with wind and solar sources. The Environmental Protection Agency also supports the biofuel initiative by labeling the harvest of forests a "carbon-fee source".

As good as biofuel sounds, Porter (2015) points out that there are still problems. The EPA argues that biofuel is carbon free because when plants grow, they pull CO_2 out of the atmosphere offsetting the CO_2 that is released when they are burned. However, burning the biomass doesn't enable the trees, for example, to keep absorbing CO_2, so the CO_2 that the biomass would have absorbed still remains. Because of this, using biofuel cannot be labeled accurately as a "carbon-free source". Also converting a plot of land to grow biofuel eliminates the possibility of using that land to grow food or to store CO_2 in vegetation that would otherwise be growing there. If more of the world's land is converted to produce biomass, which would be necessary to use biofuel as a significant energy source, then there would be a decrease in the amount of food we could produce and the amount of CO_2 that could be absorbed. Much of the land in the US that was once used for biofuel has reverted back to forests. According to Porter, it seems beneficial to keep these forests as they are and not use them to produce biofuel.

Porter, E. (2015, February 10). A Biofuel Debate: Will Cutting Trees Cut Carbon? Retrieved February 22, 2015, from http://nyti.ms/1Rfmzu9

CO_2 and Rainforests
by Jackson Cooney

Deforestation significantly impacts our world's climate. Within the last 40 years, one billion acres of tropical forests have been cleared, contributing to a massive increase in overall CO_2 levels. Because forests store huge amounts of carbon, cutting or burning them releases their stored carbon back into the atmosphere where it mixes with oxygen to create CO_2. CO_2 increases at an annual 12 to 15% due to deforestation. Although there are economic incentives to cut down these forests, for timber, farmland and mining sites, there may be a greater incentive to preserve them. Forest carbon reserves can be monetized and traded or sold to offset releases by companies that produce greenhouse gases. This benefits companies that need these reserves to stay below a polluting limit set by the government. The offsets are subtracted from their emissions, keeping them within the legal limit. Revenues can then be used to support energy efficiency or energy saving projects. Until recently, it was difficult to quantify "emissions avoided by not destroying tropical forests". However, techniques have been implemented to quantify the emissions that would be saved, specifically, a process that protects an acre of forest, even if the specific acre in question is destroyed. The proceeds of the sale would then be returned to the local communities.

Recently, the Rainforest Standard, a new system that brings into account all of these ideas, has been developed and is being tested on a 1.6 million acre forest in south America. Due to the high cost of employing people to patrol the forests, there is relatively little enforcement of forest protection. The offset method provides money that could be used to ensure that the forests are adequately protected. Protecting a million acres, for example, could stop 367 million tons of CO_2 from being released. Because of such high rewards, this offset method could be very beneficial.

Melnick, D., Pearl, M., & Warfield, J. (2015, January 19). Make Forests Pay. Retrieved February 27, 2015, from http://nyti.ms/1eoOrxZ

China and Solar Energy
by Jackson Cooney

China is the world's largest user of energy, and one of the largest consumers of coal. However, recently it has shifted to solar power and started relying less on oil, natural gas, and coal. Between January 2014 to June 2014, China added 3.3 gigawatts of solar capacity, which brings China's total to 23 gigawatts (Topf, 2015). This is the second largest solar capacity behind Germany's 36 gigawatts. The Chinese government has gone as far as to ban the use of coal by 2020. The renewed focus on the clean energy has a lot to do with the worsening smog conditions and an attempt to clean up the environment. China has appropriated $23.5 billion to finance an increase in solar panel use which is the most money assigned to solar energy.

The main reason that solar energy has blossomed so rapidly in china is the massive incentive policies and the government's initiative to undercut the competition. China was accused of selling their solar panels at a lower price then the domestic producers elsewhere putting these makers out of business. After a threat of the EU imposing an antidumping tariff China agreed to sell their panels at a predetermined price. Along with undercutting, China has also implemented subsidies to increase their use of solar energy. One of these incentives included 14 to 16 cents per kilowatt-hour applying to both ground mounted and roof panels.

It is clear that China's push for solar energy is an attempt to combat their massive pollution problem. Solar energy will improve air quality as well as decrease their reliance on other nations for fuel needs. It seems that China will continue to increase their use of solar power and be the leading nation in solar energy because of the sheer environmental need. Something has to be done differently and it seems that solar energy could be that something.

Topf, A. (2014, August 24). Why China Is Leading The World In Solar Power. Retrieved March 30, 2015, from http://bit.ly/1Ktm4vH

Governor Brown Takes Water Conservation into His Own Hands
by Jackson Cooney

California governor Jerry Brown imposed the state's first ever water restriction requirement in an attempt to preserve the little amount of water that is left. The four-year drought and the winter's record low snowfall levels were the catalyst for this executive action (Nagourney, 2015). Governor Brown mandated the State Water Resources Control Board to impose an average 25% cut over 2013 usage level in the 400 local water supply agencies over the coming year. The specifics of how the agencies will implement these cutbacks are left up to them and the federal government will not dictate how these cuts must be made. It is clear however, that it will become increasingly more expensive to have large gardens and green lawns. Governor Brown said, "The idea of your nice little green lawn getting watered every day, those days are past". This cutback in water supply is likely to have significant effects on homeowners, farmers, and other business owners. Farms that get their water from sources that are not attached to the local water agencies will not be subjected to the 25% cut. However, these farms will still be required to supply the government with detailed reports that show their water use.

State officials are ready to enforce these cutbacks through fines, but are hopeful that it will not come to that. The government has encouraged the use of dishwashers and washing machines that are more water efficient by providing rebate programs for these homeowners. Governor Brown also said that he will be imposing water restrictions on golf courses and cemeteries, which are areas that consume massive amounts of water each year. Finally, he encourages that homeowners replace their lawns with other plantings that consume less water. There will also be a raise in the rates for heavy water users, so these methods to consume less water that were presented by Mr. Brown seem favorable. Because this executive order was just implemented, it will take time to see if it will have a positive effect on water preservation.

Nagourney, A. (2015, April 1). California Imposes First Mandatory Water Restrictions to Deal With Drought. Retrieved April 13, 2015, from http://nyti.ms/1Hr6lHd

Meshing Opposing Methods of Climate Change Measurement for Accuracy
by Tyler Dean

Camille Parmesan and Gary Yohe describe the reasoning and results of the IPCC's method of measuring the fingerprint of climate change. Their goal was to "improve communication, provide common ground for discussion, and give a comprehensive summary of the evidence." The IPCC's method mitigates the result abnormality from the opposing methods and views of biologists and economists by implementing both of their techniques into IPCC's. The need for the IPCC's approach comes from both of the existing results being beneficial, but flawed to the point that citizens, readers and policy makers must remain dubious of the results. Economists focus on direct evidence, in the moment and apply time discounting in order to account for their lack of quality control. From this, they conclude that climate change is only important if it is responsible for the current biotic changes; which leads economists to the conclusion that climate change's fingerprint is weak. The reason for this is that most short term local changes are not caused by climate change, but by changes in the abundance and allocation of species; ergo economists can argue that climate change is if little importance to wild systems. The problem with this is it ignores the fact that over time, several small incidents or changes compile and yield large problems. Another problem with this is the inability to measure whether or not the changes to the environment over time are caused by climate change or by land-use change and natural fluctuations in the abundance and distributions of species. Biologists focus on minimizing the confounding factors by searching for trends in undisturbed environments and testing for the effects of climate change. Economists view this as a biased, while biologists view this as a pure analysis, free of non-climatic disruption. Biologists' methods allow them to implement a quality control that eradicates their need of the time discount used by economists. The IPCC utilizes the biologists' confidence assessment for "statistical meta-analyses of effect size and more comprehensive categorical analysis of the full literature." They then create a model of probability that considers "proportion of observations, matching climate change predictions, numbers of competing explanations for each of those observations, and casual attribution of each observation to climate change" for both the biologists' results. They use the same model and variables to consider the economists' confidence assessment. Last, IPCC explore the sign switching patterns that are predicted by and/or result from climate change. From this process, the IPCC concludes very high confidence levels, supported by their analysis results.

Parmesan, Camille, and Gary Yohe. 2003. "A globally coherent fingerprint of climate change impacts across natural systems." Nature 42. 37-42.

Climate Change and Its Effects on Human Health

by Tyler Dean

Anththropogenic greenhouse gas emissions are leading to climate changes in temperature, precipitation, humidity and/or wind patterns (Natural clmate forcing also contribute to this). Climate changes yield environmental effects that cause adaptation and health effects. The environtmental effects include: change in frequency, severity and geography of extreme weather events, ecosystem changes on land and sea that effect numerous species, rises in sea level that cause storm surges and salination of costal land and freshwater, and environmental degradation on land, costal ecosystems and fisheries. The health effects include: thermal stress that causes deaths, illness and injury from floods, storms, cyclones and bush fires (thermal stresses also effect food yields), microbial proliferation that leads to food poisoning and unsafe drinking water, increase in vector-pathogen-host relations and in infectious disease geography and seasonality, impaired crops, livestock and fisheries yield that lead to impaired nutrition, health, survival and loss of livelihood that lead to poverty and adverse health such as mental health, infectious diseases, malnutrition and other physical risks. The easiest to define climate-health relationships are related to heat waves. The harder to define climate-health relationships are from "changes in regional food yields, disruption of fisheries, loss of livelihoods, and population displacement (because of sea-level rise, water shortages, etc.)." The results from this research on climate change and its effect on future human health represent an imperative contribution to international and national policy debates.

McMichael, AJ & Woodruff, RE Climate Change and Human Health: Present and Future Risks Lancet 367.68079-3 (2006): 859-69.

Electrification of Cars and Sustainability Over the Next 40 Years
by Tyler Dean

The international Energy Agency (IEA) predicts that global economic growth over the next twenty years will double the aggregate fleet of vehicles and that over the next forty years will triple it. This is not sustainable with the limited amount of fossil fuel energy sources. The IEA has concluded that even if we were to double the efficiency of combustion engines, we still could not sustain predicted quantities of vehicles. Today, the majority of vehicles are powered by burning fossil fuels through internal combustion engine. This results in local air pollution and greenhouse gas emissions. Alternative methods of powering transport are required to clean the air in our cities, prevent the worst excesses of climate change and diversify and secure our future energy supplies. Vehicles contribute a large portion of the greenhouse gas emissions that cause climate change. Improving vehicle efficiency is an essential step in mitigating the problems we face.

According to the IEA we must electrify powertrains and utilize low carbon electricity and hydrogen. In addition, we must use automated vehicles; which are more efficient and can improve the economics of electric vehicles. This will provide economic benefits by cutting down monetary costs and environmental benefits by making electrification of powertrains more likely and in turn reduce aggregate emissions. Automated vehicles increase vehicle efficiency and change the economics of alternatively fueled vehicles. This makes them the cheapest transportation and manufacturing option in the long term.

Through automated vehicle fleets used as "point-to-point on-demand car clubs", we could increase the total availability of transport services and make the benefits of alternative fuel and automated vehicles available to a larger potion of the global population. The downsides to electrified vehicles and automated vehicles are range anxiety and the loss of the driving experience. With complete adaption, range anxiety is eliminated by specialized distance transportation. It is also eliminated by the mass majority of society adapting to method because of the benefits of utilizing their time more efficiently while transporting. The other downside is the fear that cheaper and more readily available transportation will cause the IEA's prediction to be inaccurate and over time increase the aggregate use of resources, which could yield very negative effects. No one is sure if this will happen, but the current evidence points to electrification and alternative energy methods being the best option.

Offer, GH. 2015. Automated vehicles and electrification of transportation. Energy, Environment, Science 8. 26-30. http://rsc.li/1ErZISX

Improving Food Yields in Africa
by Tyler Dean

According to an article in Appropriate Technology in 2014, climate change is predicted to increase the number of malnourished people in Sub-Saharan Africa by nearly forty percent by 2050, from the current 22 million, to 355 million. In East and Central Africa, suitable areas for growing beans could decline up to eighty percent, while areas suitable for growing bananas could decline twenty-five percent. In aggregate, climate change will severely lower crop yields by adversely affecting the length of the growing season and rainfall. It is crucial for African farmers to switch to "climate- smart agriculture"(CSA). CSA will increase resilience by allowing farmers to adapt to climate change and reduce their greenhouse gas emissions. The government has implemented monitored subsidy programs, consultants and aggregators in order to improve production and instill confidence in Africa's farmers. Farmers have been taught to utilize smarter farming and to pool their resources in order to increase efficiency, lower green house gas emissions and bring down costs. Currently, many have turned to innovations that mitigate the effects of climate change. These include improving soil health, fertilizer quality, seed systems, water management and mechanization. These activities have improved and will continue to improve the socioeconomic statuses and health conditions in Africa. In time they will help Africa avoid the complications of inevitable climate change, while lowering the global greenhouse gas emissions.

Anonymous. 2014. 'Climate-smart' approaches to increase Africa's food production. Appropriate Technology 41. 25-28. http://bit.ly/1JNWBfd

Green Computing—a Double-Edged Sword
by Tyler Dean

The colossus of computing and computer

manufacturing has a direct effect on our global environmental footprint. Our society is increasing computer usage at an exponential rate and in order to sustain this growth in an environmentally positive way, we must utilize green computing. Green computing is a responsible and effective way to mitigate global warming. It consists of the disposing, recycling and manufacturing of computers and electronic devices. The goal is to lower the use of hazardous materials, maximize energy efficiency and popularize biodegradability of outdated products and waste.

As the performance and breadth of applications of computers increase; the costs, scarcity of resources to energize and create them do as well. A positive effect of computers is the fact that they allow businesses to adopt greener lifestyles and work styles that positively contribute to environmental stewardship, protect the environment and reduces energy and paper costs.

The positive environmental effects computing have due to changes in daily operations for users combined with green computing can and will yield positive results. Steps that can be taken by everyone to move towards greener computing include: solar computing, energy efficient platforms for low and small factor computing devices, reduction in paper consumption from printing, power management software and habits, a switch to organic light emitting diodes, downloadable content instead of physical copies, storage consolidation, virtualization and the purchase of environment friendly products. These methods are becoming more globally used and are complimented by innovation in efficiency and supplemental programs.

Today, the eight programs running globally to promote green computing include the EPA's 'Energy Star' program, Dell's Plant a Tree for Me project, VIA Technologies' initiative for green computing, HP's Planet Partners recycling services, Green Electronics Council's Electronic Product Environmental Assessment Tools, The Climate Savers Computing Initiative, the European Union's Restriction of Hazardous Substances Directive (RoHS), and the Waste Electrical and Electronic Equipment

Directive (WEEE).

Saxena, S. 2015.Green computing: Need of the Hour. International Journal of Current Engineering and Technology 6. 333-335.

Using Gaming to Reduce Energy Usage
by Tyler Dean

Increased energy efficiency is a crucial factor of energy and climate strategies in our mission to reduce carbon emissions. While many efforts will resort from technological inventions and innovations, efforts in changing human behavior must compliment and match them. Reeves performed an experimental field test on the effects that media entertainment can have on energy efficiency.

The reason for the study was energy information could have been too complex and uninteresting for consumers to assimilate. Media entertainments, such as video games, offer a compelling means of engagement with energy information and can help change consumers' behaviors. Reeves built a social game about energy usage in a virtual home and designed an experiment around it. Participants in the experiment significantly increased their energy efficient behaviors after playing for 30 minutes in the lab. The game walks the player through a virtual home as an individual family member while making sure they turn off the appliances and make efficient choices. It then elevates the number members the user is controlling to increase difficulty and keep the player interested.

The results proved that the actions carried out in the game were also partially implemented into the participants' daily routine. The reason for this is games increase retention, encourage production, and provide motivation to improve. "Games enable interactive experiences that exploit several sub-processes that govern observational learning." Games also increase awareness and practice of good habits, while decreasing the complexity of making better energy choices. This makes them attractive and relevant and gives them huge advantages over the existing sensors and energy monitoring technologies existing today. Games offer a new and compelling context in which to place important information about personal behavior. "Social games tied to Facebook are played by tens of millions of people daily, and counter to stereotypes, gamers are increasingly middle-aged, gender-balanced, healthier, and well-connected socially." From this, we can conclude this benefits are invaluable. Embedding serious information involving energy efficiency is a beneficial and effective method of evoking behavioral change by millions of people.

Reeves B, Cummings J, Scarborough J, Yeykelis L. 2015. Increasing Energy Efficiency With Entertainment Media: An Experimental and Field Test of the Influence if a Social Game on Performance of Energy Behaviors. Environment and Behavior 47. 102-115.

Using Cloud Computing to Monitor Climate Change

by Tyler Dean

The department of Biomedical Engineering at the Adhiyamaan College of Engineering has proposed a system that provides monitoring benefits to a large number of users by deploying a collection of observed data over a long period of time. The system uses a combination of advanced technologies to collect comprehensible environmental data that can be accessed from any location online. The system requires sensors for air pollution, temperature and humidity of a selected place. The data acquisition system acquires the data of temperature, humidity, pollution of air including Illumination, dust, carbon dioxide, ultraviolet, wind direction, wind speed, air pressure and the altitude from remote sensing areas. The system can be used for intrusion detection, used to remotely monitor the conditions of a place, to determine the habitat of a place and to field conditions to specify which cultivation is suitable for a region. The system is designed to indicate higher pollution levels with an alarm and predict future levels of pollution and temperature change through an automated checking mechanism that also helps conserve energy because it doesn't have to constantly monitor the environment. Several projects measure these things, however most focus on one place and the data is not recorded in a manor in which it can be accessed globally. Cloud computing, the delivery of computing as a service rather than a product, allows data to be accessed anywhere in the world, which brings access to a large number of users. It relies on sharing of resources and collaboration to achieve coherence and economies if scale.

Monika R, Pranith Jain R, Salmaan N. 2014. Monitoring Climatic Changes by Cloud Computing. Science Q 1. 1-4.

3-Dimensional Printing, the Economy, and Climate Change
by Tyler Dean

3DP (3-Dimensional Printing) is an industrial manufacturing process with the potential to significantly reduce resource and energy demands as well as process-related CO_2 emissions. The Center for Energy and Environmental Sciences at the University of Groningen assessed the global qualitative and quantitative sustainability of 3DP through 2025. At present, due to limited production speeds and other technological blockages, 3DP is mainly applicable to small production volumes, especially of high-value customized products. In the near future though, 3DP has the power to generate shifts in product designs towards more complex geometries, provide incentives for the customer involvement in production processes through online platforms and reconstruct supply chains towards more digital and localized processes. 3DP's ability to lower financial and energy resource inputs into production processes could lead to total cost savings of US $170–593 billion over the next 10 years, while simultaneously decreasing product costs and lowering of CO_2 emissions. This leads to an energy saving of 1.46–5.72 EJ, the decommissioning of 0.22–0.81 EJ of power plant capacity and significant lowering of resource demands and process-related waste amounts, since the technology applies additive means of production. 3DP will positively effect the environment and the economy over the next decade; the size of the effect will be measured in time.

Gebler M., Uiterkamp A., Visser C. 2014. A global sustainability perspective on 3D printing technologies. Energy Policy 74. 158–167

Tiny Houses as a Response to Climate Change
by Tyler Dean

Tiny houses provide economically and environmentally efficient means of housing and have gained national attention. Tiny houses have become a movement that educates those who follow it by being based on green principles. Tiny Houses use eco-friendly and recycled materials and leave a relatively miniscule footprint on the environment when compared to traditional housing. Because of the minor amount of land and resources used to create and live in tiny houses, the tiny house movement gaining global popularity acts as a catalyst to a more environmentally friendly housing situation.

Yale University interviewed Elizabeth Turnbull, a graduate student about her experience in building a "Tiny House." She set out to build her tiny house in 2008 with the following list of goals: make a beautiful and comfortable home, source recycled materials, utilize a small budget, maintain sustainability, insulate well with natural materials, share the design and build process, inspire others to explore low-budget, low-impact structures, build without harmful materials, minimize my fossil fuel use, incorporate energy-efficient LED lights, use minimal appliances and weigh less than 10,000 pounds.

When planning her design she had to consider how much space she needed to live well, how minimally her home would impact the environment and the cost compared to purchasing an apartment near Yale University for two years. Throughout the building process, she received donations of both time and materials.

Companies supporting the project donated the aluminum roof, FSC-certified red oak flooring, bio-based soy foam insulation and the faux-painted interior. She also received small donations, such as windows, a door, and curtains. During the building of her tiny house, Turnbull created a blog and was written about in papers that had global reach. Over time, the project became an

Internet sensation and community-supported project. Turnbull's "Tiny house" project and similar and similar ones making small strides in educating the masses on sustainable living and inspiring other to do the same.

Turnbull E. 2015. Tiny House. Oz 31. 3-7.

Long-Term Effects of Climate Change
by Brina Jablonski

In 2006, William E. Bradshaw and Christina M. Holzapfel highlighted the unforeseen effects of climate change in an article posted by sciencemag.org. The two authors made a point of telling their audience how organisms are not directly reacting to the increased amount of heat on planet earth, but instead reacting to the resulting seasonal change due to the rising temperature. They also consistently mentioned examples of how organisms are capable of "phenotypic plasticity", the ability of organisms to alter themselves in response to a change in environment.

In one of the cases mentioned, caterpillars are maturing earlier because of the earlier spring seasons caused by global warming. This in turn is slowly killing off the European great tits' [birds'] population because the caterpillars are maturing before the tit chicks are born. This example and others mentioned throughout the article supports the idea of how the primary concern of global warming should be seasonal changes rather than how the climbing temperature directly affects the organisms.

The authors also mention their concern about how northern climates are slowly evolving into southern climates. They believe that over time organisms will acclimate to the fluctuating timing of the seasons and as a result slowly adapt to the growing temperature of planet earth. This change will therefore directly impact the genetics of many organisms and change their biological makeup. However, even with eventual genetic changes, some organisms will not be able to adapt quick enough to keep up with the rapid changes in our climate.

It was predicted that only small organisms with large populations would be able to thrive in today's modern world. Smaller population sizes and larger animals are expected to see a drop in population size or eventually be substituted by a species of animal that can handle warmer temperatures.

Sad as it is, both Holzapfel and Bradshaw agree that unless action is taken to stop climate change, the long-term effects of earth's increasing temperature could be permanent and result in the termination of certain species of organisms forever.

Bradshaw, William E., and Christina M. Holzapfel. 2015. Evolutionary Response to Rapid Climate Change. SCIENCE. 312. 1477-478.
http://people.westminstercollege.edu/departments/science/The_Natural_World/Lesson_Schedule/ev%20response%20change.PDF

What Needs to Change in Today's Health Promotion
by Brina Jablonski

Rebecca Patrick, Teresa Capetola, Mardie Townsend, and Sonia Nuttman define the threats that the world is facing as whole due to climate change and explain how there is a greater need for health promoters at the community level. Health promotion professionals are those responsible for improving and adapting the health sector to match the current climate. The authors constantly emphasize how these professionals are responsible for strengthening society's relationship with the environment and how they stand as catalysts for change.

The authors note how current climate changes are dangerous to human beings across the globe. They mention how "already vulnerable populations such as remote Aboriginal communities, Pacific Island Countries, the elderly and people with low income" will feel the rippling effects of climate change even more than they already do. This statement supports the fact that health professionals are desperately needed in today's age.

In response to the climate change and the need for more effective health promoters, the School of Health & Social Development, Faculty of Health, in Australia conducted a study that focuses on the core competencies desired in a health professional. The study determined that those working in the health industry need skills such as teamwork, communication, critical thinking, and analytical skills in order to make a change in today's world and prevent further human damage from global warming. The study also notes how these health experts need to be aware of the latest research and must be able to work across multiple disciplines instead of specializing in one area.

The personal qualities associated with an effective health promotion official were empathy, flexibility, initiative, self-motivated, resilient, and positive attitude.

The study overall demonstrated that health promotion practitioners need these certain competencies in order to carry out their job to the best of their ability and make a change in the world.

Patrick et al 2011. Patrick, R., Capetola, T., Townsend, M., Nuttman, S., 2011. Health promotion and climate change: exploring the core competencies required for action. Health promotion international, 27.4 (2012): 475-485.

Climate Change Adaptation in California
by Brina Jablonski

Climate change has always affected California but even more so now in today's current climate conditions. Problems revolving around rising sea levels, frequent heat waves, floods, wildfires, droughts, shrinking snow packs, growing water demand, changes in precipitation, hotter conditions, an increasing number of threatened or endangered animal species, and an extreme growth in human population are forcing the government of California to adapt and make plans for the future in order to minimize later damage for the Golden State. Assembly Bill 32 (the 2006 Global Warming Solutions Act) has already improved California's energy, transportation, construction, agricultural, and natural resource sectors. As California faces these issues, the state also sets the framework for potential national and even international action.

Davis and Chornesky (2014) primarily address how California is responding to rising sea levels, changes in water supply, flood risks, and weakened ecosystem resilience. They mention how California is avoiding development in future hazard zones and redesigning coastal structures in order to adapt to some of these problems. They also include how the government of California has decided to reduce per capita water use by twenty percent and improve statewide water quality in preparation for the possibility of uncontrollable flooding. Pricing, taxes, and gains in efficiency will hopefully influence water demand for the better in the long run. According to the authors, the main problem that California faces for the future is that the modifications for climate change may come up against private property rights. Although California is making significant modifications to combat climate change, the efforts are primarily centered on talk and analysis rather than action. The state has successfully shared information and made plans involving climate change but needs more political and financial support in order to take major action. Hopefully, with the help of stakeholders, California will be able to expand its' climate change policies to not only address issues in the west coast but issues across the world.

Davis, Frank W., Chornesky, Elizabeth A. 2014. "Adapting to Climate Change in California." Bulletin of the Atomic Scientists, Volume 70.5, 62-73.

Balancing the Energy Triangle
by Brina Jablonski

Frank Umbach (2012), uses an "energy triangle" to illustrate the importance of energy supply security and its' three main goals: environmental/climate sustainability, energy supply security, and economic competitiveness. Countries struggle in balancing the three areas and often lean towards one at the cost of misbalancing the other two.

Energy shocks and supply disruptions can leave individual states and countries extremely vulnerable. This highlights the increasing imbalance of the supply and demand of energy worldwide and also the dire need for supply security, or in other words, the necessity of balancing the three objectives of the 'energy triangle'. An example of this balance is the expanded usage of domestic coal. Although expanding the usage of domestic coal can increase economic competitive and strengthen supply security, it will also increase carbon dioxide emissions and as a result accelerate climate change. In contrast, reducing coal emissions by replacing coal with natural gas can negatively impact economic competitive and energy supply security. Umbach uses this idea of balance throughout the article to analyze the methods the USA and the EU are using to reduce the damaging effects of climate change.

Umbach also mentions how climate change and climate change prevention are linked through six major factors: the burning of fossil fuels and the greenhouse gases they release, the rise of carbon dioxide emissions, how human activities play a large role in climate change, how climate change is affecting global security because it stands as a 'multiplier' for potential conflict, how the substitution of biofuels for traditional fuels has increased the price of food and is thus no longer efficient, and lastly how current energy plans and policies will likely have no effect on the climate change situation in the future. These six factors link together climate change itself and the efforts that people are making to prevent further climate change.

Umbach, F. 2012. The intersection of climate protection policies and energy security. Journal of Transatlantic Studies, Vol. 10, No. 4, 374-387.

Are General Practitioners Prepared for Climate Change?
by Brina Jablonski

Human activity has led to a temperature increase of 0.75°C in the past century 0.6 degrees of which have occurred in just the last 30 years. This increase in temperature has led to increased drying, decreased precipitation and has contributed to changes in drought patterns. These changes in the environment will especially affect those residing in rural areas of Australia, and according to Purcell and McGirr (2014), health practitioners are going to need to get prepared for them.

In Australia, the droughts and high fire danger will increase in frequency, soils will be drier because of increased evaporation and heat, tropical cyclones and wet season rainfall will increase in intensity, and sea levels will continue to rise. Heat-related deaths will most likely increase and people will be more exposed to air pollutants and infectious diseases. Natural disasters, droughts, and decreased agricultural productivity will negatively affect rural communities and most likely leave them emotionally and mentally unstable. These major changes in our environment pose as a challenge for general practitioners in the medical world to prepare for climate change and the harmful after effects.

General practitioners are people who play an influential role in rural communities by improving and evolving medical care in the community. However, little is known about rural general practitioner perceptions towards climate change and their recommendations on how they are going to adapt to the changing climate.

A quantitative survey was put together in order to provide insight into adaptation strategies for the health impacts of climate change suggested by rural general practitioners. The study's ending results indicate that there can be a level of uncertainty among general practitioners about how they are going to adapt to the current climate change. Furthermore, between 33% and 44% of general practitioners are either unsure or did not agree that their health service has the capacity to provide a response to an extreme weather event. Thus, further development of disaster response planning is needed as soon as possible.

Purcell, R., McGirr J. 2014. "Preparing Rural General Practitioners And Health Services For Climate Change And Extreme Weather." The Australian Journal Of Rural Health 22.1: 8-14.

Importance of Fisheries Management in Mitigating the Effects of Climate Change on Global Fisheries

by Margaret Loncki

Fishery management plays an important role in maintaining sustainable fisheries around the world. The more effective and flexible management styles are, the better they will be able to adapt to changing fisheries as a result of climate change. The most common fishery management styles discussed by Melnychuk, Banobi, and Hilborn (2013) are harvest control and flexible season opening and closing dates.

Global climate change has brought about significant changes to our world's marine ecosystems and without proper fishery management, many fisheries will be exploited until they disapear. Climate change causes shifts in abundance and distribution, and has even been shown to effect species dynamics such as spawning times. Melnychuk, Banobi, and Hilborn suggest that the most effective way to produce long-term sustainable fisheries is the use of harvest control. Harvest control, or some other form of management that adjusts to changing abundance and conditions, is a management system that would be easily adapted to the effects of climate change on global fisheries. Melnychuk, Banobi, and Hilborn argue that current harvest control systems are only able to manage declines typically within the range seen as a result of fishing pressures. They suggest that if changes are more drastic than fishing pressures have produced, current harvest control systems will not be able to adequately protect fish stocks. Current systems may be able to manage the effects of climate change so long as pressure from fishing is significantly reduced. Harvest control also does not very adequately protect multi-specie fisheries. As the ability maximum sustainable yield decreases for one species, fishing will often be reduced for the other species due to the effect of bycatch on the declining species. Melnychuk, Banobi, and Hilborn found that flexible season dates were most often employed in locations more dramatically effected by climate change and changing sea surface temperatures. The authors continually stressed the importance of fisheries management but failed to provide many suggestions for changes that would increase the effectiveness of fishery management systems.

Melnychuk, M., Banobi, J., and Hilborn, R., 2013. The adaptive capacity of fishery management systems for confronting climate change on marine populations. Reviews in Fish Biology and Fisheries 24(2), 561-575.

The Importance of Low-Emission Vehicles To Energy Reduction in Japan
by Margaret Loncki

Prior to Fukushima nuclear plant accident in 2011, Japan had published a revised energy plan to significantly reduce carbon emission with the main goal of reducing emission by 80% by 2050. A significant portion of this goal was made possible because of the potential of nuclear power. After Fukushima, there was a significant decrease in support for nuclear power after the risks were so vividly demonstrated in 2011. In order to reach the 80% reduction goal set for 2050, Japan has been encouraged to reach these goals through other energy-efficient mediums.

Oshiro and Masui (2015) believe that the reduction plan produced in 2010 is still feasible as long as Japan acts quickly and on a rather grand scheme with the deployment of more energy-efficient technologies and the utilization of low carbon energy sources. In the recent study, Oshiro and Masui attempted to assess the impact of low emission vehicles using the AIM/Enduse model. This study was conducted using only technology that is currently available and ready for production in energy efficient vehicles. Oshiro and Masui insist that this target can be reached is if there is a significant long-term emission reduction in the transport sector through the transition to electricity and hydrogen as well as the decarbonization of electricity. A transition to battery electric vehicles as well as fuel cell electric vehicles would increase the demand for electricity in the transport sector providing more motivation to produce more renewable sources and incorporating them into the electricity system. The authors suggest a policy of dynamic pricing of electricity in order to demonstrate the true potential of smart charging battery electric vehicles. The model used in the study suggests that by 2050, the industrial sector will be responsible for 40% of the total GHG emissions due to the fuel demand for high temperature heat is very hard to replace with a decarbonized fuel source. Oshiro and Masui also emphasize the importance of the transition from electricity produced from coal to electricity produced from natural gas. The study suggests that an 80% emission reduction in the freight and passenger transport sector by switching from fossil fuel to low carbon energy. Oshiro and Masui conclude that with the integration of more energy efficient transportation, Japan can achieve 81% CO_2 emission reduction by 2050.

Oshiro, K., Masui, T., 2015. Diffusion of low emission vehicles and their impact on CO2 emission reduction in Japan. Energy Policy 81, 215-225

The Importance of Nuclear Power in Reducing Carbon Emissions and Protecting Developing Nations

by Margaret Loncki

After the recent catastrophic nuclear meltdown of Fukushima in 2011, global support of nuclear power plants has significantly decreased. Reinhard Wolf, an international relations professor at Goethe University in Frankfurt, aims to demonstrate that developed nations do not have the luxury of shutting down nuclear plants out of fear of meltdowns. Wolf emphasizes the philosophical concept of one's obligation to not seriously harm any other individual, which he believes will be the result of continuing to shutdown nuclear power plants around the world. Recent studies suggest that in 2009, climate change forced 10 million people into severe poverty and 45 million people to go hungry. The same study suggests that climate change produced 315,000 premature deaths. These affected individuals reside solely in developing countries.

Developed nations, on the other hand, released a large majority of the world's carbon emissions. Wolf mentions the three main potential dangers with nuclear power plants but concludes that they do not come close to outweighing the damage caused by carbon emissions from coal-fired plants, which emit 16 times as much carbon as nuclear plants over their lifetimes. The first of those risks is radiation; yet, background radiation from coal fired plant smokestacks exceeds this more than 100 times. The second main concern with nuclear power is waste storage. Currently, we do not have a perfect system for the containment and disposal or radioactive waste. However, many promising geological sites have been suggested that would be suitable for repository. According to Wolf, any leakage would still cause far less damage than climate change continues to cause every day. The last, and most pressing, of the three potential risks, is complete meltdown. Coal-fired power plants resulted in the premature death of around 24,000 US citizens in 2009 alone. The catastrophic meltdown of the Chernobyl plant in 1986 was estimated to result in between 9,000 and 34,000 fatal cases of cancer. But carbon emissions result in nearly as many if not more fatalities than the largest historical nuclear meltdown every year, a number that will surely continue to increase as more and more carbon is released into the atmosphere. Wolf concludes that it is the moral obligation of developed nations to prevent further atmospheric contamination, even if it means putting its own citizens in danger.

Wolf, R. 2015. Why wealthy countries must not drop nuclear energy: coal power, climate change and the fate of the global poor. International Affairs 91, 287-301.

Nuclear Power, Climate Change and Energy Security in Britain
by Sam Peterson

The relationship between climate change and present energy consumption (in addition to anticipation of future energy needs) has increasingly bordered on mutual exclusivity. Following significant revelations regarding the correlation between emissions from fossil fuel incineration and average global temperature increases, legislators have struggled to reframe alternative energy source debates in a more favorable light. A major topic in these debates is nuclear power, easily the most divisive of environmentally-friendly energy sources. Policymakers have reframed nuclear power as a low-carbon technology, but Corner *et al.* (2011) find unconditional acceptance of nuclear power practically nonexistent in a national survey in Britain. In general, "people who expressed greater concern about climate change and energy security and possessed higher environmental values were less likely to favour nuclear power." However, when subjects were allowed to express their conditional support, "concerns about climate change and energy security became positive predictors of support for nuclear power." The study concludes that acceptance of nuclear power will increase conditionally, as "other (preferred) options have been exhausted."

The study focused on a triad of points regarding nuclear power, including detection of framing impacts on nuclear power acceptance, exploration into changes of public perception of nuclear power when framed as a method of "energy security," and correlation between climate change concern and acceptance of nuclear power. While the United Kingdom currently has the most ambitious GHG emissions reduction targets of any national government (by 2050, GHG emissions must be reduced by 80% compared to 1990 levels), the government is also attempting to close approximately one-third of existing electricity production sources (mostly nuclear) over the next two decades (Department of Trade Industry, 2007, cited by Corner *et al.*)

Even after accounting for increased use of carbon capture and storage (CCS) technologies, this demand for environmentally friendly, and secure electricity production (defined in 2001 by the International Energy Agency as 'the uninterrupted physical availability of energy at a price which is affordable, while respecting environment concerns") has left legislators with the option of nuclear power. In 2010, 18% of UK electricity was provided by nuclear power stations (DECC, 2010, cited by Corner *et al.*). This number should decrease in the short- and medium-terms, as there seems to be no intent of incorporating a new generation of power plants (all

'Magnox' and Advanced Gas Cooled Reactors (AGR) are scheduled to be decommissioned). Public support has been historically divided on the subject, with some ecologists demanding the integration of nuclear power into existing infrastructure as a means to combat further GHG emissions (Black 2003, cited by Corner *et al.*), while influential NGOs, such as Greenpeace and Friends of the Earth have remained staunchly in opposition (Friends of the Earth, 2004; Greenpeace, 2010, cited by Corner *et al.*) Public opinion on this matter is well documented, with surveys showing that in 2005 and 2007, 90% of British citizens were "concerned about climate change" (Poortinga *et al.* 2006; Eurobarometer, 2007, cited by Corner *et al.*), but climate change often has significantly lower levels of concern associated with it when compared to the economy or terrorism (Upham *et al.* 2009, cited by Corner *et al.*) Previous research in this particular field has shown a strong negative correlation between concern about climate change and support for nuclear power (Spence *et al.* 2010, cited by Corner *et al.* 2011), which may "reflect the philosophy of traditional environmentalist movements in maintaining a clear anti-nuclear stance." This study shows the average unconditional favorability rating for nuclear power has not changed significantly since 2005 (35% to 36%), but finds that conditional favorability ("willing to accept nuclear if it helps improve energy security") has slightly increased (54% to 56%). These results lead to the conclusion that while public support is still highly contingent on time elapsed from previous nuclear accidents, public support for nuclear power will grow as other traditional energy sources are consumed. The authors close by noting that a country locking itself into a pro-nuclear policy may very well put itself in extremely precarious positions if there are problems either domestically or internationally with nuclear electricity production.

Corner, A., *et al.* (2011). "Nuclear power, climate change and energy security: Exploring British public attitudes." Energy Policy 39(9): 4823-4833.

Socio-Economic Status and Climate Change
by Patrick Quarberg

The agricultural response to climate change will greatly affect how the world adapts to different environmental conditions. Given that crops respond differently to differently levels of CO_2 in the atmosphere, it is important that agricultural developments are made to be able to cope with changing crop yields. A less thought of effect of climate change is how socio-economic factors influence how food is grown and distributed, as well as how different areas are able to respond to a shifting global climate. Studies on how crops respond to increased CO_2 in the atmosphere have revealed some positive effects on growth and water retention. Using this information, Parry *et al.* set out to investigate how these changes affected places of different socio-economic status.

To do this, agricultural adaptations were considered on both a local and regional scale, the regional scale being a more conservative estimate of these effects, while the local or site-based estimates are more optimistic. Using a model that accounts for biophysical changes in crops due to climate change as well as rising CO_2 levels, they found that the positive effects caused by a higher level of CO_2 in the atmosphere only temporarily offered a benefit. The boost in productivity was eventually canceled out by increased temperature and decreased precipitation. In all scenarios, certain areas benefitted more from the CO_2 boost, and others suffered heavily from lack of precipitation or suitable growing climate. The areas that benefitted the most tended to be areas with temperate climates. These areas also tended to be more developed than equatorial or tropical regions, suggesting that the disparity of food production between developed and developing countries will only be made worse in the future when climate change is taken into account. Since developing nations have less access to resources, which would allow them to adapt to the ecological changes, they suffer more than developed countries. On top of that, developing countries in equatorial regions will be most heavily and negatively affected, and will face the most difficulty in adapting.

Parry M.L, Rosenzweig C, Iglesias A, Livermore M, Fischer G. 2004. Effects of Climate Change on Global Food Production Under SRES Emissions and Socio-economic Scenarios. ScienceDirect, Volume 14, Issue 1, pages 53-67. doi:10.1016/j.gloenvcha.2003.10.008

Global Warming May be Fatal to Forests
by Chloe Rodman

Jeff Tietz (2015) reports for Rolling Stone magazine on the work postdoctoral student Park Williams has been conducting in the past decade. After surveying thousands of trees, Williams created the forest-drought stress index, which determined that, due to climate change, the average forest stress caused by drought will, by 2050, surpass what it has been in the past 1000 years. Conifer forests in the Southwest United States will die, along with many other species across the globe.

Trees are very important in mitigating climate change. Of the 36 billion tons of carbon dioxide gas that we send into the atmosphere each year, trees absorb 25%, while the ocean absorbs an additional 25%. However, in a warming world, trees are beginning to die more frequently. To trees, excessive heat is equivalent to a lack of water, so as the climate warms, trees begin to dry out and die. When trees dry out, they produce less of the sap that helps keeps insects away. Global warming will therefore result in an infestation of insects and wildfires due to the dried out trees. These insects, such the bark beetle, and fires kill trees in addition to the ones that are already dead, which is a major problem because dead trees release the their stored carbon dioxide into the atmosphere. This starts a vicious cycle; forests die, not only taking less carbon out of the air but also emitting carbon dioxide into the atmosphere. This addition of new carbon dioxide aids in global warming, resulting in higher temperatures. These higher temperatures cause more forests to die and the cycle repeats itself.

Forest fires will cause a whole other problem on their own. They are predicted to burn more frequently and severely in the north due to the continuous temperature increase. The soot and ash from forest fires settle over the Arctic permafrost causing it to turn black and absorb solar radiation from the sun. Climate change is already causing this permafrost to melt, releasing huge quantities of carbon dioxide and methane into the atmosphere, and because of soot deposition, the solar radiation absorption is speeding up the process.

Scientist do not believe the world will be barren of trees however. They predict that with every degree Celsius that the world warms, global rainfall will increase by two percent. This means that already wet areas will still thrive. However, as for the moderate-to-dry regions of the world, trees are expected to die at an increasing rate because the evaporation of water will be too great for forests to handle. Forests will be replaced with more water-efficient grasses and shrubs and the landscape will look completely different from how it appears now.

Tietz, J. 2015. The Fate of Trees: How Climate Change May Alter Forests Worldwide. Rolling Stone. http://rol.st/1eoM6mt

Seattle's Bullitt Center Sets Precedent for New Green Buildings
by Chloe Rodman

Bryan Nelson (2015) writes for the Guardian about the new trend of net zero energy buildings. The Bullitt Center, a recently constructed office building in Seattle, Washington, has earned the title of an "ultra-sustainable living building". To earn this label, the building was surveyed for a year to make sure the features promoted by the Bullitt Foundation performed as promised. The building generates its own electricity, collects its own water, and composts human waste from the bathrooms. While the non-profit Bullitt Foundation hopes to convince other corporations to construct similar green buildings, it is having a hard time proving that its new building is worth the $32.5 million construction cost. Since these types of buildings are so new, it is difficult to predict the long-term success of the green technology and whether it will eventually recover the cost of construction.

Seattle is one of the United States' cloudiest cities; however, the Bullitt Center managed to produce approximately 244,000 kilowatt hours of energy via solar panels, surpassing the 153,000 kilowatt hours of energy necessary to sustain the building. On top of this, the structural layout of the building resulted in the overall demand of energy being cut by 60 percent. Seeing this success, Pittsburg has decided to construct a similar building of its own, the Tower, at PNC Plaza. The skyscraper will be 33 stories high and is predicted to be the greenest skyscraper in the world. Pittsburg is not the only other city to begin building these green structures. The number of zero-net-energy commercial buildings has doubled between 2012 and 2015.

These green buildings have been likened to Tesla cars; everyone wants one of these trophy energy savers if they can afford it. While these buildings are in high demand from governments, as well as oil, gas, and law corporations, The Bullitt Foundation hopes long-term institutions such as universities and museums will transition to using these green structures. While investors are skeptical about the price of the construction, these green buildings, if designed properly, will recover all upfront costs via energy and water savings and could have a public benefit around $18.4 million.

Nelson, Bryan. 2015. Can the Bullitt Center prove that it pays for buildings to go 'deep green'? The Guardian April 23, 2015. http://bit.ly/1eoM9ir

Questionable Outcomes—the Real Significance of No-Till Agriculture Practices for Climate Change Mitigation
by Russell Salazar

The *Emissions Gap Report 2013* published by the United Nations Environment Programme (UNEP) may be providing a misleading emphasis on the conversion to no-till agriculture. Powlson *et al.* (2014) argues that, while there are data to support a correlation between no-till practices and increased carbon sequestration at certain soil depths, many other findings have been overlooked or understated, potentially skewing the focus of climate change mitigation initiatives. The UNEP and the agricultural sector may need to revise their action plans for the coming years.

Traditional cultivation methods, such as ploughing and discing, involve the upheaval of large amounts of soil, causing a release of carbon-containing compounds into the atmosphere. No-till agriculture and reduced tillage are arguably the greener alternatives, keeping the carbon compounds in the soil where they may contribute to the growth of crop. The practice has resulted in 'healthier' soil: greater biological activity, rainfall infiltration and hence productivity. But how significant is this alternative as a tool for climate change mitigation? The authors examine the metrics and pose several significant concerns.

The main evidence in support of further conversion to no-till agriculture is somewhat undermined by comparisons of organic carbon content at different depths in the soil. While no-till supposedly results in higher organic carbon levels closer to the surface, the total organic carbon taking into account deeper soil remains close to unchanged. Additionally, the published measurements focus on soil characteristics at particular depths, neglecting the differences in soil density between tilled and non-tilled land. Overall, the contributions of these practices toward climate change mitigation are miniscule. This begs the question: is the conversion to no-till agriculture worth promoting?

More worrying is the risk of increase in emissions of nitrous oxide, a more 'powerful' greenhouse gas than carbon dioxide. The correlation between no-till agriculture and the level of nitrous oxide is uncertain; nitrous oxide emissions may increase or decrease depending on the conditions. Careful evaluation of the effect of no-till practices on particular areas of land must be made.

The authors' insightful observations bring risks and practicality into question. The potential for misconception and oversight with the UNEP-published data is troublesome, to say the least.

Powlson, D., Stirling, C., Jat, M., Gerard, B., Palm, C., Sanchez, P., & Cassman, K. (2014). Limited potential of no-till agriculture for climate change mitigation. Nature Climate Change 4, 678–683. http://bit.ly/1ErYgQD

Leading with Green—the Future of Urban Design

by Russell Salazar

How will the urban landscape be transformed as the global climate continues to heat up? Hagan (2012) presents case studies of two city redevelopments that could be leading the way toward a new mindset for urban design. Cities, as they stand today, are both contributing to and susceptible to climate change, due to their intense consumption and dense population. Hagan stresses that "the built environment's role both in contributing to and mitigating global warming needs to be better understood by architects and urban designers, given their role in the creation of that environment." The problems are inherent in the way cities are constructed; urban planners, civil engineers, and architects may design individual eco-friendly structures, but rarely consider environmental engineering on a macro scale. Rather than having considerations of economic and social sustainability at the forefront of urban renewal, this paper highlights the potentials of having environmental sustainability act as the driver of design.

Climate change mitigation and adaption should be the goals for city construction and modification in the twenty-first century. The first case study focuses on Gothenburg, Sweden, a port and economic hub under threat of rising sea levels. Given government funding for the reengineering of city infrastructure, the city launched an "international competitive workshop" to attract innovative solutions. Team EAST/R_E_D proposed a unique network of green spaces and permeable pathways, essentially creating a transport system that doubled as a flood-preventive structure. Such "Green Networks" were devised to be integrated into the city in a way that would not only mitigate the effects of rising water levels, but would also abridge the social and economic segregation caused by the industrial nature of the city.

The second case study introduces R_E_D's "parametric Seed Catalogue", which, in an almost game-like fashion, considers urban design as a combination of interlinked "tiles". The project suggests that, just as an ecosystem contains mechanisms whereby the waste of one species is of benefit to another, cities can be designed with metabolic and self-improving concepts in mind. For example, "instead of the city's wastes being exported, and energy imported, they are handled as much as possible in situ by 'artificial ecosystems': water filtration systems, biogas systems etc." *Tiles* would assist in sustaining one another in a way that reduces waste and encourages economic productivity.

The warming climate has added an element of urgency to the need for urban renewal. The marriage of environmental engineering and urban planning could lead to future where the environmentally oriented approach to socio-economic reforms in an urban setting becomes commonplace.

Hagan, S., 2012. Urban Design in a Time of Climate Change. Design Principles and Practices: An International Journal 6, 73–96.

Delay Your Trip to China—the Effect of Climate Change on Fall Foliage
by Russell Salazar

Landscapes and the natural environment are invaluable tourist attractions for many countries. Regions in China and Japan, in particular, have been known for the mesmerizing red coloration of their fall foliage, reeling in tourists from all around the world. How, then, does their tourism industry transform with the average rise in global air temperatures? Ge, Dai, Liu, Zhong, and Liu (2013) study the effects of climate change on the fall foliage in Xi'an and Beijing, identifying potential changes to peak dates for tourism and sightseeing.

Beginning with measurements from 1960, their study measured "the beginning, best, and the end of the fall foliage vacation season", defined as "the dates of start coloring, full coloration, and leaf fall, respectively." More specifically, their study outlines specific guidelines for the measurement of said dates: the start coloring date occurs when 5% of leaves on a specified observation tree turn yellow or red; the best date, or full coloration date, occurs when 90% of the crowns of observed trees are completely red; the end date occurs when 95% of leaves fall off from the observed trees. The consistent measurement criteria allows for comparable data over the long study period.

The data collected very clearly show a few trends. First, the total delay since 1960 for the beginning of leaf coloration is 21 days in Beijing, and 15 days in Xi'an. Similar sized delays have been recorded in the measurements of the best color and the end of the fall foliage vacation season. Comparing these results with the temperature increases in the studied regions, it is shown that increases of 1°C led to delays of about 3 days.

This poses some interesting points for the tourism industry—consumers and companies alike—to consider. As an adaptive technique, providers of service to tourists should plan for later peak weeks to take full advantage of effective pricing mechanisms. Tourists should also be aware of such changes and plan vacations accordingly. Without proper planning, the wellbeing of the tourism industry in Beijing and Xi'an, along with the associated culture and social climate, may experience significant deterioration over time.

Ge *et al.* (2013) have shown through their research that subtle differences to the environment could amount to somewhat significant shifts in tourism-heavy economies.

Ge, Q., Dai, J., Liu, J., Zhong, S., and Liu, H. 2013. The effect of climate change on fall foliage vacation in China. Tourism Management 38, 80-84.

One World—Climate Change, Globalization, and Human Health
by Russell Salazar

Modern technology has granted us the ability to access populations across the world, adapt to diverse landscapes, and intensify economic growth and development. Globalization has caused fundamental changes in our ecosystem, not only changing climate, but also altering the ways we are affected by changes in climate. McMichael (2013) looks at the relationship between globalization and human health in a warming world. His paper identifies particular outcomes of globalization that are intimately related to the health and well-being of the world population.

He points out that "population growth is often overlooked in the discourse on global change". Our numbers are expected to grow by a remarkable 2.7 billion by 2050, which is made possible by the economic growth that globalization provides. Such an exponential increase will create severe pressures on the dwindling resources available, "not only exacerbating various ongoing worldwide environmental and ecological changes, but also [entrenching] conditions of poverty and disadvantage" as groups under such conditions face higher fertility rates. From a human health perspective, an even clearer disparity with regard to healthcare access can be expected, and the level of treatment currently available to the general public will be divided amongst much larger populations. The same scarcity applies to all goods, including food and fresh water. Such a large population would experience much more severe responses to changes in the global climate. Combined with the crop-reducing, resource-damaging effects of climate change, population growth poses severe threat to human health.

Given our interconnectedness and ability to travel, we also face much faster transmission of infectious disease. Given the ecosystem damage generated by the changing climate, as well as warmer weather in general, changes in microbial ecology are expected that may result in our susceptibility to infectious diseases increasing.

However, McMichael suggests that there may also be groups that benefit, to some degree, from the changing climate. In some areas, milder winters may lead to fewer cold-related health issues, while in others, hotter conditions may reduce survival of pathogen vectors such as mosquitos and other insects. These, however, are minor short-term benefits that do not outweigh the severities to be expected.

Ultimately, McMichael argues that globalization has given rise to a highly dynamic ecosystem; increased human activity is accompanied by increased volatility, and different groups must develop adaptation strategies to match the dynamic environment. Climate change

mitigation strategies will also work to reduce such
volatility, providing a more stable future.

McMichael, A., 2013. Globalization, Climate Change, and Human Health. The New
England Journal of Medicine 368, 1335-1343.

Evaluating the Environmental Impact of the California High-Speed Rail

by Abigail Schantz

Chester and Horvath from the Department of Civil and
Environmental Engineering at UC Berkeley determined
that a life-cycle environmental inventory was necessary to
fully understand the pros and cons of the proposed
project. The life-cycle environmental inventory reviews
emissions resulting from use of this transportation
method as well as the environmental costs of building and
maintenance. Presently, people traveling in this corridor
rely most heavily on automobiles, secondarily on
airplanes, and lastly on heavy rail transit. Because we are
unable to predict the precise usage of a high-speed rail
system, when comparing the environmental impacts of
each of these modes of travel, it is critical to take into
account differences between low-demand and high-
demand scenarios, and to account for an expected initial
transition period of low-usage. Additionally, relatively
small differences in the design of the rail can make drastic
differences in the environmental impact, such as use of
smaller cars seating approximately 600 passengers as
opposed to larger ones seating approximately 1,200, which
require more energy than smaller cars. Using this kind of
information about components of the system, a return on
investment (ROI), calculated at 9.7 million Mg CO_2
emissions, model can be created. Chester and Horvath
found this model estimates that with other travel modes at
low occupancy and high-speed rail at high occupancy, the
ROI for energy and green house gas (GHG) would be 8 and
6 years respectively. In the opposite scenario, with other
forms of transportation at high occupancy and high-speed
rail at low occupancy (as is probable during the initial
transition period), neither energy nor GHG would ever
return the investment. Lastly, with all transportation at

mid-level occupancy, the ROI for energy would be 28 years and for GHG, 71 years. These estimates suggest that under optimal occupancy, the high-speed rail would lower both energy and GHG emissions. On the other hand, it is likely that construction of the high-speed rail would greatly increase other emissions such as SO_2 due to the system operating primary on electricity, which also must be taken into account. Decision-makers will have the opportunity to increase the environmental benefits of the rail during construction, for example, by utilizing lower-CO_2 concrete mixes or minimizing concrete usage in the design, as the production of concrete is energy intensive and releases large amounts of CO_2.

Chester, M., Horvath, A., 2010. Life-Cycle Assessment Of High Speed Rail: The Case Of California. Environmental Research Letters, 014003-014003.

Reducing the Environmental Impact through Building Certifications—LEED, ASHRAE, and IGCC

by Abigail Schantz

Sangwon Suh, Shivira Tomar, Matthew Leighton, and Joshua Kneifel (2014) analyzed the environmental benefits to be gained from three major building certification systems: LEED, ASHRAE, and IgCC. The final analysis showed that GBCC-compliant buildings reduce environmental impacts in major categories by 15%–25%. But, because LEED permits consumers to selectively choose which measures to adopt rather than maintaining strict baseline requirements, it is possible for a LEED certified building to show no reduction. The estimates also assumed proper use of the buildings, whereas after construction, occupants' behavior can significantly decrease the reduction potential. The authors concluded that overall, with 40% of US energy consumption stemming from buildings, a 15–25% reduction can have a major impact and, therefore, implementing these certification systems should be seriously considered.

It is currently estimated that 40% of United States energy consumption comes from residential and commercial buildings. Efforts to reduce the environmental effects of this consumption include making changes in materials, building structure, uses of insulation, and more. There are already numerous efforts to do this, as demonstrated by the 44,270 LEED-certified projects in the US as of August 2013. In this article, the authors did not attempt to determine the best system but rather used Green Building Code and Certification (GBCC) as a standard basis for reviewing the three.

As a base model, the researchers used the life cycle assessment (LCA) developed by the National Institute of Standards and Technology (NIST) and a model building from the National Renewable Energy Laboratory (NREL). GBCC used both inputs (materials, services, etc.) and outputs (waste, emissions, pollutants, etc.) to quantify and generate life cycle inventories (LCIs) for all three systems, as well as for a baseline building. The baseline building, a 3-story office building, which is consistent with the national average for office buildings, was estimated to emit 9.9 tons of CO_2-equiv/per square meter.

Bills of Materials (BoM), comprehensive inventories of all products needed in construction, were also generated for all four buildings (baseline, and three GBCCs). The three systems all involve similar requirements, with slight variations. LEED is a voluntary program that assigns points to various potential features, allowing consumers to choose any number of options for impact reduction so long as the total number of points meets certification requirements. ASHRAE and IgCC both use minimum requirements that all buildings must include, as well as supplemental options. These two systems can be either offered as voluntary opt-in strategies or adopted by local governments as building requirements.

The quantifiable components used in the LCA do not encompass all benefits or faults of the buildings, but this study ignore these variations because they currently cannot be measured. The unmeasured factors include, though are not limited to, indoor pollutants, light pollution, and improvements in occupants' productivity.

The buildings were analyzed at three stages: preoccupancy (construction), occupancy (use), and post-occupancy (end-of-life, demolition). Results were analyzed for twelve categories: global warming; acidification; human health-criteria pollutants; eutrophication; ozone layer depletion; smog formation; ecological toxicity; human health-cancer (HHC), human health-noncancer, primary energy, land use, and water consumption. Due to the large number of assumptions made in order to analyze the data generally, the team conducted an analysis to determine how responsive each result was to slight alterations in the unmeasured variables. The authors noted that a small number of the inputs represent a large share of the LCI while the majority have negligible effects. For example, of the 380 inputs measured, 13 comprise 99% of the HHC impact.

Suh, S., Tomar, S., Leighton, M., Kneifel, J., 2014. Environmental Performance of Green Building Code and Certification Systems. Environmental Science & Technology. DOI:10.1021/es4040792

Al Gore is Ready to Win the Battle of Climate Change
by Abby Schantz

In the New York Times article, "The New Optimism," published on March 16th, 2015, John Schwartz explains a change in action by Al Gore regarding climate change. Gore has a long list of achievements; former vice president of the United Sates, environmental activist, and investor. He is also the recipient of a Nobel Peace Prize for his work on climate change, including his Academy Award winning film, "An Inconvenient Truth." These efforts have focused on showing the magnitude of the problem of climate change, instilling concern for the issue around the globe. Recently, however, his viewpoint has transformed to cast a more optimistic light saying, "We're going to win this." Gore uses the history of cellphones as an analogy to changing energy sources. In 1980, AT&T estimated that 900,000 cellphones would be sold by 2000. In fact, 109 million were sold by 2000 and, by- today, around 7 billion. Gore says the mis-estimation was due to the rapid increase in technology and decrease in costs, which turned giant blocks (old cellphones) into miniature computers (new cellphones). This same trend is apparently holding true in renewable energy. In 2000, it was predicted that worldwide wind-generated energy would reach 30 gigawatts. In fact, wind generated energy reached 200 gigawatts by 2010 and by 2014 it was nearly 370. In 2002, it was estimated that by 2010, one new gigawatt per year would be added by solar power. In fact, the amount was seventeen times higher in 2010 and, by 2014, fifty-eight times higher. The statistics continue to support Gore's claim. Two homes install rooftop solar panels every minute in Bangladesh, and Dubai's state utility is building a solar power panel which will cost less than six cents per kilowatt-hour, less than almost anyone pays anywhere. To aid the rapid growth, Gore is working on spreading the word through training programs. Gore presents 164 slides on climate change over the course of eight and a half hours, accepts questions from scientists throughout the presentation and then has the newly educated create local forms of the presentation to help educate their local communities. Al Gore also demonstrates the possibilities for home renovation through his own house, which has 32 solar panels, insulating windows and LED lights. His driveway hosts 10 geothermal wells and all of his electricity comes from a utility plant that generates power from wind and solar sources. To Gore, winning the fight against climate change is possible, it is just a matter of time. His biggest obstacle; his former political persona. To democrats, Gore is a great symbol of change, bringing many on board. But to conservatives, he is working to "undercut the scientific consensus on the human role in global warming". As Gore works to educate people on climate change, he is constantly reminding conservatives of his past as one of the most divisive political leaders.

Schwartz, J., 2015. The New Optimism of Al Gore. The New York Times, March 16th, 2015. http://nyti.ms/1lY0q0s

The Beans that Will Survive Climate Change
by Abby Schantz

Concerns about climate change are high on peoples' minds around the globe, but not many consider the changes it is already beginning to cause in food production. Dan Charles of NPR discusses bean production in his article, "Meet the Cool Beans Designed To Beat Climate Change." It is estimated that approximately 400 million people globally rely on beans for nourishment. This is problematic because most beans, including the common ones–pinto, black and kidney– cannot survive in temperatures that remain above 66 degrees throughout the night. A Colombian scientist, Alvaro Mejia-Jimenez was intrigued by a bean indigenous to communities in the American Southwest, the tepary bean. Though this bean is not widely planted anymore due to its small size and the few produced per plant, it has a remarkable ability to survive through both heat and drought. Mejia-Jimenez set out to combine the genetic traits of the tepary bean with those of common beans. He fertilized the flower of a common bean using pollen taken from a tepary bean plant, forming an embryo, then removed the embryo and raised it in a laboratory dish. Through several generations of cross-breeding, he created seeds with the combined genetics traits of both beans. His work went unnoticed until the problems of climate change began to become more prevalent. The Consultative Group of International Agricultural Research researched how the rising temperatures would likely affect bean production. They found a potential loss of 50% crop area in one generation, by mid-century. This gave Mejia-Jimenez's work a practical application. The Center for Tropical Agriculture (CIAT) began testing more varieties of the genetic combination and experimentally planting the beans to see results. In Nicaragua, farmers planting these beans produced twice the quantity of farmers planting the common beans, showing just how great the temperature limitations already are. CIAT is continuing to experiment with other bean varieties and plans to make the variations available globally.

Charles, D., 2015. Meet The Cool Beans Designed To Beat Climate Change. NPR, March 25th, 2015. http://n.pr/1cdncVm

California Water Rationing — Wake Up!
by Abby Schantz

Tom McCarthy in the Guardian's recent article, "California governor tells climate change deniers to wake up," writes on California Governor, Jerry Brown's speech about the newly imposed water rationing regulations for the state of California. He points to climate change as the cause of the ongoing drought. The state relies on snow melt to refill reservoirs each year. Today, the snow pack is at levels just 8% of what is expected each year and reservoirs are running dry. Brown's reduction plan calls for reducing water consumption by 25% through ceasing to water lawns, limiting toilet flushing, and reducing shower times along with many other small lifestyle changes. Regarding enforcement, local water districts will be able to track water usage and then fine households going over the limit.

Many complained that with 80% of California's water usage going towards agriculture, especially crops with high water demand such as almonds, other nuts, and many fruits, the focus should be on limiting water in that sector. Brown believes that the small changes people can make in their daily lives can reduce the severity of the issue without putting hundreds of thousands of people out of work. He did recognize, however, that if the problem continues at this level, reviewing policies that reduce agricultural water usage may have to be considered. Dianne Feinstein, one of California's Senators, also acknowledged the severity of the issue, particularly for farmers. She announced plans for emergency legislation to help those whose livelihoods were affected, such as farmers.

McCarthy, T. "California drought: governor tells climate-change deniers to wake up." The Guardian. April 5, 2015

You Might Die From Climate Change
by Abby Schantz

In the CNN article, "Obama: Environment has effect on public health," Ben Tinker writes about the new approach being taken to get people to act against climate change: public health. The goal is to take an issue, which to many seems distant and theoretical and make it applicable to their own lives, especially the health of their families. In a study released by the American Thoracic Society, seven out of ten doctors cited climate change as increasing health problems in their patients. In 2012, pollutant exposure accounted for approximately one in eight deaths worldwide. Three million deaths were attributed to under-nutrition and more to malaria.

The effects of climate change will amplify these epidemics as food security is compromised and floods increase breeding ground for insects. The World Health Organization has predicted an increase of 250,000 deaths per year between 2030 and 2050 due to climate change. Over the past century, earth's average temperature has risen by a mere 1.4°C, and the EPA estimates an additional two degrees over the next 100 years. Even these small changes are responsible for drastic changes in climate and weather, causing floods, droughts, intense rains and heat waves.

President Obama is getting on board the new approach, describing climate change as a health concern. He recently participated in a roundtable discussion on this issue with US Surgeon General Dr. Vivek Murthy and EPA Administrator Gina McCarthy during National Public Health Week. Obama reflected on his move to Los Angeles in 1979 to attend college. He recalled being unable to play outdoor sports, frequent of air quality alerts, and people with respiratory problems being stuck inside. He noted that when people took action, the air quality improved, and the health effects diminished, showing action is possible.

Obama hopes that companies like Google and Microsoft will design apps that enable families to monitor their air quality on a real-time basis, providing information people will be able to utilize pressure elected officials to work on reducing the effects of climate change.

The biggest setback to action: Close to half of the American population still denies climate change. A March Gallup poll found that no more Americans believe in the effects of global warming than did two years ago, indicating a significant lack of progress. Obama is hopeful that recognizing the direct heath concerns associated with climate change will motivate people to get involved.

Tinker, B., 2015. Obama: Environment has effect on public health. CNN, April 8th, 2015. http://cnn.it/1GxABnW

Changes in Measuring Air Quality
by Emily Segal

Particulate Matter (PM) is an air pollutant that when large enough can be seen as soot or smoke, and when small enough, can only be observed using an electron microscope. Particles less than 2.5 micrometers in diameter ($PM_{2.5}$) are especially dangerous because they can be inhaled into the respiratory system and can lodge in the lungs. Scientists have been studying the quantity of particulate matter in the air for a while, but between 1988 and 2013, the system for monitoring this air pollutant underwent many changes. Essentially, the old way of measuring $PM_{2.5}$, through traditional filter sampling, was replaced by the more effective method of using Beta Attenuation Monitors (BAM). It is important to have a monitoring network that operates frequently and in many areas because this data can then be compared to data from various hospitals in order to draw conclusions about the connections between $PM_{2.5}$ concentrations and health consequences. Additionally, the real-time nature of BAM can help make short-term forecasts for air qualities in different regions. This was not possible previously because traditional filter sampling had many delays caused by transporting, conditioning, and weighting filters before any conclusions about the actual $PM_{2.5}$ measurement could be made.

In their paper entitled "Changes in fine particulate matter measurement methods and ambient concentrations in California," Ling Tao and Robert A. Harley analyzed the available record of filter-based and BAM measurements of $PM_{2.5}$ concentrations in California. There was much more PM2.5 data available from BAM then from filter measurements which they found were often checked once every third or sixth day or had missing samples all together. For example, in 2013, records showed that in the San Joaquin Valley, an average of 89% of days had BAM data compared to only 38% of days that had data from filter-based methods. Tao and Harley concluded that overall, $PM_{2.5}$ levels in California have been reduced greatly over the last two decades. Especially in Los Angeles, the amount of $PM_{2.5}$ in the air decreased by 50% between 1988 and 2013.

Tao, L., Harley, R., 2014. Changes in fine particulate matter measurement methods and ambient concentrations in California. Atmospheric Environment 98, December 2014, Pages 676–684.

Complications of Climate Engineering and International Law
by Emily Segal

As anthropogenic climate change continues to become an increasingly discussed social, political and environmental issue, some people are turning to climate engineering as a way to supplement the pre-existing strategies of mitigation and adaptation.

In the paper reviewed here, Winter (2011) explores its relationship to international law. Geoengineering, or geological engineering, refers to the application of geoscience to shape our interaction with the earth. Some forms of geoengineering that have been around for a while are detrimental to the health of our planet. Examples include deforestation, the method of clearing forested land to create arable land for monocultures, and burning fossil fuels, a process that releases toxic substances into the atmosphere, which contribute to the greenhouse effect and speed up global warming. New forms of geoengineering, however, are different from these older forms because they do not encourage side-effects that are harmful to the environment. Instead, they have intended consequences that will help reduce climate change. Carbon capture and storage (CCS), a way of capturing CO_2 after it is emitted and storing it in land, is an example of a more recent form of geoengineering that would aid in decelerating climate change. Solar Radiation Management (SRM) is another form of geoengineering intended to reduce climate change. SRM increases surface and cloud albedo, a kind of weather manipulation that could be effective if used on a large scale.

Unfortunately, there are expenses for these beneficial methods of climate engineering as well. Stratospheric aerosols and space reflectors, part of the SRM strategy, could be a quick and moderately priced way to cool down the planet; however, the safety for this is very low, and there would be a greater risk for adverse side-effects on both human and environmental health. Even trials for climate engineering projects could be dangerous because they would have to be performed on a large scale to see whether or not they are effective.

Legal barriers complicate the use of climate engineering as a way to reduce climate change; some international laws enable state action, while others regulate each state's ability to act as it pleases in order to protect the global public interest. International law gives states sovereignty over regulating the release of particles into the stratosphere, but it also ensures that activities in outer space, such as the insertion of reflectors (as would be used in the SRM method of climate engineering) are not subjective to each state but rather are part of the common freedom among all states to explore and use outer space together. So, a state does have the sovereignty to decide what amount of toxic gas it will release into the atmosphere, taking into account whether it has signed any international treaties regarding air pollution. It also has the free but not exclusive legal power to implement a form of climate engineering that takes place from outer space, though this is complicated, because one state does not have jurisdiction over another state in influencing how to utilized outer space. These examples only brush the surface of the complicated legal issues that surround climate engineering and its obstacles.

Winter, G., 2011. Climate engineering and international law: last resort or the end of humanity. Review of European Community & International Environmental Law, 20 (3), 277-289.

Consider the Mushroom as a Companion Species
by Emily Segal

Species interdependence describes how various species in an ecosystem interact with and either benefit or hurt one another. Anthropologist Anna Tsing (2012) in her article "Unruly Edges: Mushrooms as Companion Species," relates this idea to scientist and historian Donna Harraway's concept of companion species which looks at how animals and humans interact together, though perhaps not entirely comfortably. Mushrooms can be thought of as a companion species for a variety of organisms, including humans, because they take part in symbiotic relationships with numerous plants, help enrich soil, act as pathogens or parasites, and break down dead forest wood, among other things. They play a crucial part in ecosystem renewal, which highlights their importance as a companion species and also how interdependence is a natural and essential part of how ecosystems operate. As Tsing (2012) explains, we as humans are blinded by the superior status we feel we can assume in nature. Instead of thinking about the interdependence between humans and the environment, we polarize our views, thinking about either human control of nature or human impact on nature. In reality, however, there is interdependence between humans and nature that deserves attention. An example of this is how the cultivation of cereals like wheat and barley encouraged domestication of the human species. State development and cereal agriculture evolved together because the government had control over a specific portion of the harvest, which was then used to benefit the elite. Cereals high in carbohydrates allowed women to have more children. These children were beneficial because they could then work in the fields to cultivate more cereals. With more children, women were needed to run households, and their options aside from childcare became increasingly limited. Meanwhile, fungi, considered the enemy of monocrop farms, prospered with tons of new grain fields. What is interesting is how the history of mushrooms correlates with human history, showing a continued relationship between the species from the very beginning. More recently, fungi have posed threats to genetic manipulations of crops. Plants grown from a single clone are susceptible to the same kind of fungi, which is dangerous to their survival as a species. Tsing (2012) claims contemporary developers in favor of replacing destroyed natural environments with these uniform crops are really proponents of European conquest and expansion.

Unfortunately, environmental degradation reaches even the strongest mushrooms. Some fungi are dying from air pollution and acid rain, while others growing near sites of nuclear accidents transfer radioactivity to animals who then feed it to human herders. Mushrooms have been and will continue to be companion species for humans. As Tsing (2012) writes, "We can ignore them, or we can consider what they are telling us about the human condition," (152).

Tsing, A., 2012. Unruly Edges: Mushrooms as Companion Species. Environmental Humanities 1, 141-154.

Major Climate Change Problems Closer than Most of Us Think
by Breanna Sewell

Retired NASA astrophysicist and former leader in humanist organizations, Jordan Stuart, discusses the willingness and ability of people to counter the effects of climate change in his 2014 paper, "Is Action to Mitigate Climate Change Possible Today?" He introduces the topic by addressing the unfortunate state of our planet in regards to increasing amounts of natural disasters, and then continues on to state that global climate change is undeniably caused by human activity. Stuart writes that scientists have done enough to prove that global warming is the cause of climate change and that anthropogenic greenhouse gases are the cause of global warming, therefore we, as a people, should admit that we are the cause of climate change.

Despite this certainty, very little action has been taken to reverse or even slow down the process of climate change. For this inactivity, we can thank those opposed to the idea of reducing carbon dioxide emissions. With only profit in mind, from Stuart's perspective, they do their best to convince voters that there is great debate surrounding the tie between carbon emissions and climate change, when in actuality, there is not.

Later on, Stuart explains that if all major carbon emitters do not cooperate soon in trying to reduce emissions, it will not be possible to stay at the proposed limit of a two-degree Celsius increase in global temperature. This is a serious dilemma considering that recent studies suggest a 21-foot increase in sea level if the global temperature were to increase 3.5°C. This shocking truth calls for cooperation on a global level.

According to Stuart, these facts about global climate change are known by few, which is the root of the problem. Stuart points out the necessity that action be taken quickly, but realizes the difficulty of this due to the general ignorance of the public when it comes to climate science. We can't expect to see progress until the truth about climate change is made clear to the public.

Stuart, J., 2014. Moving Past A Warm-Up: Is Action to Mitigate Climate Change Possible Today? The Humanist.

Reasons Why NGOs Aren't Tackling Meat Consumption Issues
by Phoebe Shum

Meat consumption is one of the largest contributors to greenhouse gas emissions. Reducing the number of meat eaters in the population would provide massive benefit to our environment. So why aren't climate change non-governmental organizations (NGOs) assertively pushing for reduced meat-intensive diets? Laestadius *et al.* (2014), with the support of Johns Hopkins Bloomberg School of Public Health, studies the reasons behind the lack of campaigning done to decrease meat consumption

Apparently, NGOs are hesitant to adopt campaigns that vouch for lower meat consumption as they feel that targeting individual behavior can lead to uncontrollable backlash. People are creatures of habit and when their individual behaviors are attacked, there are bound to be adverse reactions. Culturally, many people hold in their minds that a proper meal consists of meat, vegetables and carbohydrates. Telling them to change their diet due to reasons of what people perceive to be a distant issue such as climate change will not be effective and might actually distance supporters of NGOs.

According to Laestadius *et al.*, while most NGO's have information on ideas such as Meatless Mondays on their websites, most do not have active campaigns advocating for the importance of meat reduction in climate change. Only animal rights NGOs and food focused NGOs have constructed public education campaigns to encourage decreased meat consumption. Contrastingly, those with an environmental focus have not. Meat consumption is a popular personal choice, and NGOs fear that diet-related messages will waste already-limited NGO resources. Some NGO staff members also commented that reducing meat consumption would "challenge the American dream." Others say that individual personal change requires more effort than other climate change mitigation efforts, such as shutting down coal plants, which "is relatively easy and wouldn't create lifestyle changes." The issue of decreasing meat consumption seems to be facing a negative feedback loop. When the problem is brought up and people are not interested or doesn't elicit response, NGOS place their efforts on other issues, thus forever prohibiting the issue to rise in popularity.

Laestadius L., Neff R., Barry C., Frattaroli S., 2014. "We don't tell people what to do": An examination of the factors influencing NGO decisions to campaign for reduced meat consumption in light of climate change. Global Environmental Change, 32-40.

Environmental Costs of High-Density Cattle Farming

by Sarah Whitney

A dramatic increase in the density of United State's dairy farms has created a cause for concern across the nation. The number of cattle per farm has jumped from 1000 to more than 15,000 cows. Dairy producers are easily able to increase their production and thus their profit with access to cheap fuel and feed. The State Department of Natural Resources states that dairy farms containing 500 cows or more have increased by 150% in size, but the number of dairy farms in the United States has decreased by a third. Such an increase in high-density cattle farms has generated a major issue with proper manure disposal. On small-scale farms, roaming cows naturally fertilize the pasture with their manure. Yet on large-scale cattle farms, where cows are confined to a barn, the ratio between cattle and land is extremely out of proportion and thus the significant amount of manure in a small space poses a huge environmental problem.

Manure is primarily composed of nitrate, phosphorus, and excess hormones fed to cows to foster growth and prevent diseases. Improper disposal of such material has led to many cases of groundwater and surface water contamination. For example, in February of 2014, there was a 1 million gallon spill from a manure lagoon into local waterways causing a 5-mile plume across Michigan Allegan country. Runoff from dairy farms seeps into aquifers used for drinking water, elevating nitrate concentration to unsafe levels and possibly adding estrogenic compounds from the hormones. Additionally, contamination to surface water increases and promotes algae blooms creating dead zones. A dead zone is a habitat void of life caused by the loss of oxygen in water and thus the death and migration of marine life.

Many environmentalists, residents, and policy makers are protesting the expansion of dairy farms because of the repercussions of improper manure disposal. Members of Kewaunee County in Wisconsin are protesting the permit for the expansion of Kinnard Farms because of the increase in nitrate and bacteria levels in local drinking water and soils. Erin Fitzgerald, senior vice president of sustainability of the Innovation Center for US Dairy, states that organization and regulation of cattle farms is the key to success. However, the EPA suggests a switch from Holstein cows to Jersey cows, which produce half the amount of manure. The true solution may lie in the opinion of small-scale farmers such as Jon Bansen of Double J Jerseys, who says we should value sustainable quality products over large profit.

Grossman, E. 2014. As Dairy Farms Grow Bigger, New Concerns About Pollution. Yale Environment 360. http://bit.ly/1AocXJB

A Public Health Policy Approach to Rising Sea Levels
by Sarah Whitney

Robin Kundis Craig (2010) concludes that it is absurd to expect governments to put policies in place now that predict and manage the long-term effects of rising sea levels. Craig argues that governments can prevent the extent of damages caused by rising sea levels by implementing a policy focusing directly on public health. She notes that scientists are still unsure exactly how high the seas will rise. Their predictions, she states, are uncertain as they are based upon scientific assumptions and factors like the effect of current and future mitigation methods, (the methods combating greenhouse gas emission). Craig also states that it is unreasonable to define adaptive measures to govern climate change almost three centuries from now as new information will inevitably arise. One can reasonably assume however, that humans will still retain the same basic desires such as health and comfortable living conditions in the distant future. This assumption can be used to form a preventative policy that benefits society without the need to fully comprehend all the uncertainties of rising sea levels. A public health approach aimed at the needs and concerns of humans is an adaptable policy that can remain stable as the discoveries and effects of climate change arise.

In general, rising sea levels are caused by an increase in global temperatures. This increase melts polar ice caps and glaciers, which in turn causes an influx of freshwater into oceans and adds to the total body of water. While rising sea levels may not be consistent around the world, in general seas are increasing at an accelerating rate. Rising sea levels cause the erosion of shorelines, mass flooding, and an increase of salinity in water quality. These effects destroy coastal habitats, contaminate drinking water, and increase the force and damages caused by coastal storms.

One of the main public health concerns of rising sea levels is saltwater intrusion upon drinking water. Instead of focusing on the effects of increased salinity on estuaries and biodiversity, governments can focus on the humanities as a more stable approach that will additionally benefit the environment. Coastal communities depend largely upon local freshwater from aquifers, lakes and rivers for drinking water, which will all be affected by climate change. Current management deals with saltwater intrusion by storing freshwater in reservoirs and releasing it during droughts. This method is likely to become impractical in the future where there are decreases in the supply of freshwater. The government needs to begin to prepare for these effects by implementing methods for water conservation, identify and construct proper water supply infrastructure, and identify alternate sources of water.

An increase in sea level in tandem with increasing global temperatures threatens the public health of humans by the immergence and spread of diseases. Mosquito born diseases, like dengue fever and malaria, are projected to become rampant as shallow water transforms into greater, stagnant, warm bodies of water, aka the ideal breeding ground for mosquitos. Water born diseases like Cholera and *Vibrio vulnificus* are projected to be exposed to a new and extensive population through the rise of sea levels. As these communities are currently unequipped to deal with such epidemics, a policy to promote doctoral training of such diseases will allow coastal communities to implement control measures if problems arise.

Finally, due to the impacts of rising sea levels on the landscape of coastlines it is imperative that governments create policies addressing the control of damages caused by an increase in the force of coastal storms. Rising sea levels causes erosion, eliminating protective barriers for infrastructure and coastal communities, and also increase vulnerability to flooding. As seen in disasters such as Hurricane Katrina, floods transport toxins from local industries causing air quality and soil contamination issues directly affecting human health. Requiring industries to have waterproof storage facilities for toxins, and focusing on the cleanup of coastal Superfund sites can reduce the health effects of strong coastal storms.

By focusing on public health through water quality, disease prevention, and limiting health concerns of natural disasters, governments should be able to control the harmful effects of rising-sea levels without full knowledge of their effects. While politicians debate or ignore the issue of climate change, governments can implement these precautions to protect the public from the more predictable effects of rising sea levels.

Craig, R.K., 2010. A public health perspective on sea-level rise: starting points for climate change adaptation. Widener Law Review 15, 521-540.

Human Adaptations to Climate Change Further Jeopardize Biodiversity
by Yijing Zhang

Even though the science community has increased the awareness of the human impacts on climate change and biodiversity, Watson (2014) argues that conservation scientists still have not addressed how humans' adjustment to climate change has further adversely influenced non-human species. Some ecological degradation includes the impacts of oil and gas mining in Arctic due to the retreat of sea-ice, which harms the already vulnerable polar biodiversity. In Africa, the irrigation in the valleys of the Congo Basin has negatively affected the local biodiversity. For instance, a devastating drought can force the human population to migrate, resulting in an unfavorable change for the ecosystem, which relies on the human population. In addition, the human population might change their own behavior, which in turn, further affect biodiversity.

In southern and southeastern Asia, there was an increase in hunting of tiger and deer species during a flood. As a result, there might be an increase in flooding frequency in the area where most tigers and deer inhabit. Sometimes the motivation of human adaptation is well defined, but it might also bring unexpected and unwanted outcome. In Papua New Guinea, the construction of seawalls destructed the coral reefs in the sea. Therefore, to prevent all the tragedies listed above and to obtain better mitigation policies, Watson suggests a clearer understanding of planning strategies. This means further research on not only climate change impacts on biodiversity, but also how human response to climate change can have an effect on biodiversity. The most effective response will allow species and humans to rapidly adjust and adapt. To do that, an integration of ecology and climatology with social, economic, and political sciences is needed to study human responses to climate change.

Watson E.M. James (2014). "Human responses to climate change will seriously impact biodiversity conservation: It's time we start planning for them" Conservation Letters 7: 1-2.

About the Authors

The authors of this book are first-year students at Claremont McKenna College. The book is a work product of a Freshman Humanities Seminar—*The Human Response to Climate Change*—taught by Dr. Emil Morhardt, the George R. Roberts Professor of Environmental Biology, in the W.M. Keck Science Department of Claremont McKenna, Pitzer, and Scripps Colleges.

The students' task was to write journalistic summaries of interesting academic technical papers having something to do with climate change, but not written by natural scientists (*i.e.* not written by anybody who might be housed in the W. M. Keck Science Center). A way into the project, the criteria were relaxed to include pieces written by journalists and fiction writers, as well as writing about art and theater projects—all obviously important aspects of the humanities. The summaries were due weekly and were returned with editorial comments shortly thereafter.

The editor remembers how difficult it was for him to learn to write as a freshman at Pomona College (another member of the Claremont Colleges), and suspects he was not nearly as good at it as the students who wrote this book. They have done a terrific job.

www.ingramcontent.com/pod-product-compliance
Lightning Source LLC
Chambersburg PA
CBHW031425270326
41930CB00007B/572